A Swim *Against* The Tide

A Swim *Against* The Tide

*The fight to adopt
children into a loving home*

David R I McKinstry

White Knight Publications
2003 Toronto, Canada

Published in 2003 by White Knight Publications,
a division of Bill Belfontaine Ltd.
Suite 103, One Benvenuto Place
Toronto Ontario Canada M4V 2L1
Telephone: 416-925-6458 Fax: 416-925-4165
e-mail <whitekn@istar.ca>

Ordering information
Hushion House
c/o Georgetown Terminal Warehouses
34 Armstrong Avenue, Georgetown ON, L7G 4R9
Tel: 866-485-5556   Fax: 866-485-6665
e-mail: bsisnett@gtwcanada.com

National Library of Canada Cataloguing in Publication

McKinstry, David R. I.
A swim against the tide / David R.I. McKinstry.

ISBN 0-9730949-5-8

1. McKinstry, David R. I. 2. Gay adoption—Canada. 3. Gay parents—Canada. I.
Title.

HV875.72.C3M34 2003   362.73'4'08664   C2003-902230-7

Cover and Text Design: Karen Petherick, Intuitive Design International Ltd.
Editing: Bill Belfontaine
Editing consultant: Lindalee Tracey
Cover photos: Photodisc @ 2003

Printed and Bound in Canada

Dedication

This book is dedicated to
the countless millions of orphans in the world
who may never find a loving family.

Message from the Publisher

It is most unusual for me to move my remarks from the back page of a book to the front, but this time it is well justified.

When I chose to publish this story of heartache, frustration and its message of hope as a leading social concern, I made the decision to involve myself in the very broad issue of homosexual men adopting children.

This book, by a new Canadian publisher of social issues, White Knight Publications, is but one person's involvement in that larger milieu of adoption. Members of the heterosexual, gay, lesbian, single parent and international communities live as close as next door and in the far corners of the globe. It is a complex world ruled by bureaucrats, martinets, social workers and politicians – and in many countries, people on the take. Problems range from the backsheesh (bribe or payoff) in far off lands to the roadblocks presented by the mixed ethnicity of children.

David R I McKinstry, a new author we are introducing to write on social issues, will continue to express his deep concern that the playing field needs to be levelled so that the letter of the law, service and interest be applied equally and to all. As a gay man, with his partner Michael, McKinstry determinedly slogged up and down the halls of government, adoption agencies and orphanages in Canada and foreign lands for twenty years before success honoured his endeavours.

At the end of his swim against the tide, desiring to provide a loving home for a child from India, David became the father of not one but two sons, and he and his partner Michael hope their sons will someday be joined by a little girl, or even two.

The Rattenbury/McKinstry family is one of the happiest and most loving I have had the pleasure of knowing closely – in any genre. As a straight man, I endlessly thank the wisdom and help of many members of the gay community, and my personal humanistic development, that I have been able to understand "The Community." Apprehensive as I may have appeared at first, I was openly welcomed into a loving gay family, and treated equally as a confirmed heterosexual male by the larger gay community.

Allow me to appeal to you, especially if you are straight; read this book, understand it with an open mind, let yourself start to comprehend and come to respect the wonderful qualities I have found in the relationships of the gay families I have come to know.

Bill Belfontaine
Publisher

Contents

Acknowledgements

I would like to acknowledge the talents, friendship and efforts of the people who believed in my desire to adopt children, without whom this journey would have been ten times more arduous.

To Karen Petherick of Intuitive Design International Ltd. for her talented rendition of an appealing and pertinent cover and interior design.

To Lindalee Tracey for her phenomenally precise and intuitive editing and well-timed encouragement for my writing.

To Bill Belfontaine of White Knight Publications, without whom this book wouldn't have been professionally published, I want to thank him for his boundless energy, guidance, friendship and professional support.

I boldly asked friends in the arts, journalism and film industries to be part of a round table discussion one Sunday afternoon in February 2003. With their talents freely given and their hope for my success as their guide, they showed me that rage and therapy had no place on the pages of this book. Their generous, no-holds-barred approach to critiquing my third draft challenged me to dissect and redevelop my writing. Many heartfelt thanks go to Lindalee Tracey, Kelly Walker and Ray Harsant, Kevin O'Keefe and Paritosh Mehta, Anne Hainsworth, and Darlene Montgomery.

My sincerest appreciation go out to some very special readers and supporters of my writing: Susan and Tom Harpur, Mike and Chris Rickaby, Barbara Stewart, Elizabeth and Jonathan Streeter, Joan Hill, Deb Reid, Joyce and Sandy Gammie, Vivian and Bill Heinmiller, Joyce and Joe Roberts-Mathews, Jamie and Laurie Chapman, Philip Lowry and Jeff Flamm. Thank you for your unconditional support, love and fellowship with me and our family throughout this often daring process.

To Paul and Clara for welcoming me back into their lives and being loving, attentive grandparents to Nicholas and Kolwyn. To know you is to love you.

To my mother, Dorothy McKinstry, for her endless love, support and encouragement of me throughout my life, especially while I was blindly trailblazing the paths of great resistance on my journey toward adopting children. I'm thrilled she survived the mayhem and today has two grandsons who adore her. Mum's patience, love and respect for others makes her a lighthouse in the storm for us to follow.

To our two sons, Nicholas and Kolwyn who are the joy of our labour. They have impacted and blessed our lives with their unique personalities, charm and unconditional love beyond my wildest expectations. This love our children give so easily and readily to us, has made our lives complete. I was naïve to think our children would be spared prejudice in the new millennium because it still exists. It was heartbreaking the first time we witnessed them being taunted by classmates about having gay fathers. However their loyalty, love and zealous protectiveness for their parents prevailed and they have become our heroes.

The person who needs to be acknowledged most is left for last. Michael Rattenbury, my spouse is truly an earth-bound guardian angel for me. Michael spent countless months editing, reviewing and spell-checking my manuscript on his computer. He lets me know in subtle ways that I am the light of his life. Michael's love for me and our sons continues to grow stronger day by day, regardless of the challenges I present to him hourly. He's a phenomenal parent who personifies wisdom, charm and grace under fire even as I continue to drag him along on my nightmarish adventures. Together we make a great parenting team. I look forward to growing older with Michael laughing and sharing the joy and pain of the teenage years which lie ahead of us.

David R I McKinstry

Introduction

The title of this book is a metaphor for the many attempts made to adopt children into my home from 1979 through 2000. Having been a competitive swimmer for most of my pre-adult life and attempting to swim the 32 miles across Lake Ontario, I felt swimming had to be in the title of my book.

I was born into this world in 1954 without the usual fanfare that most often accompanies hospital births – no hoops and hollering for joy, no comments about the happy healthy baby – just bright antiseptic lights hovering over the unwed teenage mother who bravely carried her fetus to term and gave me up for adoption. Shortly after my birth, I was adopted and became known as David Ross Irlam McKinstry, son of Dorothy and Eric McKinstry.

I grew up as part of a large loving and extended family, a child with many close ties to the community. It was a childhood wherein my sister and I felt like we were the richest kids on the block. Although my father worked his entire life at Outboard Marine Corporation (OMC) and never earned a huge salary as the company's purchasing agent, we owned a cottage with a ski boat on Stoney Lake; my parents took us to Toronto regularly to stay at the Royal York Hotel for weekends away; our family went on an annual winter ski holiday with two other families; and we had seasonal downhill ski memberships at a local ski resort. I thought my Dad was rich. Little did I understand during my childhood that my father, one of the middle-management team at OMC, got lots of perks, such as a brand new Evinrude 125 h.p. motor each summer and complimentary hotel weekends from his suppliers.

That set the stage for me to want to make something of myself. I grew up in the YMCA learning to swim at an early age. I became very competitive and worked hard to gain a modicum of acclaim. My favourite cousin Elizabeth ran off to Hawaii and got married in 1970. The following summer she invited me to Hawaii. We became best friends and my eyes were opened to adventure and travel. When I left my hometown of Peterborough bound for the University of Toronto in 1973, I had already travelled to Europe and Australia.

Toronto made me feel like I was a minnow in a huge ocean. I joined the Varsity swim team, became a member of Alpha Delta Phi Fraternity, and vowed I'd become a big fish in that ocean. I always had a need to be someone special, to make my parents proud, most likely a result of being an adopted kid and subconsciously feeling I had to validate my parents' decision for choosing to adopt me as their son.

By the time I was in university I knew I was not like other men. I knew the terms homosexual, queer, puffter, nancy and dorothy but I just couldn't come to terms with being categorized as one of them. After all, I kept telling myself, "I'm David McKinstry. I'm going to be famous, wealthy and important. I'm going to have a pretty wife and lots of children just like all my friends. I AM NOT GAY!"

Not wanting to own my secret sexuality, I made a supreme effort to show that I couldn't possibly be gay. I stood alongside my fraternity brothers and pitched rotten tomatoes at the transvestites who rallied outside the St. Charles Tavern on Yonge Street at Halloween. I accompanied the U of T swim team to Christmas training camp in Florida, met Becki and we had sex on the beach at New Year's Eve, she got pregnant and nine months later delivered a healthy boy who was given up for adoption. Strange how the cycle continued! At the time I gave little or no thought to the fact that I had just set in motion a second generation child, born to teenage parents, who had to be placed for adoption, yet again the burden occurring of another innocent baby.

During my third year in Jockdom (pet name we had for those of us in the Physical Education program), I met Matt, a new fraternity recruit and a varsity water polo player. Our friendship blossomed into best buddies within a short period of time. Both of us having been recently dumped by our girlfriends, we spent most of our free time together between and after classes. It was heaven on earth to know Matt and looking back, we were star-crossed lovers without ever having touched one another sexually. It had been an exceptional year of fellowship with

David R I McKinstry

Matt; our fantasy destroyed when a drunken fraternity brother remarked at a party that Matt and I were always together and loudly suggested that we must be a pair of queers. That was enough to have me nailing shut the closet door! I deliberately pulled away from Matt. Within a month Matt committed suicide, leaving letters and poems expressing his undying love for me and his bewilderment over my abrupt and often mean-spirited rejection of him. I hadn't had the guts to stand up for what I knew was true and real, and blamed myself for his death. It made me feel a sadness I had never experienced before.

I resolved to prove myself physically. In 1978 I attempted to swim Lake Ontario from the south shore at Niagara-on-the-Lake to Toronto. Within five miles of completing the 32-mile swim I was two hours ahead of the existing speed record. Huge crowds had gathered at Ontario Place to watch David McKinstry swim into the history books as the fastest man to ever swim the lake. The last few miles of water passed over the deepest and coldest portion of the lake. With no fat reserves, I passed out due to hypothermia. I awoke the next day in hospital once again the loser and left wondering if losing or coming short of my goals was becoming an all too familiar and comfortable pattern of behaviour in my life. One month later I tried again but colder waters at the end of August forced me out of the water twelve miles into the swim.

I moved to Vancouver, became a student at the University of British Columbia, fell in love with a second-year medical student named Jason. We skied together at Whistler on weekends and studied hard all week, dreaming of the day that I'd get high enough marks to be accepted into medicine. We lulled ourselves into thinking we could be the perfect medical team to settle into a small town in BC's interior, be part-time village doctors, spending the rest of our time skiing and hiking in the mountains. I shared my dream to adopt children with Jason and he enthusiastically made my dream into our dream. Our intertwined lives were the realistic embodiment of what I wish I'd had the courage to share with Matt. Less than twelve months was all I could have with Jason, his life ended on the highway to Whistler on a wintry Sunday

A Swim *Against* The Tide

morning. I grieved for months. I was determined to continue our dream to adopt children. It was left to me to adopt children alone, but no agencies would consider me, as a single man, regardless of my sexuality, to be a suitable adoptive parent.

I spent seven years in Vancouver. Coming out as a gay man in a strange city was all too easy for me. I didn't have to look over my shoulder to see if someone I knew was watching me enter a gay bar. I worked my way through school, switched from the pursuit of medicine to an MBA, took part time jobs, launched entrepreneurial pursuits and spent three summers working as the Cruise Director on an Alaskan cruise ship. Life had been fun and carefree, but late in 1986 it was time for me to return to Toronto and establish some roots.

I was 34 when I returned to Toronto in late 1986. Within a year I started to train for one more attempt to swim Lake Ontario. This time I upped the stakes – I wanted to be the first man to swim a double crossing. After thirteen months of training, three hours into the swim my calf and thigh muscles became gnarled with severe cramps. My swim ended in failure by the silhouette of the distant city's nightscape.

Several months later I met Nick, a Jesuit priest on a leave of absence from the Jesuits to decide if he should leave the Jesuits or stay on. Nick had just returned from a doctoral program at Yale and he was HIV+. I fell in love with Nick before he told me he was infected with the dreaded virus; a virus that every urban gay man in the 1980s feared would be the kiss of death.

We lived a wonderful life. We married in 1993 when it wasn't in vogue for gays to marry, and forged our own paths in life, despite mounting homophobia during the height of the young AIDS epidemic of the 1980s.

Nick had encouraged me to seek out and find my biological parents. I had, like most adopted kids, a hankering to know what my biologicals were like, from who did I get my athleticism and which of them gave me a gene pool that constantly led me into complicated maverick adventures.

A Swim Against The Tide tells my story of reuniting with my bio-

David R I McKinstry

logical parents 37 years later, meeting half-siblings, and discovering the answers to the constant questions of who, what, when, where, how and why that accompany many adopted kids into adulthood. As a result of my searching out Clara and Paul they rekindled their love after 37 years apart. This tryst continued for three years before they mutually agreed to abandoned their 40-year marriages to other people and join as husband and wife. How unique and exciting to see them acting like two teenaged lovers as they entered the last chapter of their lives. From the moment I learned of their rekindled love affair I imagined their story becoming a Hollywood screenplay starring Jack Nicholson and Shirley MacLaine.

With dignity, compassion and education, Nick helped me come to terms with my sexuality. We became a couple, raised five dogs, lived in nice homes, entertained and actively pursued alternate ways to have children. Adoption wasn't going anywhere fast, so we investigated surrogacy for several years. We spent tens of thousands of dollars on wild goose chases across the USA in an effort to adopt or find a surrogate to carry our child. Just as we became more and more encouraged that getting a child might actually happen, Nick's health took a turn for the worse. We bought a large cottage on Sandy Lake, two hours from Toronto, and lived our dream to own a Bed and Breakfast facility. We named our new business Woodhaven. After arranging for Peterborough's AIDS physician, to handle Nick's healthcare, we settled into life in rural Ontario.

One year later, only seven hours before Nick's death, we received the long awaited call from a USA lawyer who assisted gay couples to adopt. One of her clients had chosen us to be the parents of her baby when it was born. Nick died February 2, 1995 and one week later our lawyer called to say her client had been in a terrible car accident and her six-month-old fetus hadn't survived the crash. Once again, factors beyond my control prevented me from becoming a parent.

Twenty months later I met Michael Rattenbury, the Mathematics Department Head of a Toronto private school. Ironically, Michael and I had attended the same high school (albeit four years apart) yet we hadn't known of one another during our teen years. Michael remembered me having taught him swimming at the Peterborough YMCA back in the 1970s. We fell in love, renovated the former Bed and Breakfast into a larger facility, renamed Woodhaven Country Lodge and became more determined than ever to see adoption through to completion. As per God's design, Michael was the person with whom I was to finally share parenthood. We adopted two sons. One son came from an orphanage in India while our other son dropped into our lives because his Toronto mother was dying of AIDS and needed to find a home for her four-year-old son.

A Swim Against The Tide is about my efforts to adopt children. As a gay man I had many obstacles to overcome, not the least of which was rampant homophobia within the Children's Aid Society (CAS), the provincial and federal governments of Canada during the 1980s and 1990s and from the scores of family and friends who consistently refused to understand our desire to become parents.

Thankfully Michael and I were blessed to have guardian angels on our shoulders in the form of a close knit community of Sandy Lake neighbours. We had superb friends who put no limits on their friendship and my grandmother-in-waiting mother, who stood guard over us to be sure we felt supported each time an obstacle temporarily blocked our path on the road to parenthood.

The first draft of this book was full of rage and therapy. But it was cathartic to spend two years raging on about injustices done to me as a gay man wanting to adopt children in a country that refused to see past my sexuality to the anxious parent-in-waiting I had become. People and organisations that assuaged the egos of decision-makers (mostly out-of-touch male heterosexual politicians), tried to thwart my efforts and discourage me for more than 20 years. Yes, I was full of rage when I wrote the first draft. However, the wisdom of a select group of mentors wisely convinced me that rage and therapy subtexts shouldn't have top billing, burying the real issue of my fight to provide a loving home for our two adopted children. It was a revelation to me that I had infused so

David R I McKinstry

much rage onto the pages of my book. I wanted to extract my pound of flesh from all those who persisted to defame my good intentions and thwart my effort to become a loving father. In doing so I was reducing myself to the low level of those who tried to crush my spirit and enthusiasm. I hope my first foray into authordom will do my mentors justice and tell my story inspirationally to those who read it.

It is with utmost humility and candour that I share my story of swimming against the tide of prejudices, which fought to prevent me from adopting destiny's children into a loving family.

David Ross Irlam McKinstry

Daddy and Nicholar, Dad and Kolwyn at Sandy Lake.

A Swim *Against* The Tide

CHAPTER ONE

The Search

Suffering exhaustion from the cloying heat made lying in bed with the blanket over my head seem almost necessary on my first day in India, January 22, 1998. I slept soundly until 10:30 a.m. when I was startled by the strange ring of a telephone. Sleepy eyed, I jumped out of bed and grabbed it. Janice McCann, from the Canadian High Commission in Delhi had tracked me down. "How about coming over after lunch?" she suggested. We chatted about my luggage being routed to Moscow, the expense of the hotel room and being shafted by the airport taxi driver. Janice laughed over me having flown on the Russian airline Aeroflot.

"Typical of that airline. You must put in a claim for the luggage immediately and hope that it is returned to Delhi by the end of this millennium," she said half-seriously. Janice said a Consulate car would be sent along shortly to bring me to the Canadian compound.

I spent thirty minutes with Janice that afternoon reviewing the names on the list of Canadian-approved adoption agencies in Delhi. She asked if all my paperwork was in order and I told her "not yet," but that I had come anyway in order to do the necessary fact finding and introduce myself personally to the executive directors of different orphanages in Delhi. I reminded her about Blair Hart, who had worked at the High Commission until a year ago, and how he and his wife had counselled me to "Just go to India and let your presence be proof to the Indian authorities of your desire to adopt." Janice felt that this was a wise bit of advice.

I returned to the hotel and began to arrange meetings with personnel at the fifteen orphanages on my pre-approved list. Four were operated by Catholic missions and the rest were a hodgepodge of state-run and privately-operated institutions. Most orphanages had one particular country with which they had a special arrangement. In exchange for donations, that country would get first dibs on the orphans deemed acceptable by international standards. Children with deformities or those of poor health were never considered. The lighter skinned orphans would be first offered for adoption to infertile Indian couples domestically then to Indians living abroad. Darker skinned children were always offered to non-Indian international families. Considering India's population of nearly one billion people, 160 million are referred to as untouchables or the lowest class or caste of people. They do the menial jobs of cleaning out public washrooms using their bare hands, sweeping streets and removing animal and human corpses randomly discarded around every shantytown. Many orphans from this untouchable caste end up in orphanages and are first on the list to be adopted internationally. Muslim refugees from Bangladesh and Pakistan lived in makeshift camps around the city. If very young refugee children became separated from their parents they would either die as abandoned waifs unable to fend for themselves or be placed in state-run orphanages. Medical care for refugees was practically non-existent. Therefore if a single parent of three children died in a back alley of tuberculosis or any other disease, those children would either live on the streets as beggars, perish from malnutrition or, if *very* fortunate, become wards of an orphanage with a long list of international couples desperate to adopt children.

It became apparent from telephone calls to set up interviews, that a group of kind-hearted, wealthy Indian matrons had established several

David R I McKinstry

orphanages around the city, which were shown on my list. My interviews were to begin the next day and continue until I had seen every possible site of available children. Around supper I hailed a taxi and headed into the centre of Delhi to check out some inexpensive hotels in the Connaught Circle district.

Connaught Circle was in the hub of the downtown business and financial district. It had been a well-known marketplace for tourists for over a century. It had lavish five-star hotels for business people, smaller hostels used by backpacking vacationers, and everything inbetween. India's Independence Day celebrations would soon be happening on January 26th making New Delhi alive with revellers. Many of the hostels I viewed were full and those that had a room looked so seedy that I couldn't trust the locks on the doors. One place, the Jagoso Inn, provided breakfast coupons to overnight guests. The price was about $50 US per night for a bedroom with a TV that had two Hindi and one English language channels, a bathroom with cockroaches and an open air hallway that ran across the side of the building. The bed looked comfortable enough but the slate floor looked grungy and in need of a good scrub and disinfectant. I paid a deposit and said I would be back the next day to check in around noon. The woman behind the registration desk reminded me of Yvonne DeCarlo's character Lily in *The Munsters* TV show of the 1960s. Herman had to be around somewhere, I thought, as I walked back to the street for something to eat. Connaught Circle had a plethora of eateries to choose from but I wanted something familiar. My choices were Indian style Kentucky Fried Chicken or Pizza Hut.

The Pizza Hut line-up was ten deep when I put my name in the reservation book. Standing in line gave foreigners an opportunity to find someone that spoke their language for a shared dining experience. Of all the possible languages being spoken in that line up, I heard no one speaking English. The waitering staff were all fair skinned young men who resembled a group of happy university students working their way

A Swim *Against* The Tide

through college. There were no women on staff and it brought home the strangeness of this land where women's rights remain draconian.

I saw no sign of anyone gay in the shops or restaurants but I did see a small group of young men from Australia wearing T-shirts that read "THE KINGS CROSS and so is this Queen" who came into Pizza Hut a while after me. They were so overtly feminine and were queer as three-dollar bills! A modernly dressed Indian family seated near my table just stared at them as they sashayed past our section of the restaurant, leaving many of the waitering staff chuckling and commenting amongst themselves. I smiled at the thought of their youthfulness and laissez-faire attitude to onlookers yet I sensed the looks of disdain from the locals to be worrisome and threatening.

After a wordless supper sharing a table with an older Italian couple I couldn't communicate with, I paid my bill, left the restaurant and headed back to the hotel in a yellow taxicab. I asked the driver if he would take me on a tour of the city before we got back to the hotel. Vinod was 30 years old and had been driving a taxi for three years. He told me his brother had moved to the United States and was a computer technician in Seattle. Vinod was trying to save enough money to visit his brother within the next few years. I chatted readily with Vinod about my reasons for coming to India and he said he had driven many times for foreigners who had come to Delhi to adopt children. While driving around to see the parliament buildings and the rich districts of Delhi, we passed many open-air markets lining alleys and main thoroughfares. One street reminded me of Forest Hill Road in Toronto. It was lined with at least fifty huge palatial compounds each a foreign consulate. The architecture of the Canadian Consulate reminded me of a bland 1960s style three storey insurance building from the suburbs of Toronto; the vast colourful gardens and stately looking lawns being its only redeeming feature. Each compound had its own wrought iron fence or concrete six-foot high enclosure, closely guarded by military personnel.

Vinod stopped the car at a roadside bazaar and I got out to watch a snake charmer working his skills on a huge cobra. A small crowd of

David R I McKinstry

internationals had gathered to watch his act and was mesmerized by his control over this venomous snake. After five minutes of teasing and taunting the snake, the act was over and all of us in the crowd put rupees down on the blanket beside him. I returned to Vinod's taxi feeling weak from the heat, and asked him to take me to the hotel without delay.

Vinod asked if I had found any children to adopt. I explained that this trip was really just a fact-finding mission and I had interviews arranged with orphanages in Delhi for most of the following three days. Vinod suggested I hire him on a daily basis to take me to all my appointments, as it would be far cheaper and faster than hailing new taxis to each destination. Vinod also asked if I would be interested in meeting some of his academic friends who were social workers and could help facilitate finding children for adoption. I said that I was very interested in any leads he could present and that I would pay him handsomely for any introductions to people who could help process an adoption. Vinod told me he would be waiting for me at the front entrance of the hotel to help with my move to Connaught Circle in the morning and then he would drive me to my orphanage meetings. I asked him for a daily rate and he said 2000 rupees would be fair (which I later discovered was twice the municipality's legislated rate for taxis to charge).

I packed my bags and wrote the addresses of my appointments for the following day in bold print. After a shower I turned on the TV and watched a *Law and Order* rerun on the English channel. My stomach had been upset for the past 24 hours, and before I got into bed I had my first of many dates with the porcelain throne. Aeroflot had not returned any of my numerous calls about my lost luggage. I was tired of washing my underwear, socks and shirts by hand nightly. My carefully packed medications for diarrhea, upset stomach, ulcer problems and simple headaches were in Moscow.

At breakfast I'd eaten fruit and toast, and during the day I had consumed two cups of coffee. I'd been told not to eat soft-fleshed fruit or drink unboiled water. I had bought bottled water to be safe but discovered later that it was often tampered with; locals filled non-sterile

A Swim *Against* The Tide

bottles with unpurified water. I'd consumed at least four bottles that day and it was obvious that my guts were churning because of something foreign in my system. I had been sick all night. By the next morning I was exhausted and my face had the pale look of someone who hadn't slept in days. Suffering from diarrhea, upset stomach and the heat, I was not in great humour when Vinod buzzed my room to say he was there to help me move to the slum hotel. I checked out and told Vinod that I wasn't feeling well. He asked if I needed to go to a clinic but I told him that I would just need to stop frequently. I managed through sheer desperation to make it to my new hotel without soiled underwear. I fled down the hallway to my room and prayed the key would open the latch quickly. Unfortunately it didn't. I spent the next forty minutes sitting on the toilet watching trapped cockroaches running around the interior of the cracked bathtub and a hundred flies hovering around. The heat was searing in this room and by the time I was ready to head back downstairs my washed underwear was dry enough to wear again.

Vinod was standing outside my bedroom door when I emerged looking ashen. He handed me two tablets and told me he had bought me some medicine to help the diarrhea. He said it was safe to swallow the pills and that they would help me almost immediately. I asked him how much I owed him for the pills, half thinking that he would just say, "Don't worry about it." But Vinod told me he had paid 50 rupees for the pills and I angrily told him to tack it onto my bill at the end of the day. I handed him the list of five orphanages I had appointments with that day and after scanning the list Vinod indicated he knew where each of them was located, except for one Catholic run orphanage. He stopped for gas at a downtown station and discovered that the unknown Catholic mission was only a few blocks away from my previous hotel.

Traffic and an upset stomach dogged my day. The diarrhea stopped immediately, just as Vinod had said it would. What a relief. The thought of having to stop and squat in one of the roadside outdoor toilets made me want to wretch. Farm animals walked everywhere and traffic some-

David R I McKinstry

how managed to swerve and avoid collisions with cows meandering on roadways.

The first orphanage was a state-run facility, Delhi Council for Child Welfare. The building rose up in front of us as we drove into an upscale neighbourhood with white stucco houses, each lot divided by rows of 50-foot high canopied trees. The narrow streets of this cul-de-sac were cobblestoned and many labourers swept the streets spotless, taking home only a few rupees for their daylong effort.

Nisha, the director of this facility, was a stunningly beautiful thirty-ish woman. Her kind and gentle demeanour was much appreciated as she greeted me and then led me to her office. She was the first Indian to genuinely smile at me since I'd landed in this country. Most of the locals I'd met had their agenda set to rip me off as much as possible and I was becoming impatient and annoyed by their efforts.

Nisha had just placed a child the previous month with a family in Ottawa and she was happy to see more Canadians coming to India to adopt. She scanned my file and asked me thought-provoking questions while frequently making felicitous observations about my readiness to adopt children. However, after thirty minutes of discussions, she announced that she wouldn't be able to help me as the orphanage's Charter denied single people, widowed or not, to adopt their children. She suggested I visit Mother Teresa's Missionaries of Charity Orphanage just up the road. I told her it was the next orphanage on my list. Nisha asked if I was Christian and gave me a warm bright smile when I replied, "Indeed I am." After a short walk around the compound full of nicely dressed and happy looking children playing under shade trees, she bid me goodbye and good wishes for a successful adoption.

Vinod drove me directly to the Missionaries of Charity compound. A garden worker opened the gate for the taxi to enter and fifty pre-school children and two nuns instantly surrounded us. Vinod spoke to the first nun who motioned him to move the car forward and for me to follow her to the office. The taxi drove slowly through the crowd of excited children playing tag with the car. Once inside the building, I was

A Swim *Against* The Tide

directed to sit down in a small waiting room at the far end of a dimly lit corridor. As we entered the hallway leading to the waiting room, I gazed into a large room on my right filled with cribs housing at least 50 cooing or crying babies. The dank cool air of this old cinderblock building was a relief from the oppressive heat outside in the courtyard, yet I was left wondering if these babies had ever seen the moon and the sun or had the chance to breath fresh morning air.

The Mother Superior, known as Sister Joyce, an Indian Christian in full habit, came to greet me. I mentioned Nisha's name from the orphanage down the road and told Sister Joyce I'd come to see her about adopting children. She showed no facial expression and her locked tight lips gave me the impression I was in the presence of a no-nonsense nun who wouldn't waste time on niceties. She motioned for me to follow her into an office. She sat down at a huge desk, looked at the paperwork I'd handed her and after five silent minutes said, "What you want?"

I told her my well rehearsed story (the version that the Canadian adoption officials had dreamed up) – that I was a widower. I said that my deceased wife, Nicci, begged me prior to her death to go ahead with plans to adopt children from India. I told Sister Joyce that I loved children and was able to afford to give children a wonderful, loving home in Canada. After twenty minutes talking about my reasons for wanting to adopt she began to loosen up. However, she said that being a widower still meant I was a single man in the eyes of the courts and very few orphanages would go through the hassles in order to give me a child.

"Why not you get married again?" she asked. I just shrugged my head and handed her photos of Woodhaven and my life in Canada. After a quick gaze at the pictures and a chuckle over the dogs she said, "I think you good man. Want to see children?" I stood up and nodded eagerly.

She walked in front of me and led me into a room like the nursery I'd passed when I first entered the building. Sister Joyce informed me that three helpers were preparing lunchtime formula and pablum for 60 babies and if I wanted to help feed one or more of them I could. I was overjoyed at being asked to help care for these youngsters.

David R I McKinstry

"Are these babies to be adopted? Would I be able to adopt one or two of your babies?" I asked her wide-eyed with joy at holding these precious bundles.

"These babies orphaned at birth and it OK for Canadian to adopt our babies. Maybe you like one of these children?" she smiled up at me, nodding her head a few times. It sounded like I had made a first good impression and she might be considering me to adopt one of her wards. My gosh! I had no idea it would be this easy. One of the helpers motioned for me to follow her into the kitchen and she put a bowl of pablum in my hands. Sister Joyce handed me a baby from one of the cribs and told me to feed this little boy. I spent the next hour feeding children from the cribs amidst the smiles and chuckling of the nuns and helpers. I wondered what they were saying to each other about this Canadian man who wanted so fervently to adopt children.

Vinod was brought into the nursery by the nun who had greeted us at the gates of the compound. He wondered how I was doing and saw me feeding a baby. While he stood there watching I had two or three youngsters crawling up my pant legs and another two children scrambling up my arms. They just didn't want to let go of a prospective parent. As I fumbled to try and balance all the children, the supervising nun walked past me toward a young boy, who looked about three years old, trying to escape from his crib. She smacked him across the face and pushed him back into the crib. He didn't cry or wince. I was horrified but I knew if I confronted the nun, I would be told to leave and not to return.

Vinod smiled as he stood beside me in the nursery and asked if one of these children was going to be my baby. I could feel my smile widening from ear to ear and I told him that I thought the Mother Superior liked me and she had invited me to visit the children and help feed them. Vinod smiled and said, "You look happy with baby." He told me that if we were going to make the next appointment we had to leave within thirty minutes or be late.

I placed each child back into its respective crib. Each one in succession shrieked and cried while reaching up to be held again. It was

A Swim *Against* The Tide

painfully obvious that these institutionalized children didn't have much tender time in human arms on a daily basis, except for ten minutes of feeding three times each day. I walked back through the long inner hallway past an office where Sister Joyce was talking with a very blonde haired Caucasian man and woman.

"They from Norway," she said as I peaked my head into the room to say goodbye. I told her I had to go to another appointment but asked if I could come back later to help with suppertime. She smiled and told me to come back later to help feed the children. As I left the building and entered into the compound, I was swarmed by a hundred children all looking to be less than five years of age. They were playing in the dirt piles of the compound and when they saw me they rushed over and grabbed at me to pick them up. On one hand it was exhilarating to have all this attention from so many adoptable children, but Vinod came over and pulled the children off me so I could get into the taxi.

"They want to go with you," he said. "These children always do this to foreign people who might adopt them." To actually experience clinging children trying to climb up my pant legs into my arms was emotionally painful and I could feel tears welling in my eyes. The taxi drove out of the compound amidst wails from the children who hadn't yet touched me. I wondered how the nuns and helpers managed to maintain such calm demeanours surrounded by orphans clamouring for constant attention.

Vinod finished the rounds of orphanages on time and by 5:00 p.m. I had visited five different institutions. Only the Missionaries of Charity orphanage had given me any indication that I might be considered as an adoptive parent. Two Catholic missions had bluntly and curtly refused to consider me as a single parent for their children. Another state-run group told me that due to infertility being on the rise in India, that Indian couples and those Indian nationals living abroad were given first right of refusal of their children. I would be a last resort due to the light skinned children they adopted out of that orphanage.

David R I McKinstry

I returned to Sister Joyce's compound and told Vinod that I would stay for a few hours feeding the children and he agreed to wait when I told him I'd treat him to supper.

I entered the nursery and found several older nuns helping to feed the children and change diapers of those standing at the sides of the cribs. If a child wasn't being fed, he or she was crying alone. Some cribs had two babies sharing the same space. Without delay I grabbed a bib and a bowl of stew from a large pot in the adjoining kitchen area and began to feed babies in the row nearest me. Some of the nuns were quite brisk in handling the babies. I watched one nun walk down a centre aisle of cribs and slap 18-month-old babies on the cheeks for standing up in their cribs. I was appalled by this abuse and again had to grit my teeth in silent horror.

I began to cradle and sing to a pair of crib-sharing babies simultaneously. Two nuns walked by and smiled like angels looking down from on high. I was desperately seeking to make a good impression on the nuns and Sister Joyce. As I looked into the eyes of the babies, known as Elsbit and Lampai, cradled in my arms, I whispered, "I'd take the two of you home to Canada tomorrow if Mother Superior would let me."

Mother Teresa's Orphanage. Lampai and Elsbit standing in crib.
These were the two children I hoped to adopt.

The babies smiled up at me and then nodded off to sleep. Several attempts to put the babies back into the crib failed as they awakened with one hell of a sound every time I tried to place them back in the crib. My arms were falling asleep and I knew Vinod was waiting for me. Finally the babies were sound asleep and I quickly placed them into the crib at opposite ends. I bent down and kissed them goodnight and told them I would like to be their dad. I said a little prayer to God and sent a silent prayer to Nick that if these two babies were to be mine would he please let me have a sign.

As I passed through the hallway leading out to the compound Sister Joyce walked around the corner surprising me. We were both taken aback at almost running into one another. "You are good with babies. Someday you be good father," she smiled and walked past me into her office. I hopped into Vinod's taxi absolutely alive with my wonderful experience and told him to head to a restaurant where we would share a grand meal.

Over supper Vinod told me he had made some good contacts with adoption officials who wanted to meet with me the next day. I asked if they were on my list and he said they worked for the state and babies could be placed through any of the state-approved orphanages on my list. The catch was that it would cost me $2,500 US dollars up front to bribe the assistant of the man who would make the decision about me adopting a child. I was blown away by this suggestion that I pay some guy's assistant such a ransom just to put my paperwork on the top of the day's pile of adoption papers. "Well, lets wait until I know if Sister Joyce will give me some children. Hopefully I will know by the end of tomorrow if I will get two of her children," I naively said to Vinod as he stuffed his mouth with food. With supper quickly over, Vinod drove me back to Connaught Circle and dropped me at the hotel. I was barely out of the door before I was swarmed by a dozen men and women begging for food or money. I yelled back into the cab to Vinod and asked him to pick me up after breakfast for another day of visiting orphanages.

I was too excited to sleep right away so I wrote a two-page letter to Michael which I faxed the next morning. My room wasn't air-conditioned

David R I McKinstry

but it had a big ceiling fan that whirled constantly and kept me comfortable. The hot water taps didn't work so I shampooed my underwear, socks and shirt in cold water under the tub faucet. I had barely settled into bed and turned out the light, my mind whirling with the day's emotion, when my doorknob jiggled. I was so stunned that for a split second it seemed like I must have been dreaming but ten seconds later it rattled again and I heard someone pushing against the locked door. I bolted upright and yelled, "Hey, stop that," in a loud deep voice. Someone ran down the hallway and disappeared. I put a chair in front of the door and braced it under the doorknob to further decrease any risk that someone could break in during the night. I fell asleep wondering if $50 US per night was worth it. Staying in a better hotel would give me a heightened sense of security that I wouldn't get here. But I had to be prudent about saving money for important adoption costs and paying for me to stay in Delhi for up to four more weeks. My luggage still hadn't been traced and I was sceptical about ever seeing my belongings again. But the humour was that any thief would find it slim pickings in my room if he did break in. I had my money pouch practically shoved up the crack of my butt just in case I'd have to make a run for it in the middle of the night.

Vinod drove me to three orphanage appointments the next morning. Not one gave me any hope of adopting children from their organizations. Around lunchtime we drove into the compound of the Missionaries of Charity and were met by the Sister Joyce alone in the courtyard. As if she had been waiting for us to arrive, she walked up to the taxi window and said, "You healthy man. Go find new wife and make babies. You don't get any of our children. Sorry but you go now."

I was stunned. She turned to walk away but I flung open the door of the taxi and ran around in front of her and stood looking down at her. I could feel a swell of mucus-like anger rising in my throat. She halted immediately and looked up at me with an expressionless face, reminding me of the first time I'd met her a few days ago.

"I want those two babies I cradled last night. My paperwork is good

A Swim *Against* The Tide

and I have shown you my sincerity. Why won't you give me children to adopt?" I asked, trying not to appear too confrontational.

"You go find new wife, these babies for infertile people, you make babies of your own," her brows furrowed as she repeated herself. "Now you go out in taxi." She slipped past me and into the side door and I could hear the latch lock.

I stood alone in the compound in shock. Vinod had witnessed this scene and put his arm around my shoulder, "I will find you children to adopt." I allowed him to usher me back into the taxi and we drove off leaving a cloud of smoke behind. I was devastated. I really had believed that those two babies would be mine today. Had I just been an extra pair of hands to relieve nuns from two days of feedings in the nursery? Had she somehow figured out I was gay? How could she be so cold and heartless to dismiss me so crudely?

Vinod kept me in a constant supply of anti-diarrhea medications, which kept my bowels intact during the day. I still got up once or twice in the night feeling that I wanted to throw up.

Vinod was driving quickly along the street leading back to the highway and barely missed colliding with the calf of a cow that suddenly jumped out into our traffic lane. "You want to meet adoption official I told you about yesterday?" he asked gingerly. He knew my emotions were raw and I was on the verge of dissolving into a pool of anger and tears. I didn't even get to say goodbye to Elsbit and Lampai, I kept saying to myself.

I agreed to pay the $2,500 US to get my paperwork into the hands of a state adoption official. We stopped at a State of India Bank and I got $2,500 in US funds from the $10,000 in US traveller cheques in my waistband wallet. Vinod drove me to a very officious looking office tower near the parliament buildings and told me to follow and bring my backpack full of paperwork that I took wherever I went. I was led into the air-conditioned lobby and we took the elevator to the sixth floor. Other than most of the people working behind desks being Indian, the elevator opened up into an office area that could easily have been located

David R I McKinstry

in any downtown Toronto office tower. Vinod took me down a long corridor to a small lobby and told me to sit and wait for him to return. I held the wad of money tightly and stuffed my hand deep into a pocket of my trousers. Within a few minutes Vinod returned with a pleasant-looking man, about 40, who had a somewhat nervous smile. Vinod introduced us and then bluntly said to give the man the envelope. I understood this to mean to give him the money discreetly. I had looked around and as no one was near us, I nervously shoved the money into his waiting hand. It disappeared quickly into his pocket as he smiled and waved us into an adjoining office. He followed us in and went on the opposite side of the desk and asked to see my paperwork. It took him several minutes to examine my documents and he asked if he could take copies of them. He excused himself and left Vinod and I alone to ponder what would happen next. It didn't take long for him to return with copies of my documents and he began to write notes on my copied material. "How will this work?" I asked politely. "Can you guarantee me a child to adopt?"

Introduced to me as Mr. Vasnani, he looked up and stopped writing on the documents long enough to say that I would get one chance on the pile for each $2,500 given to him. He explained that it was really the luck of the draw. If his boss picked up my documents, one of only five to six he would examine in a given day, my chances were very good that I'd be given immediate clearance to adopt a child through CVARA, the Indian child welfare offices. He asked how long I would be staying in Delhi and I told him as long as it would take to find children. He made a sinister smile loaded with greed which gave me the creeps but I couldn't let on that I was nervous about being milked for more money than the $2,500 US. He told me he would contact Vinod by phone twice each afternoon and tell him if I had won the prize. If my documents weren't chosen, Mr. Vasnani would put them in front of a different official and put them on the top of the pile and so on until someone gave me the clearance. This was hardly honest but I felt trapped and didn't have many other options. I kept telling myself that I had to do everything possible

— 15 —

A Swim *Against* The Tide

to prove my 100% commitment to this task of finding a child. I wasn't going home a loser this time. $2500 seemed like a drop in the bucket if it meant saving a child from the iron grip of this god-forsaken city.

I learned quickly that in India money talks and without "backsheesh" (Indian word for a bribe) you get nowhere fast. I was extremely apprehensive about how long it would last, but most of all, would I be successful?

Vinod drove me to the six remaining orphanages on my list. I decided to drop in rather than make appointments, as it didn't seem that appointments were necessary. I wanted answers now and didn't want to have to find a phone booth and make a dozen calls to arrange appointment times. The first four places on my list were unprofessional looking dumps and I was almost glad to discover that they didn't have any available children for overseas adoptions. The last place was an hour's drive away. Vinod asked me if I really wanted to continue on and I told him we had to check it out. He stopped at a garage and filled the car with gas, then used his cell phone to call Mr. Vasnani. It didn't come as any surprise that Vinod was told that I hadn't been approved but Vasnani would put me on another official's pile if I paid another $2,500 bribe. My options were dwindling and I felt I had no choice but to keep trying with the government insider. I agreed and before we headed off to the last orphanage on my list, we went to a bank to exchange traveller's cheques for US dollars and deliver the money to Mr. Vasnani.

It was 3:00 p.m. and we were getting caught in heavy traffic. We stopped at a set of lights and I became absorbed by the sight of the hundred or so beggars milling around the cars and taxis asking passengers for money. Some of the young mothers carrying babies in their arms couldn't have been much older than thirteen or fourteen. With horror I watched one young mother thrust the hand of her baby into the car window and wave the child's bloody hand, missing two fingers, in front of my face. Vinod opened his door and cursed and shouted to chase the beggar away. He saw the look of amazement in my eyes and told me that often these refugee beggars would routinely

David R I McKinstry

mutilate the hands of their babies because foreigners would take pity on them and give a lot of money through their windows. I looked for signs of this barbarism and at every traffic stop I witnessed ten to twelve babies with recently chopped off digits, blood still bubbling and oozing from the wounds as they screamed in pain. The agony of the mutilated babies seemed to fall on deaf ears as the young teenaged mothers raced between car windows at every stoplight. Using well-rehearsed pathetic winces they showed off their wounded children to the mortified foreigners in hopes of getting a few rupees with which to buy food.

Vinod told me we were entering Vasant Vihar, a wealthy area where very rich people lived. The orphanage office was located in the home of a wealthy matron. It didn't take long to find. We rang the bell at the gated entrance and a woman appeared to open the gate. Vinod said he would stay with the taxi. I told the lady that I was here to see Mrs. Raghunath and she smiled and told me in broken English to follow her.

Mrs. Raghunath had only received her approval status from the Canadian Immigration one month prior to my arrival. She was thrilled to have her first Canadian consider adopting one of her children. She presented herself as a warm and lovely lady in her traditional sari, her graying hair cut short and a shawl draped over her shoulders. She said she found it quite chilly these days as she caught me gazing at the shawl, "I know you think it is hot today but I find January weather in the late afternoons to be chilly."

From the moment we met, Mrs. Raghunath was kind, gentle and encouraging with her remarks. She gave me an overview of the Indian adoption rules and told me I would probably never be allowed to adopt more than one child at a time. The staff at her orphanage had been rebels over the past few years in their fight to standardize and legitimize adoption procedures in India. Mrs. Raghunath told me she was on a judicial board that attempted to make reforms and she had received a slap on the wrist recently, basically being told to lay low and stop being a radical reformer. She offered me tea and asked me to tell her about myself. Between the facts and fiction behind my efforts to adopt

A Swim *Against* The Tide

children, she informed me that should I be eligible to adopt from India. She wouldn't be allowed to offer me a daughter, but perhaps a boy about five years-old. I asked why I wouldn't get a daughter and she said too many wealthy businessmen from Thailand and Saudi Arabia had come to India over the years to adopt little girls who ended up working in the sex trade. The Indian government had passed a law stating that no single men, Indians or internationals, would be allowed to adopt daughters. I was horrified.

All the time we chatted she was scanning my documentation, making notes and asking many questions. "Would you consider adopting siblings? How old a child would you consider? I have a little boy who is ten years old and his mother can't keep him. She has asked me to find him a home out of India. He is a nice looking boy, lighter skinned and very smart. Would a boy like this interest you?" she inquired. I told her I really felt fate had brought me to her doorstep and I would follow her instinct. I said I had hoped a younger child might be best for me, but I would entertain all suggestions from her. After an hour her secretary came in and spoke quietly to her in Hindi. Mrs. Raghunath said a Spanish couple was here to formalize the adoption papers for a daughter they were adopting.

"I am glad you came to see me today. I can tell by looking into your eyes that you would be a great father. My best advice to you is to go back to Canada now. Don't spend any more time or money in Delhi this trip. Guaranteed, I will call you within three months about a son. Get your paperwork in order and send me all the documents when you receive your final clearances," she said looking deep into my eyes. I was dumbfounded by her candour, warmth and suggestion that she would call me in three months to come back for a son she would find for me. I thanked her profusely and for the first time since arriving in Delhi I was calm and happy. I was so dizzy with elation that I felt a tear slip from the corner of my eye. Mrs. Raghunath came and put her arm on mine and walked me to her gate. As she paused she turned to me and repeated again the words that I still hear so clearly in my mind, "Go home David.

David R I McKinstry

I will call you. Be confident that I will call you soon. And one word of advice, do not try to buy off public or government officials in India. You will lose your money and it could work against your efforts to adopt a child." I wondered if this woman had telepathic powers. I wanted to hug her but thought I shouldn't be too forward. I smiled and clasped her hand in mine and said I believed her and I would go home and await her call. She turned and walked away and I watched her return to her lovely house, awestruck by the peace I felt in my heart for the first time in longer than I could remember.

Vinod noticed the difference in my demeanour the moment I entered his taxi. I told him what Mrs. Raghunath had said and how good I felt about her. We had one more orphanage in this area I wanted to check out. I told Vinod to drive to The Church of North India Orphanage, about seven miles from Mrs. Raghunath's office. There I met Mr. Akeday. This visit lasted less than ten minutes as he explained that in the last year ninety percent of his orphans went to Indian families, and international adoptions were always arranged with pre-determined Catholic homes. I thanked him kindly and put a $20 US bill in the collection plate inside the door of the Church and told him to buy the children ice cream as a treat.

I returned to the taxi and told Vinod to drive me back to the hotel. Vinod looked into his rear view mirror and told me that Mr. Vasnani had just telephoned him while I was out of the car and said that my paperwork was not among the pile chosen for his boss to read the next morning. If I wanted to continue it would require another repeat of the $2,500 bribe. Vinod could tell without me answering that I was through with that rip-off artist Mr. Vasnani and his bogus efforts to help me adopt. I was beginning to wonder how much kickback from my $5,000 US went into Vinod's pocket. I really felt like a fool and the warning words of Mrs. Raghunath echoed loudly in my head. If only I'd started at the bottom of the list! I would book a flight out of this god-forsaken country as soon as possible.

I returned to the hotel, paid Vinod his wages and asked him to check

A Swim *Against* The Tide

back with me in the morning, as I would need a ride to the airport when I got a confirmed flight. As I passed by the receptionist of this dive of a hotel, I noticed a sign saying FAX Machine. I asked if I could send a fax and what the cost would be for a two page fax to Canada. The cost was reasonable and I sent Michael the two-page letter I had written the night before. It had been one hell of a day filled with wildly extreme emotions. This morning I felt like crawling under a rock because Sister Joyce had refused to consider me as a prospective parent for those two beautiful children, now seven hours later, I knew that Mrs. Raghunath was my ticket to parenthood.

Knowing Janice McCann often worked late at the High Commission office, I telephoned her direct number. She answered and I gave her an update of my week so far. I mentioned that I had met a man at CVARA who said he could help me find an adoptable child. I didn't mention the bribes.

"That man doesn't have any authority to get you a clearance, nor is his office responsible for international adoption paperwork. He is totally bogus, David," she said. "I'm surprised he didn't hit you up for a hefty fee referred to as backsheesh." She laughed heartily in the phone and I was glad I hadn't divulged how easily I had been swindled by Mr. Vasnani. I really didn't care at this point. I asked if she had any contacts with travel agents that could get me the hell out of Delhi really quick. Janice gave me two numbers for travel agents she regularly used for international flights. I thanked her for her warm and friendly help over the past few months.

For supper I went to a small café next to the Pizza Hut for real Indian food. The meal was terrific and after 45 minutes I left and headed back to the Jagoso Inn. The cooler night air was a welcome relief from the heat of the day. I found myself walking along unfamiliar streets, and became unsure where I was within the fog settling over the city. I hailed a rickshaw and asked the skeleton between the shafts to take me back to the inn. After twenty minutes of riding through back alleys and

David R I McKinstry

unfamiliar streets, we arrived at the opposite corner of Connaught Circle. I had been duped again, obvious to me that I had just taken one wrong turn and was only minutes from the Jagoso Inn but the rickshaw driver, like everyone I met with their hand out, had taken me on a long tour just to get a higher taxi fee out of me. I shook my head in dismay as I paid him and went upstairs to my room, closed the door and prayed I'd get out of this city in one piece.

By late the next morning I was confirmed on a flight out of Delhi in two days, just prior to the Independence Day celebrations. I put in time walking around Connaught Circle and repeatedly making calls to Aeroflot's office at the Delhi airport about my luggage. To my amazement I got a return call from Aeroflot informing me that my luggage had been re-routed from Moscow and could be picked up on my next trip to the airport. What could be more fitting in the upside-down world of India, just as I'm leaving Delhi I'll get my bags back. How I longed to feel a different shirt on my back, to have clean underwear on again, and be able to use my medications. It hit me sitting there at that moment, that what I had experienced for the past four days, with only one shirt to my name, was exactly the way many of the street people of India experience 365 days of every year. I felt a twinge of conscience at the opulence of having luggage full of a variety of clothing waiting for me at the airport.

I faxed Michael saying I was leaving Delhi the next afternoon for the long return trip across the Pacific. I told him I would be home within a few days and gave him an overview of my meeting with Mrs. Raghunath and her orphanage Children of the World. My diarrhea returned with a vengeance the night before I departed Delhi and I wondered if I'd make the hour-long ride to the airport without soiling in my pants.

I decided to spend my last day in Delhi visiting temple sites and the zoo. It was a hot afternoon and I didn't stray far off the shady winding paths throughout. I met a young Irish businessman also killing time. Ironically this was his last day in Delhi before heading off to the airport

A Swim *Against* The Tide

for a late evening flight home via Europe. We decided to share a cab to the various temple sites. He was a computer specialist in Delhi to recruit a few talented Indians for his company. He was very intrigued by my adoption trip and at 7 p.m. we stopped for supper back in Connaught Circle at Pizza Hut. By 8 p.m. we were in a cab bound for our separate journeys.

My passport and other documents were hidden in my waist pouch. I claimed my bags from the Aeroflot counter and bid a heartfelt goodbye to my Irish friend. Once alone, I immediately checked things over to see if anything had been stolen from my luggage. Nothing was disturbed and I grabbed for my Imodium pills and tossed two back without a second thought. I had three hours to wait until my check-in time so I just walked and walked through the many terminals of this sooty, humid airport. Check-in time finally arrived and I nestled into the departures line-up. I gladly flounced my ticket down on the counter and the agent laughed and asked if I was happy to be heading home to Canada. We exchanged pleasantries while she finished stamping my ticket and checking in my luggage. She directed me to the departure gate a hundred feet away and told me to present my documents to the duty officers. I walked hurriedly toward the departure desk with my carry-on bag slung over my shoulder and documents in hand. I couldn't believe I was actually heading home.

After five minutes in the waiting line, it was my turn to hand documents to the officer. Being suspicious of potential screw-ups I felt nervous as I waited for him to hand back my documents and direct me through the gate to the waiting lounge. Not a minute later, he looked up and said, "Passport please." I was sure I had handed him my passport with my ticket. It wasn't in my document pouch. I could feel beads of sweat beginning to flow down my forehead. I frantically looked on the ground around me and then ran back to the baggage check-in counter to ask the agent if I had left my passport with her by mistake. She immediately looked as distraught as I felt.

Without any further hesitation I yelled loudly, "Police! Police!

David R I McKinstry

Someone has stolen my passport!" Within seconds everyone around me was double checking to be sure they had their passports and two police officers came over and asked what had happened. I told them my flight was leaving in 45 minutes and my passport had been stolen between checking in my bags and walking 100 feet to the departures gate. Several junior officers came running over and in Hindi the senior officer told them something which sent the junior officers running off at high speed.

"You had better retrieve your baggage from the plane because without your passport you won't be leaving tonight," the senior officer said. "We must file a report in the office quickly. Please follow me." He touched my arm and indicated that I should go with him. I couldn't believe this was happening to me. I was returning to Canada with less than $50 in my wallet. My VISA card was well over its $5,000 limit. I'd spent all of my money and had nothing but the bills in my wallet. Now I was within inches from getting out of this god-forsaken country and my passport is stolen. Could I afford to spend even one night here? My remaining money wouldn't get me back into the city, give me accommodation for a few more days, food and taxi fare to get around to the various offices I'd need to visit to have a new passport issued. I cursed this country – I just wanted to get the hell out!

The senior officer escorted me silently and quickly to the airport security office. I knew I'd be sick to my stomach as I could feel the urge to puke getting stronger. He directed me to a washroom 100 feet away. All I wanted to find was an empty stall but when I walked in and found myself looking at rows of men squatting over holes in the floor I was sure I'd arrived in Hell. I hung onto the wall and puked in a corner hole. I wasn't going to linger waiting for another bout. I knew if I stayed in this rudimentary public bathroom a second longer I'd end up fainting and falling into the hole head first. I returned quickly to the security office feeling destitute. I sat down and noticed the officer behind the counter speaking in Hindi but looking directly at me. A moment later, a burly looking man walked out of a side office and asked in perfect English, "Are you Mr. David McKinstry from Canada?" Stunned, I looked up at him and said I was.

"We found your passport on floor of the terminal by the exit doors. It was probably dropped by accident by whoever stole it," he said. He opened my passport and examined the photo for a moment and then told me I should be more careful and if I hurried I would still make my flight. I flew out of his office after thanking him and his staff. I made it through the departures gate and down the ramp onto the plane with ten minutes to spare. I was either the luckiest person in the world that day or it had been another one of God's tests to see how much more angst I could withstand.

The return trip across Southeast Asia and over the Pacific Ocean to Canada was physically exhausting yet emotionally I was on a real high. Janice McCann said to be sure to communicate daily with Mrs. Raghunath at the Children of the World orphanage.

"Keep in constant contact with her office by fax or email to show them just how eager you are to adopt a son." I couldn't wait to get home and begin writing letters to Mrs. Raghunath. I'd send her enough daily correspondence to choke a mule if it was the best way to demonstrate my enthusiasm for becoming a father.

Michael met me at the Toronto's Pearson Airport and he could tell I had been to hell and back when he ran to hug me. My bowels were rumbling with dissent and my gut was in constant turmoil. Michael said he was thrilled to have me home again. It was Tuesday night and he had to turn around and drive two hours back to Toronto so he wouldn't miss a day of school. JC, who had been running the lodge in my absence, greeted us at the door with our pack of dogs. I had missed everyone so much. My two and a half weeks away had felt like an eternity. I was so glad to be home in Canada. I threw my bags in our bedroom and said goodnight to JC. Michael kissed me goodbye and left for Toronto. The dogs swarmed around and on the bed and we curled up together for a good night's sleep.

I was a changed man. I was so glad I'd followed Blair's advice and just gone to India on a fact-finding mission. Meeting up with Mrs.

David R I McKinstry

Raghunath was like finding an earthly guardian angel. There was no doubt in my mind that I would be a dad, hopefully sooner than later. I sensed Michael was aware of the tenacity brewing in my soul as I fell asleep that first night back in Canada. I had complete conviction in my heart and soul that Michael and I had been destined to be a couple. I loved him more today than when I left for India and I felt that parenthood would soon be within our grasp. I fell asleep immediately when my head hit the pillow, the dogs already snoring softly around me.

CHAPTER TWO

And Then There Were Two

U pon my return to Woodhaven I had to concentrate on making money to pay off our debts. Building a country lodge meant putting our profits back into the business for advertising costs, upgrading facilities and providing perks to our guests.

Phone calls to let family and friends know I was back from India took up most of my first morning home. It was almost noon before I noticed two of my dogs, Tyler and Dylan, were sporting stitched snouts. JC, our part-time manager, sheepishly told me that a week into my trip he had been throwing tennis balls out in the snow for the dogs just before bed. Tyler and Dylan had both grabbed the same ball and neither would let go. Tyler let go of the ball and grabbed hold of Dylan's ear and a 30-minute dog fight ensued.

JC said he remembered me telling him that if the dogs got into a fight just let them fight it out. It was well known in dog breeding circles that attempting to pull fighting pets apart was dangerous and would cause the dogs to rip and tear one another even more. Tyler won the fight and Dylan had let go. Both dogs sustained major wounds on the neck and face. At 10 p.m. JC had loaded them into the Explorer, Tyler cloistered in the back and Dylan up front, and headed off to the Bobcaygeon

Veterinary Clinic. Four hours later he returned with two very sore and semi-anaesthetized dogs. Tyler's face looked like he had been through a lion fight and a long stitched wound ran down one side of his snout. Dylan wasn't as bad but he was still looking like the walking dead.

Business had been brisk during my absence and JC had handled two full weekends and two half-full weeks of guests. He had booked in two groups which totalled a few thousand dollars in upcoming revenue, and the next weekend was full as well. This had to be a good sign that one way or the other I would be able to complete my adoption quest.

Michael had emailed my cousin Elizabeth about my recurring bouts of diarrhea while in India and JC had saved two of her messages on the answering machine. She rhymed off a list of drugs I should have my doctor prescribe the minute I got off the plane. I called her over lunch and we chatted for an hour about my impressions of India and the opportunity of adopting a child. Always encouraging, forever grounding me with reality checks and balances, it was wonderful to hear her voice again. We both shared similar views about doing whatever it takes today to make tomorrow's dream come true.

By late afternoon on my first day I had typed a thank you letter to Mrs. Raghunath at Children of the World and faxed it off to her office about 9 p.m., knowing that there was a twelve hour time difference between Delhi and Lakehurst and that one of her assistants would be in the office to receive the fax. Every day of that week I sent a letter to Mrs. Raghunath to keep my name at the top of her adoption list and my enthusiasm evident. Michael arrived home on Friday night and we had a full house of guests milling about so it was late in the evening before I could sit and have a private conversation with him. The entire weekend was a hard slog with JC away and Michael and I attending to our guests, while trying to find quiet moments together so we could share India.

My guts were still rumbling madly, and symptomatic of some virus or bacteria I'd picked up from the water or food while in India. I had spoken with a physician twice that week about my concern and he said I'd have to just let it run its course as some of the drugs were preventative

A Swim *Against* The Tide

and wouldn't work now to correct the problem. I tried taking more Imodium but it made my stomach really upset. By the end of that first week home with good food and rest, my guts settled down and the diarrhea abated.

I had lost fourteen pounds while in India, which to me was the only bonus of my bout of diarrhea. I continued to send a fax off to Mrs. Raghunath daily and every few days I'd forward a written note with pictures of the dogs, Woodhaven and me. Michael couldn't be mentioned and I had to choose photos without him. Mrs. Raghunath said she had a file, appropriately named "The McKinstry File," in which she was keeping all my correspondence and pictures for the child I would adopt. She was forever encouraging me to press onward with my crusade and faxing her every day was like getting a daily boost of enthusiasm which in turn fuelled my vigilance.

March flew by with seminars on how to own and operate a Bed and Breakfast at Woodhaven. With over 200 guests at $30 per person, we added a substantial amount towards my next trip to India and paid bills but we still had a mountain of debt to overcome.

Clara and Paul, my biological parents, had found life in Port Perry together to be a dream come true. They lived in a condo overlooking the lake. Their honeymoon nest had Clara's decorating signature in every corner. The rose and maroon accents to her maple furniture gave their condo an elegant femininity that seemed to suit them. They were as happy as any newlywed couple and it was cute to watch them interact. Unannounced to me, however, they had been out looking for a house and had just bought one on Lake Simcoe. They told me they were moving into their townhouse at the end of April. Clara was concerned about me going back to India because she felt I would be susceptible to all sorts of diseases and return home deathly ill. Paul made his usual array of off-colour jokes about Blacks, Chinks, Punjabis and gays. I made it clear that one day soon he would have a grandson of Southeast Asian descent and those jokes would no longer be spoken in my home if he wanted to be part of our lives.

David R I McKinstry

The athletic prowess of Paul's youth had been replaced by insecurity in his elder years that manifested itself in rude jokes. I felt more sadness than anger over his brash behaviour. Paul was a mix of contradictions; he was very kind-hearted yet twenty years earlier he'd allowed his ex-wife to move their teenage sons into one bedroom so the second bedroom could be used as a kennel for prize-winning dogs. Paul and his former wife had been dog breeders who kept breeding and show stock locked up in small cages 21 hours of the day – yet Paul considered himself a kind loving pet owner. He was well liked on his own merits but still felt he had to make people laugh telling crude jokes that always left someone somewhere feeling maligned and hurt, as most jokes do. It was evident that Paul just couldn't see the forest for the trees on this joke issue. Heart attack and stroke greatly impacts judgement and discernment in many patients, and Paul's cardiac problems made him no exception.

Most often Clara laughed at his jokes and rolled her eyes at some of his behaviours. However, her love for Paul continued to grow in leaps and bounds, unfettered by anything embarrassing he said or did. She was in her glory just being by his side. Clara was a church-going Anglican with a deep faith and I could tell Paul's frequent improper use of words like Jesus Christ and God-damn grated on her sensibilities. Only occasionally had I overheard her firmly telling him to cool it with such language.

Clara had reclaimed her true love after nearly four decades and her appetite for his closeness was insatiable. Her experiences in life appeared to have hardened her to other people's frailties. We were at opposite ends of the political spectrum, me a die-hard NDP who voted Liberal and she a card-carrying member of the ruthless Conservative Party of Ontario. She felt that she had made it in life despite many difficult obstacles, none the least of which was becoming an unwed teenage mother who had given her baby up for adoption. She was a very attractive woman with a wonderful heart and soul; her jadedness was palpable and I understood why. The three of us had only reunited a few years before but with each passing year I appreciated and loved them

A Swim *Against* The Tide

more for the people they were. I was just as pleased that they had grown to love and accept me with all my foibles, irritations and bad habits.

By April I still hadn't fully recovered from my trip to India and I had bouts of strange fatigue, stomach upset and shortness of breath for most of the late winter and early spring. Jenny, our sick Golden Retriever, was maintaining her own. Cool winter weather was good for her lungs and the blastomycosis (fungus growths) was kept at bay. Unfortunately as the warmer weather of mid-April arrived, Jenny's health began to deteriorate rapidly. Her breathing was noticeably compromised. We didn't have a lot of available cash for vet bills, and every cent we spent at the vet was on our line of credit. It was pre-season and from mid-April to mid-May guests would be few and far between.

Michael was worried night and day about our finances and kept raising the issue of selling Woodhaven. The very thought of selling this "Shangri-La" would put me into a fierce mood. I wanted to live here the rest of my life. I wanted us to raise our children at Woodhaven, and owning and operating this small hospitality business was what I wanted to do with my life. From day one, Woodhaven had offered unused bedrooms free of charge to people and not-for-profit groups who couldn't afford a lakeside holiday. Michael was on line in spirit, but in reality this benevolence kept us on the brink of bankruptcy. Knowing that Jenny's health was worsening and vet expenses could easily double, I finally relented and agreed that we should sell. I called a local real estate agent and Woodhaven went up for sale. I was sick at heart showing the agent all the nooks and crannies of my home and signing the realtor's agreement of sale. I told her I wanted it priced high and she agreed. I hoped that once our summer season began and money began to pour in during June through September that Michael would see that we had a gold mine and Woodhaven was worth keeping.

On Wednesday April 29th I awoke around 5 a.m. and just lay in bed wondering about India and how long I'd have to wait for Mrs. Raghunath to call me about a child to bring home. I had many thoughts of Nick that morning, thoughts of how happy he'd have been if we'd

David R I McKinstry

adopted a child before he died. I must have lain awake thinking about Nick for almost an hour. The dogs were sprawled across the bed and beginning to stir, a clear signal that they needed to go outside for their first morning break. With the dogs in sight of the kitchen window I began to prepare my first pot of coffee. The dogs headed down the path to the water and I decided to follow them, knowing when I came up from the dock the coffee would be ready.

It was 6:30 a.m. when five soaking wet Goldens and I wandered back into the kitchen. I towel dried them then poured myself a cup of strong coffee. I had just stirred in the packet of sweetener when the phone rang. It was obvious from sound of the voice on the phone that it was a long distance call. The caller asked for me and after a few seconds delay on the line, I heard, "David, this is Mohini Raghunath. Am I calling too early in Canada?" I was absolutely stunned to hear her friendly voice and my heart began to pound. I told her I had been up for hours and without any further hesitation I asked her if she had found a child for me.

"David, we have a little boy that I would like to talk to you about. He came into our care just three weeks ago. He is a healthy, happy boy who is very considerate of his playmates in the orphanage. We call him Toni because he wouldn't tell us his name and seems to enjoy being called Toni by our staff. I think this little boy would be a good match for you," she said, pausing until the echoing on our line ended.

"Yes, yes," I said, "He sounds delightful. What else do you know about him? Please tell me everything," I pleaded excitedly.

"Toni is about five years old. We don't know his real age but the dentist and our doctor have examined him and by the size of his teeth they estimate that he is probably just turned five. He is a tall boy for his age. He is darker skinned and circumsized. Would you want a son that was circumsized?"

I couldn't believe she felt it necessary to ask about this. What would circumcism have to do with my decision whether to adopt this little boy to be my son?

A Swim *Against* The Tide

"Of course, circumsized or not circumsized, it doesn't matter to me. I am circumsized as are most of my peers in North America but it certainly isn't an issue for me whether he is or isn't circumsized. I just want a son!" She continued to tell me that being circumsized meant that Toni was most likely born of Muslim parents and in a Hindu orphanage, that meant that Toni would be put up for international adoption as no Hindu family would adopt a Muslim child.

I asked her, "How long until I can bring him home to Canada?"

"There is much to do before he could be placed with you and taken to Canada. Probably another four months if the paperwork goes smoothly. But there is a lot to do before that may happen. You must first get a "Letter of No Objection" completed by the Canadian Immigration

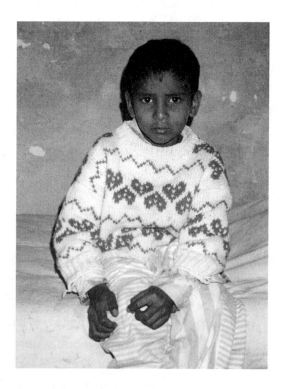

Nicholas when the police brought him to
Children of the World orphanage, 1998.

— 32 —

David R I McKinstry

authorities. This must be in our hands before I can present Toni to CVARA for their approval of this application. There is still much to be done by your authorities. I will send you a list of documents you will need to proceed. Call Mrs. Johnston, your social worker and tell her I will be sending the documents to her address. I will enclose a photo of Toni and all available information in our files on him. Knowing how slow the mail can be you won't receive this package for a few weeks. Once it arrives you will be able to discuss the details with the Canadian authorities and start sending us all the necessary documentation we require to process your application. I think you and Toni will like one another. Oh, I see in your file that you would want a son to be called Nicholas. We will consider Toni to be your Nicholas from now on." She paused again to let the echo on our line catch up with the silence.

"I have waited a lifetime to hear those words from you, Mrs. Raghunath. I want him and I will do everything possible to get the paperwork done in two months. I don't want my son to stay in an orphanage any longer than necessary. I want him home with me so I'll do whatever it takes to expedite matters from this end."

She said she would fax me the details immediately regarding Toni but the original documents she would put in the mail along with the colour photographs of Toni. I could tell she was smiling on the other end of the phone and I thanked her profusely again and again, much to her amusement.

"You have waited a long time for the right child to come into your life. I hope it will be this little boy. Please call us if you or Mrs. Johnston have any questions about the documents we require from your immigration officials. Goodbye David."

I was beside myself. I yelled, "Oh thank you Heavenly Father!" and the dogs came running to me, sensing my over-the-top excitement. I immediately thought of lying in bed a few hours ago and thinking about Nick. Had this been Nick's sign to me that a child was coming? I had to call Michael and tell him the news. It was 7:30 a.m. and he'd be enroute to school. I called the school where Michael taught and left a call-me-

A Swim *Against* The Tide

quick message on his voice mail. It took twenty minutes for me to stop walking around in a daze with a smile stretching from ear to ear. I poured another cup of coffee and silently told Heavenly Father that I was the happiest man in the world and how thankful I was for His faith in me.

Michael called at 8:10 and asked what was wrong. I told him about my call from India about a son for us to adopt. He was thrilled to hear the news and told me to get on the phone to my social worker immediately. I told him I had a list of people to call first. We laughed together on the phone and I could tell Michael was relieved to hear we would be parents. He always had a cautious edge to his enthusiasm as if not wanting to celebrate too soon in case something went wrong. I was already celebrating Nicholas' arrival into our family but risk-averse Michael wanted all the T's crossed and I's dotted before letting his excitement bubble over. No matter, I thought, I have enough excitement and confidence for us both. I spent the next hour calling Mum, Elizabeth and close friends, and left a score of excited adoption announcement messages on the voice mails of the DiCicco clan.

I drove to the Lakehurst General Store to get the mail and told the owners, Marlene and Harry, that I had finally received good news from India. They had been watching the mail for me and every time I got a letter from India they would call immediately. I knew the event would spread far and wide once the general store owners got wind of my good news. I was anxious for everyone to know of my good fortune as the more positive thoughts I had coming my way the better I'd be. I knew Nicholas would be coming home to Canada, it was just a matter of how long until the paperwork could be finalized.

No one could have prepared me for the bureaucratic homophobia, deliberate fumbling and mean-spirited delays in the eleven months ahead of me.

Sadly by mid May our golden retriever Jenny joined Nick in the land beyond and we buried her ashes alongside Nick under the Maple tree. At the end of June Michael started his summer holidays. With Woodhaven having more advanced reservations than ever before, we looked forward

David R I McKinstry

to a very profitable season. We felt on top of the world. News of getting a child from India spread around the lake quickly and we'd been inundated daily with inquiries about the progress of our adoption.

In early July, our neighbours Joyce and Sandy Gammie called to invite Michael and I over for supper at their home across the lake. We assumed it was just to be a quiet, casual barbecue for the four of us. When we arrived at the Gammies we found ourselves in the midst of a baby shower which sixty of our neighbours had organised. Most of these people were retired year-round residents of the lake, some we know well and others we hardly knew. It was as overwhelming to see this gathering of well-wishers as it was wearing funny hats of ribbon, usually worn by mothers-to-be at baby showers.

Michael and David cutting cake at the baby shower, July 1998.

A Swim *Against* The Tide

In absentia, Nicholas received all manner of toys, books and clothing. Many of these pensioners had spent a fortune buying wagons, videos, OshKosh clothing, teddy bears, skates and water skis. We were so proud to have these wonderful people in our lives. If only the tardy federal and provincial adoption officials could see all this support being given to us from this community, it might motivate them to jump into high gear to get our paperwork finished faster. Homophobic Tory parliamentarians should have been there to bear witness of this extraordinary outpouring of human kindness for a gay couple. How utilitarian of those public officials to have forced me to spend 18 years and $90,000 in American funds for the privilege of being able to provide a loving home for one orphan from overseas.

We were full to capacity every day that summer. I'd barely get rooms cleaned and changed when another group of guests would arrive for a vacation. July was a busy month spent preparing for the Woodhaven sponsored cross-the-lake swim and the summer regatta held annually on the August 1st Long Weekend. We had cancelled our real estate listing and taken Woodhaven off the market because money was flowing like water as guests clambered to have holiday time on Sandy Lake.

I had received many unsettling faxes and phone calls from Mohini Raghunath who was extremely concerned that Immigration Canada hadn't forwarded to her the documentation that she needed to have processed by the Delhi judiciary. By late July Mohini telephoned to say that the courts had closed for holiday until early September and that Nicholas' file hadn't been submitted for approval because it lacked necessary documentation from Canadian officials. Regrettably I was informed that his file couldn't possibly be presented to the courts until late September.

The Case Processing Centre (CPC) based in Mississauga, is every international adoptive parents' nightmare. All documentation bound for overseas adoptions must be approved by the CPC. Unfortunately, the CPC didn't have a phone number (odd for a government office) and the only mode of communicating with them was by fax. I would fax URGENT

David R I McKinstry

MESSAGES daily, hoping someone would respond personally to me. On more than a dozen occasions I'd be outside on the lawn or doing chores when the CPC official would finally telephone. They'd leave a message saying, "Sorry we missed you but we'll try another time." And the cycle of frustrating faxes would begin all over again. The CPC didn't give out its mailing address, other than a BOX NUMBER so when I sent them a letter by courier it was returned ADDRESS UNKNOWN. I called Laura Wen at the Ontario Adoption offices at 2 Bloor Street West in Toronto and begged her to find me a phone number for anyone on staff inside the hallowed walls of the CPC. She told me her boss had a phone number but he wouldn't release it to me.

I was irate and Laura knew it. I told her exactly what was wrong, corrupt and mean-spirited about these adoption procedures. Why would the CPC and Immigration Canada subject prospective parents attempting to adopt international children to unnecessary delays and unimaginable obstacles? Laura politely listened to me ramble on about these injustices, just as I'm sure she listened to others fed up with the Fort Knox attitude of the inaccessible Case Processing Centre. She was on my side but said her hands were tied by the bureaucrats at Queen's Park.

The day before the Sandy Lake Regatta I received a phone call from Paul Landers at the AIDS Committee of Toronto (ACT). Paul knew of Woodhaven's benevolence program and inquired if we would give one of his clients, a woman with AIDS and her young son, one last holiday together before she became too ill to travel. A recent cancellation allowed me to book them in for a three-day mid-week holiday after the weekend. Paul told me Susan was the mother of three older children in their late teens or early twenties and one who was only four years old. They had tried to get a trip to Disneyland through the Children's Wish Foundation but unfortunately the USA denied foreigners with full blown AIDS from entering their country. I told Paul if she wanted to bring all her kids we would accommodate them in a two-room suite. He said the elder son was estranged from the family but that the two teenaged daughters would probably love to come along with Susan, and the dates were confirmed.

Regatta weekend was a hoot as usual. Record numbers of neighbours participated in the early morning cross-the-lake swim and the afternoon canoeing, swimming and paddleboat events of the Fifth Annual Sandy Lake Regatta. A corn roast and barbecue followed the awards ceremonies and I was thrust back in time to happy childhood memories on Stoney Lake watching all my friends proudly exhibit dangling medallions and ribbons draped around their necks. I yearned for the moment our son Nicholas would participate in the summer regattas and be a part of this community.

The long weekend had been full of activity and guests around Woodhaven, so when ACT called with an estimated time of Susan's arrival I was just regaining my usually high energy levels. Susan wasn't well enough to drive her own car so a good friend of hers had volunteered to drive the family up.

Shortly after lunch I lay down to read a book in the library with a fresh cup of coffee. It was sweltering hot outside and I had cranked up the air conditioning to HIGH. I was just dozing off when I heard a car beep its horn in the parking lot. I yelled to Michael upstairs and asked him to don his Porter's Cap and help me carry in guest luggage.

We met Susan as she stepped out of the front seat of the car, looking very gaunt with dark circles under her eyes. Regardless of her ill appearance it was obvious Susan was an attractive woman in her early forties. Her light brown hair was long, and hung in a ponytail down her back past her waistline.

She smiled at me as I walked toward her and asked, "Are you David or Michael?"

I introduced myself and in turn Susan introduced her two daughters, Emma and Courtney, good friend Sylvia and last but not least, Kolwyn, her young son holding tightly onto the collar around his dog's neck. I suggested that they let the dog run free so it could have a bathroom break after two hours in the car. It was so hot that we didn't

David R I McKinstry

waste time chatting outside before Michael and I carried their five pieces of large luggage inside and checked them into their suite. We left their dog Patsy, a fourteen-year-old English Setter outside to become acquainted with our dogs who had already begun to lavish her with sniffs and happy whines of hello and follow me.

Susan was mobile but slow and she shuffled as she walked around the lodge. She asked if she could smoke inside and I told her we had a screened and shaded side porch where she could smoke outside. I apologised that she had to share a suite with her children but that we had been fully booked for months and this suite only became available through a last minute cancellation. Susan replied that she was absolutely thrilled with their accommodations and the opportunity to be out of the

Kolwyn, age four, arrived with his mother sporting a shaved head, August 1998.

A Swim *Against* The Tide

city for three days on Sandy Lake. Her two daughters had changed into bathing suits and were ready to go for a swim, whereas Kolwyn was obviously thrilled to be the centre of the dogs' attentions and being licked all over. Sylvia, Susan's volunteer driver, said she had to get back to the city immediately and that she'd be back on Friday to retrieve Susan and the kids.

With Kolwyn in tow, her daughters headed down to the dock while Susan sat down to rest in the library. She wrapped a cosy quilt over her shoulders, obviously feeling the chill from the air conditioning, and I asked if she like a cup of hot fresh coffee. Her eyes lit up at the sound of me pouring caffeine into a mug and we sat and chatted while the children were off with Michael swimming.

Susan thanked me profusely for giving them one last family holiday together. She said Kolwyn was still angry that they weren't going to Disneyland but that Woodhaven would cheer him up. I asked her about Kolwyn, "Where did you find such a unique name?"

Susan told me she had been born in Colwyn Bay, Wales and when he was born she decided to masculinize the name with a K rather than a C and that was how he got his name. She laughed heartily and said he'd probably never meet anyone in Canada with the spelling of that name. She told me about being raised in England and then immigrating to Canada as a young adult. She was very chatty about her life, marriages, children and travels.

Five wet Goldens suddenly ran into the room followed by Kolwyn chasing them. Patsy was in close pursuit of Kolwyn and his smile of delight told us he preferred Woodhaven to Disneyland. Susan wanted to take a nap so I suggested I take her kids to Bobcaygeon for a Kawartha Dairy ice cream cone, the best cones anywhere.

Kolwyn was quite unruly in the car, causing me to wonder if he ever got disciplined at home. I had to tell him three times each way just to sit in his seat and remain buckled up. Then he discovered the electric window button and insisted on dropping his window down letting my precious cold air escape. He spilled his ice cream cone on the fabric of

David R I McKinstry

the car seat and tried to pick it up which only smeared it deeply into the fabric. By the time we arrived back at Woodhaven, Susan was up from her nap and talking with Michael and a few other guests who had assembled to watch him prepare supper.

I reported that the ice cream trip had been a success and when she asked if Kolwyn had behaved, I told her, "He was a normal four-year-old in the car, all hands and feet." Many a truth is told in jest, I thought to myself as everyone laughed and continued to watch Michael's culinary expertise unfolding before them. Kolwyn asked for a cookie and I said it was too close to supper. He immediately went to his mother to ask for a cookie. She reached into her sweater pocket, pulled out a wafer and handed it to him. Pleased by his efforts to get what he wanted, he ran off to find out what was on the TV upstairs. Susan noticed me staring. I must have telegraphed my disapproval by the look on my face and as Kolwyn ran off, she said to me, "Being tired and sick, I find it easier just giving him what he wants."

Knowing Courtney and Kolwyn were upstairs watching a video, Susan went outside to have a smoke with Emma. The other guests dispersed to the library to enjoy an impromptu cocktail party. I looked at Michael and he smiled and asked, "How rough was the trip to Bobcaygeon?" I told him that Kolwyn had been a real handful of energy in the car and how he had only finished half his cone when Courtney egged him on to throw paper around the car.

"That little lad has a mind of his own," I said, "and what he really needs is to be taught that NO means NO. I was ticked off watching Kolwyn manipulate Susan into giving him a cookie after I'd said he couldn't have one. Considering her health status it probably is easier for her to just give in to his demands. It must be so hard for Susan to temper her need to discipline him with just holding him close, knowing it won't be long before she dies. Did she say anything about a present husband or lover to you?" I asked.

Michael was busy. I could tell he was preoccupied making supper but he managed to answer my question, saying simply that Susan hadn't mentioned anyone in particular. Michael was marinating ribs, boiling a big pot of corn on the cob and was in the midst of creating his famous Pad Thai salad. Mum was being dropped off at Woodhaven within the hour and would be bringing a dessert.

"Why don't we put on some hamburgers and hot dogs for Courtney and Kolwyn and let them sit upstairs and watch videos while we eat supper," I suggested. I asked Susan if Kolwyn and Courtney would prefer to eat earlier and she agreed.

Kolwyn was very fussy about his supper. I put a hot dog on his plate and some salad along side. He didn't want any salads and asked instead for potato chips. Susan told him he could go into her room and get a bag of chips if he ate two hot dogs. That seemed to appease him somewhat and off he and Courtney went to finish their movie.

At 7 p.m. after wine and cheese in the library, everyone filed into the dining room to have supper. I asked Susan to sit beside me at one end while Emma sat at the opposite end to help Michael dish out the food. Susan was very chatty and I hoped I could find out more about her over supper. She intrigued me. She had a look in her eye that gave me the impression she wouldn't take any nonsense from anyone.

Several of the guests had heard bits and pieces of my recent trip to India, and over supper I was asked many questions about that country, the orphanages and the difficulties I was encountering as a gay man wanting to adopt. Susan listened intently to my saga about wanting to adopt children for seventeen years and being thwarted by the Children's Aid Society (CAS) too many times to count. She didn't say a word during my account of India, meeting Mrs. Raghunath and now waiting for Nicholas' paperwork to be completed so I could go back to Delhi and fetch him home – hopefully by Christmas. I told our guests about the recent baby shower the neighbours had thrown for Michael and me, and how open and receptive Sandy Lakers had been toward us and our adoption of children.

Mum kept interjecting comments about how Nick would have been thrilled to be a father but it just wasn't in God's plan. While coffee was

David R I McKinstry

being passed, Susan asked me quietly if Michael liked children. I smiled and told her that I wouldn't be with him if kids and dogs weren't highest on his priority list. "Michael will be a superb role model for our kids." I laughed and said that without a doubt our kids would be computer literate, considering Michael was the computer science and mathematics department head at an upscale independent boys' school.

Other than Mum, Michael, Susan and myself everyone else scattered from the table after finishing dessert and coffee. Susan seemed quite content to just sit and watch dusk envelope the lake from her bird's eye perch in our dining room. Emma had gone off to check on Courtney and Kolwyn.

"Susan, how long have you lived with HIV," I asked her candidly.

"I became infected back in '83 or '84 from a guy I was seeing at that time." Then she asked, "How long did your Nick live with full-blown AIDS?" She was very interested to talk about Nick's health and the deterioration he experienced prior to death. Michael asked Susan if she had a boyfriend in her life presently and she laughed and said, "Before Kolwyn was born I was quite a babe. Never had any trouble finding good looking men, but since Kolwyn's birth my health has steadily worsened. I'm only 95 pounds soaking wet – you should have seen me at 120 pounds," she smiled naughtily. "I could have had any man I wanted. But now I look like an old woman about to die. Who'd want me now? Besides I wouldn't be interested in a man at this point. I know my days are numbered and I just want to be around my young son and the girls as much as possible."

I could tell Susan's candour had made Michael wince in his seat. Mum asked Susan if she had a faith to fall back on and Susan said she was a reformed Catholic but wasn't really into institutionalized religion any more.

"I have my own thoughts about God and I'm comfortable knowing God will look after me when the time comes," she said.

Susan asked me about Nicholas' health. "There is lots of HIV in India, isn't there? Do you know if he's been exposed to it or anything else?"

I told her that he had been found on the street by a cop, clutching the corpse of his mother and that his health background was completely unknown. The Canadian High Commission had put him through a battery of tests and I suspected he had passed what he needed to pass to be considered adoptable. Other than that, I told her, "We know nothing about his health history." I went on to say that his health really didn't matter. I felt I had waited so long for a child that I was letting God do most of the paperwork and I had to trust that everything would work out as it should. Susan asked if not knowing about his exposure to various diseases worried us and I told her it didn't.

"Nicholas is our son with or without whatever diseases may crop up in his future," I said. "No point in worrying about what might be, I just want to get him home on Canadian soil."

Kolwyn came running into the dining room and I instinctively looked at my watch and saw that it was 10 p.m. Susan greeted him with a big hug and kiss and said, "It's time for bed, Kolwyn," and excused herself from the table and took him upstairs. I soon followed and called up the stairs after her to say the coffee urn would be on by 6 a.m. if she was an early riser. She smiled back at me and said thanks for a great day and she'd see us in the morning.

It was obvious from the noise coming from behind the upstairs bedroom door that Susan wasn't having an easy time putting Kolwyn to bed. Mum, Michael, and I sat in the library after Susan went upstairs and we were all aware of the noise.

Mum wryly smiled at Michael and said, "That is typical behaviour for a stubborn four- year-old boy. I should know," she said, "David was the most stubborn child I'd ever encountered. Just hope that Nicholas isn't stubborn or that noise could just as easily be the two of you trying to put a five-year-old down to bed."

Michael looked over at me and said, "If Nicholas is like Kolwyn then we'd be in big trouble." I just laughed and told the two of them that no child of mine would be allowed to act up like Kolwyn had today. I was tired and said goodnight to Mum. Michael said he was going upstairs to

David R I McKinstry

watch a sci-fi show he'd videotaped a few days earlier and would be to bed in an hour or so. My head hit the pillow and I went out like a light.

Michael nudged me awake at 6 a.m. and said he could hear someone out in the kitchen clanging pots. "It must be one of the guests trying to make coffee so you had better see what's up," he said perfunctorily. I should have been up by then so I threw on my shorts and a T-shirt. I brushed my teeth and let the dogs out through our bedroom door and followed them onto the lawn. I walked with the dogs around to the main entrance and briskly walked in, hoping that whoever was in my kitchen would think that I'd been up and out for a walk with the dogs.

I saw Susan at the coffee bar making a pot of tea. "Sleep well, Susan?" I asked as I entered the kitchen with the dogs.

"Actually I didn't sleep that well. I never seem to be able to get more than a few hours sleep at one time. I've been up for two hours waiting to see the sun rise," she said continuing to make her tea.

"Would you like something to munch on with your tea?" I asked. Susan said she was going to have one more smoke outside and then she'd come in for a piece of toast. I made a pot of coffee and joined her on the front lawn. Being August the mosquitoes weren't bothersome early in the morning. Susan was in a talkative mood and she told me about her life, her husband's, her family back in England and she shared some of the horrors of being a mother about to die of AIDS. Her candour, under different circumstances, could have been unnerving but I sensed a deep need for Susan to speak about her health and impending death.

Susan asked me many questions about why Nick and I had moved to the country. Had I enjoyed operating a Bed and Breakfast and how long had Michael been in my life? I could hear rustling inside the dining room so I excused myself and went to see who was up. It was only 7:15 a.m. yet Mum was making toast when I opened the screen door to the kitchen.

She asked if Susan was alright, having noticed us sitting on the lawn talking.

"I didn't want to disturb the two of you. I went to bed thinking about that girl and her children. How horrible it must be for Susan's

Woodhaven Country Lodge on Sandy Lake, 1998.

David R I McKinstry

older children watching their mother's health deteriorate like this." Seconds later Susan followed me into the kitchen, greeted Mum with a warm hello and said she would be back for a cup of coffee after she had taken her meds.

I had almost finished my second cup of coffee when Susan came down and wandered over to where I was sitting beside Mum at the coffee bar. A few other guests had begun to mill about the coffee room, too. Two couples asked if they had enough time for a morning canoe ride before breakfast and I told them they had at least ninety minutes. As I got up to pour myself a third cup of coffee Susan asked if she could talk to me privately in the living room. Mum started to wander away to give us some privacy but Susan said, "Dorothy, why don't you join us, I'd like you to hear what I have to say."

Once seated in the living room Susan reached over and put her hand on my knee, turned to face me and said, "David, how would you like to have a little brother for your son in India? My reality is that I am going to be dead in a few months and I'd love for you to adopt Kolwyn so he could live here with you, Michael and Nicholas at Woodhaven."

I was shell-shocked. I wasn't sure I'd heard her correctly. I am sure my face had a look of incredulity. Before I could say anything Susan saw that she needed to repeat what she'd asked.

"I am serious, David. What about you, Dorothy, would you like to have another grandson?"

Mum's face broke into a smile a mile wide and she said, "Susan, I'd feel fortunate to have Kolwyn as my grandson." Susan looked at me with worried eyes waiting for me to answer.

The next twenty seconds became a mental newsreel reminding me of all the near misses I'd endured on the adoption trail. The total lack of humanity of independent social workers who had asked irrelevant and intrusive questions, mostly about my sex life, were a thorn in my side. Two of the worst questions had been, Who is top and who is bottom in your relationship? At what point in the sex act do you put on a condom, before or after pre-ejaculate?

A Swim *Against* The Tide

I sensed in my soul that this was to become one of those rare, once-in-a- lifetime moments that happen to so few. I desperately wanted to believe in angels, opportunity knocking and destiny. I considered grabbing Susan firmly by the arms, looking deep into her eyes and saying don't mess with me. I couldn't afford to have her wind up my emotions only to have my hopes squashed by bureaucrats shouting, "Never on my watch!" and her acquiescing. I was bruised and beaten having lived every day with an anchor of scepticism around my neck regarding anything to do with government adoption officials. Disappointment could turn into rage whenever I recalled the string of fly-by-night social workers who had taken my money and repeatedly walked me down the garden path only to leave me stranded and alone under an arbour of devastation. Although reasonable reactions given my history, it wasn't fair of me to question Susan's motives or good intentions. Was she wishing aloud for a perfect scenario in an ideal world while I was hearing a perfect solution in an imperfect world that didn't want gay people to adopt children? Susan looked serious and my gut told me to trust her sincerity.

"Susan, if you're serious, you don't have to ask me twice. The answer is yes. I'd love to adopt Kolwyn and have him live with us here on Sandy Lake. Are you really sure about this, Susan?" I asked cautiously, feeling my heart rate accelerating rapidly.

She had been awake most of the night pondering how she'd phrase this question to me.

"I knew at supper last night that God brought me here for this reason. I'm very sure about this. If you and Michael agree, then I'd like to discuss it with the two of you before lunch." Her eyes were smiling in relief.

I could tell a weight had been lifted off her shoulders. Susan told me that none of her siblings had agreed to adopt Kolwyn without him first having an HIV test, and her mother lived in England and was too old to start parenting all over again. Susan said that when she asked me about Nicholas' health last night and I'd said his status was unknown and wasn't a big concern to me, she knew I'd be right for her son.

David R I McKinstry

"It upsets me so much to think of Kolwyn calling anyone else Mummy. But having two fathers would preserve me as Mummy in his memory for all time." Susan barely finished speaking when her hands rose up to cradle her face and she began to sob uncontrollably. I reached over and hugged her close. My heart felt like it was being ripped apart. After a few minutes of consoling, she sat back in her seat and looked me closely in the eyes, "I never thought I'd have to find a home for my little son. I don't want to die but I know in my bones that it's going to happen soon. I can't die before I make arrangements for him."

Susan gave me an autobiographical sketch of her life while Mum left the room to get us all some juice and Kleenex. She had been just as maverick and strong-willed in her approach to life as I had been. She immigrated to Canada from England as a teenager. She married young and had her first two children, Austyn and Emma, back to back. Unfortunately this marriage ended, Susan said, because her husband walked out on her into the arms of another woman. During the early 1980s she decided to take her two children to Jamaica for a holiday. While on holiday she met a wonderful Jamaican who fathered her third child, a daughter she named Courtney. Three years of living in the hills with her Jamaican lover was all she could stand and Susan and her three children returned to Toronto. Susan had many careers and it was while working in real estate that she met and fell in love with the man who gave her HIV. Unfortunately he died of AIDS related infections eight months afterward.

Mum returned with a tray of juice and settled down in the sofa beside us and Susan continued to tell her story. Over the next few years of returning back into Toronto living, Susan had several long-term affairs. In the early 1990s, through real estate friends, she met a successful Toronto mechanical engineer, who was also HIV+. She fell deeply in love with him yet he remained on the sidelines unsure about committing to a fulltime relationship. In February 1993 Susan found herself eight weeks pregnant with twins. Her lover and some of his medical friends tried to convince her that this high-risk HIV+

pregnancy was wrong. Eleven weeks into the pregnancy Susan succumbed to his demands and had an abortion. The abortion devastated her for months and she clung to her boyfriend for whatever occasional scraps of love he'd throw her way. Their hot-cold relationship continued to sustain her into the summer of 1993 but when she found herself pregnant again in August her boyfriend abandoned her and flew to Thailand to work for an international engineering firm. Susan said she felt the child growing inside her was more about God giving her a second chance than about her having been irresponsible regarding birth control measures. At this point in her life Susan still hadn't told her family about being HIV+.

Her son Austyn thought she was stupid to think about having a baby at her age. Susan said he called her a slut and a whore and refused to have anything to do with her for months. He finally came around but was never again someone she felt she could rely on. After Kolwyn was born, Susan told us that her health began to decline, just as her Wellesley Hospital team of caregivers had warned her. Susan worked hard to mask the signs of HIV ravaging her body. She was steadily losing weight and jokingly told concerned family and friends that having a baby at 39 was the easiest way to regain a great figure.

Two years passed and Susan was becoming frequently ill and for longer periods each time. She finally had to tell her children, mother and her extended family. Austyn was furious and told her she was just a huge whore and deserved to die for being such an embarrassment to the family. Emma and Courtney gave her comfort and were much more forgiving. Susan said she wrote in her diary that night that she no longer considered Austyn to be her son, vowing that she wouldn't let him upset her again.

Fifteen minutes had passed since Susan began unfolding her life before us. I could hardly believe this story and wondered how any son could be so callous and hateful of his mother. The three of us just sat in silence looking out the window at the mourning doves feeding at the birdfeeder. I broke the silence and asked what provisions she had made for the older children

David R I McKinstry

"My older children will be fine. Emma and Austyn are out on their own now and Courtney will be taken into the home of a friend of mine. I just can't imagine leaving Kolwyn alone at four years of age," she said. "I think that is why I've ended up here, to ask you to be Kolwyn's fathers and adopt him into your family."

Just then Michael came out of the bedroom. He didn't seem startled to see me holding Susan's hand in mine. He sat down beside us and put his arms around her shoulder. I gave Michael the short version of what Susan had just asked. His eyes watered as he looked at Susan and said, "We would be honoured to take over raising Kolwyn." Mum moved from across the room to sit on the stool in front of Susan and patted her forearm reassuringly.

We could hear the sound of Courtney bringing Kolwyn downstairs and his familiar yell "Mummy" as he searched the kitchen, dining room and library. Susan wiped her eyes and broke our huddle formation by standing up and walking to greet her young son with a kiss and a hug. I followed her and began to prepare breakfast for the guests, hardly able to concentrate on chopping the red peppers for the frittata. Was this happening? Could I be dreaming? I was watching Kolwyn with his mother and sister out on the lawn throwing tennis balls for the dogs.

Michael joined me in the kitchen and gazed out the window at Susan and her children. "Imagine this," he whispered, "you're denied the right to adopt children for two decades and within three months we have two sons being offered to us. I'm speechless. I can't imagine how good you must feel." I told Michael that I was in awe of Susan's strength to do what she had done this morning.

"I can't even begin to fathom how gut-wrenching that must have been for her. Imagine Susan knowing she's about to die and searching desperately to find the best possible replacement parent and home for her little boy. I hope I'm never faced with that dilemma. I don't know if I'd handle this same situation with the grace and dignity Susan just did. Nick must be looking out for us upstairs, Michael. This sort of thing just doesn't happen spur of the moment. God's involved in this, somehow, I just know it," I said.

Susan, Michael and I sat down later that morning and further discussed what she had proposed earlier that day. Susan said she didn't have the physical strength or the money to find a lawyer to make this legal. We told her not to worry about a lawyer and adoption fees, that we would gladly handle all costs. I told Susan how thankful I was for this opportunity to be her son's father and that I hoped knowing Kolwyn would be well loved and cared for, might give the end of her life some peace. Several more times that day we spoke about Kolwyn, his biological father not wanting anything to do with Susan once he found out she was pregnant, and how Susan had lived her life as a maverick who enjoyed every hour to its fullest.

I was curious to know more about Kolwyn's sire and asked Susan if he'd ever inquired about her or the child she'd given birth to in April 1994. It was sad to hear that it took two years for him to make contact during one of his vacations back home in Canada. They arranged to meet in a Toronto harbour park one afternoon so he could meet Kolwyn. The visit hadn't lasted long and they parted as strangers. Susan said that she had heard recently that he had disappeared mysteriously in Thailand and his parents and the Canadian authorities presumed he had died in solitude of AIDS.

Susan asked Emma to join us in the living room later that night and told her that she had asked Michael and me to adopt Kolwyn. Emma seemed void of any emotion and simply said, "Oh that's good for Kolwyn," and sat beside her mother expressionless. I wasn't sure if Emma was stunned by this news or if she simply couldn't let herself think about her mother's impending death.

The next thirty-six hours flew by until Friday morning when Sylvia arrived to taxi Susan's family back to Toronto. Emma and Courtney wanted to go for one last swim before leaving and Susan told them to take Kolwyn down to the dock with them. Once the kids had left the house, Susan explained to Sylvia that she had found a home for Kolwyn with Michael and me. Without hesitation Sylvia grinned said she thought

David R I McKinstry

this would be a great place for Kolwyn to grow up. Before Susan left I told her I would call a lawyer and arrange for us to meet in Toronto to finalize our arrangement.

"Just let me know when and where but we should do this real soon," she said.

Sylvia's car had only been out our laneway but a few hours when my dear friend Halldor arrived for a two-day visit from Vancouver. I couldn't wait to share the news about Susan wanting us to adopt Kolwyn. He was barely out of the car when I had spilled the beans. Halldor, himself a lawyer, told me to hire a lawyer and have a joint custody agreement signed by Susan as soon as possible.

"If her health is as precarious as you say, then its imperative that you do this tomorrow. Do you know of a family lawyer in Toronto?" he asked. I told him a friend of mine had a family law practice. He urged me to call her that minute to make an appointment for the following Monday with Susan. Luckily my friend was still in her office cleaning up paperwork that Friday afternoon when I called. Flabbergasted by my story, she agreed that a joint custody arrangement should be done quickly before anyone could contest it by saying Susan wasn't of sound mind when she agreed to Kolwyn being adopted by us.

It was unbelievable that just five months ago I didn't have one son to show for my two-decade fight to adopt children, yet within a span of twenty weeks we now had two sons being offered. I was in awe of it all, while Michael remained in total shock. I'm sure I had more confidence in his ability to be a fantastic father than he had in himself. It was both humorous and sad to watch him shake his head in disbelief over recent circumstances resulting in us being on the threshold of adopting two sons. Humorous because Michael obviously hadn't been prepared for the moment when my quest would come to a happy conclusion, and sad because Michael was such a super human being, so kind and so loving yet he went through life feeling insecure about himself. Michael had everything going for himself, he was a strong, handsome man with character and an enormous heart of gold, yet it seemed to me that he was

A Swim *Against* The Tide

walking through life without the confidence to step up to the plate and at least try to hit a home-run. Almost daily I would find myself wondering how I could help Michael unlock his soul to discover his hidden innermost passions. Now we were on the verge of having two little boys arrive into our lives. I knew he would step up to the plate and be a home-run father.

I don't recall a moment in my life when I wasn't pre-occupied with thoughts of my future children. Even as a young child I knew I wanted to be a dad. I'd had such incredible parents and I had recurring daydreams throughout the years of my childhood about the type of father I would be to my children. Being a father was just something I knew I'd be someday.

Had someday just arrived?

David R I McKinstry

CHAPTER THREE

The Peterpatch Years

I realize now that growing up in Peterborough (known as Peterpatch by locals) was a unique experience. At three months of age I was placed for adoption and ended up in the home of the McKinstrys, a hard working, honest, south-end family. The town had a reputation for being like the television show Happy Days of the 1950s, a somewhat staid and conservative town where the divide between the haves and have-nots was important. Religious affiliation played a major role in everyday life. I remember walking to Grove Public School on the south side of the street whereas most of the Catholic kids (whom we called Micks) walked to St. Pias School on the north side. Frequently snowballs filled the air, the occasional yelp being drawn when the buried chunk of coal or stone centre found its mark.

I remember when a Catholic Grade 7 girl fought with a Protestant girl from Grove Public School on the lawn of St. Alban's Anglican Church. Anglicans were considered Protestants but more in the middle like Jews and Mormons. The girls were having a dispute over a boyfriend and the Catholic girl pulled out a penknife and took a few swipes at her opponent. Police were called, the knife was confiscated and both girls got five-day suspensions from school. I am not sure how this religious strife got started (probably much the same way as in Ireland), but it probably had to do with the fact that Catholics couldn't build churches within the city perimeters prior to 1893, or so we had been told by a Catholic friend on Stoney Lake. Even at an early age I knew my parents would have been very upset had they known we were pitching coal-laden snowballs at our Mick contemporaries but this was life in the south end of Peterborough in 1960.

It wasn't until I attended Kenner High School that I acquired a Catholic friend by the name of David Hickey. Until then only a few Catholic families had come into my life at Stoney Lake where my family owned an island and we spent our summers. David and I became the best of friends throughout high school and after a while religion finally faded away as a concern.

I had spent most of my time at the YMCA growing up. The uncircumsized kids in the shower were Catholics. I always thought being uncircumsized meant you were Catholic, until high school when I saw David and some of his Catholic buddies in the shower and was surprised to see they were all circumsized. From the look on other faces, I wasn't the only circumsized Protestant in the shower that day who was amazed to see circumcised Catholics, but of course no one ever discussed it. We all tried not to be caught peeking comparatively at another's genitalia.

I lived where everyone knew their neighbours from one end of the street to the other. Most of the older homes were inhabited by distant family relations. Orpington Road had been named after the Black Orpington chickens which my great grandfather brought with him when he emigrated from England in 1906. All the old elm and maple trees with 40-inch wide trunks were planted by my ancestors in 1911. Dad had taken over his parent's home when he and Mum got married. I grew up knowing who had planted each of the older trees on our street and who was a distant cousin twice removed or a first cousin. In the late 1950s and early 1960s, neighbours looked out for one another. All parents took a proprietary interest in the neighbourhood kids so that

David R I McKinstry

when a child was found to be out of line, he or she could expect a scolding from any adult in the absence of the parents. We couldn't do anything without someone knowing, so we just got used to the fact that parents and neighbours all had eyes in the back of their heads and doing anything naughty meant you would surely be caught!

I remember horse-drawn milk and bread carts delivering door to door along Peterborough's streets. Mr. Doig's horse-drawn flatbed wagon lumbered slowly up the side streets during the summer from which he would sell fruit and vegetables. The neighbourhood kids fed carrots to teams of horses and watched their tails lift to let out huge brown balls of scat squeezed from their behinds, which fell with a splat on the road to the fascination and delight of all! Until I was in Grade 11, many sidewalks were still cleared of snow by horse-drawn snow removal equipment.

Looking back from today's frenetic pace, I realize even more that growing up in small town Ontario during the 1960s was a real blessing in terms of the opportunities my parents provided to my sister and me. In thirty-five minutes we could be at our cottage door, we had a family membership to the YMCA, the ski club, and we dined well at Roland's Steak House, Peterborough's finest restaurant. We visited Toronto regularly for a weekend staying at the King Edward or the Royal York so we could see hockey games at Maple Leaf Gardens or attend a stage production at the O'Keefe Centre. It seemed like a life of privilege.

The YMCA was the sports hub of the city and being a member of a sports team automatically helped me to garner respect from people I didn't know. The *Peterborough Examiner*, our local paper, always featured pictures of sports events; our Y swim team was ranked as one of the top teams in the province and probably in the country during the mid-1960s. Peterborough's gymnastic, lacrosse and hockey teams were also nationally recognized. Several others on the Y swim team and I became well known in competitive swimming circles provincially and nationally.

The sports community was like an extended family. I attended the Y almost every day for swim team practice or for Red Cross life-saving

A Swim *Against* The Tide

programs. A fast game of ping-pong was always in play in the lobby and we'd often would sneak upstairs to the residential quarters, where rooms were rented out for $5.00 a night to travellers, and where we'd run and yell with careless abandon until someone snitched.

Beside the locker rooms was the cage where old George handed out towels and a bar of soap to the Health Club members. It was his duty to push the secret buzzer to open the door to the adult facilities. Kids weren't allowed into that room. Being told we could not go in there by old George was just the catalyst needed to dare us to try to sneak in. Every manner of diversion was used to get George away from the cage. We'd yell, "Toilets overflowing!" or "Fight in the shower!" and he would come running out of his cage. A scout was always hiding nearby ready to reach into the cage window and push the buzzer so we could gain access while George was off putting a damper on the imaginary problem we'd caused him. Once inside we headed for the sauna that was off limits to kids. It was always hell to pay whenever we'd barge into the sauna and meet up with one of our father's sitting in the buff in the sauna.

Peterborough was so much like Andy Griffith's *Mayberry, SC* on TV. Mum stayed at home, baked cookies, was an active member of United Church Women's group, canvassed for every cause going, made me thick peanut butter and banana sandwiches for an after-school snack and then shooed me out the door to catch the bus to the Y. Jell-O with fruit was a staple in our fridge, bushel baskets of apples from Mr. Doig's orchard lined our cold cellar walls and gallons of Central Smith orange-pineapple ice cream was never missing from our freezer. Mum shopped at Sturdy's Market. When Mr. Sturdy died in 1964, his butcher bought the business. The butcher had a thick Dutch accent and his entire family worked in the store. Every Saturday morning Mum walked to Sturdy's and left her shopping list to be filled. One of the butcher's sons would deliver it an hour later and take the frozen meats and ice cream down to the freezer in our cellar. It didn't matter if we were at home or not as we never locked our doors. It wasn't that we tempted thieves but that we went through our daily routines with a measure of small-town

David R I McKinstry

innocence. My father's attitude about locking doors at home and at the cottage was that he'd rather someone walk in and use our things than break down the door and clean us out.

Frequently children attempt to block out the negative influences that happen to them during their early years. Such was my case. A neighbour's 19-year-old son and his 18-year-old girlfriend, sexually molested me when I was just six years old. His parents weren't home and I still remember them taking me upstairs to a bedroom to play. The game was to undress each other and lie on the bed. I remember feeling this was wrong, but I felt helpless. Even at that young age I felt shame. I felt I couldn't tell these teenagers that this activity made me want to tell my parents. The awkwardness of this situation and my naïve assumption that I'd caused this to happen somehow, made me keep it a secret. As the abuse continued, I felt more and more guilt as if I had somehow been the perpetrator instead of the innocent victim. It was not a daily thing but it happened probably a dozen times during an eighteen-month period. They were naked and forced me to touch and see their bodies. I did not like this stuff and tried to avoid them. I always seemed to fall prey to them just when I thought this couldn't happen again. Thankfully by the time I was eight, this abuse ended. I had a tough time handling this secret and was desperate to tell my parents but just couldn't get up the nerve to say anything or even hint at what had happened. I remember wondering if I was the only one in the neighbourhood who had experienced their abuse.

When I was twelve, a Y friend and I were showering after our nightly swim team practice. I finished showering and headed to my locker to get dressed. Peter was lingering in the shower. Since his father was waiting to drive us home I returned to the shower room and yelled for him to hurry up. Through the steam I saw Peter talking to a strange man at the end of the shower room. It didn't mean anything to me so I just walked back to the dressing room to wait for him. Peter entered a while later, followed by this unknown man, and proceeded to get dressed. Our fathers alternated driving us to swim practices and it was his dad's

A Swim *Against* The Tide

turn to drive us home that night. As Peter got dressed he said that he'd met a man in the shower who was a talent scout for a Toronto magazine. Peter said the man told him he had a good body and asked if he could take some photos of him for an upcoming magazine. Peter asked me to stall his dad for a while so he could go upstairs to the men's residence to have his photo taken. The man was going to give him $10 for the photo. I had a gut feeling this wasn't a good idea but Peter was proud of his pubescent muscles and would do anything to show them off.

I stalled his dad and finally Peter arrived in the lounge and said he was ready to go. His dad was ticked off and asked where he had been. His excuses were fumbled and it was obvious to his father that Peter was hiding something. By the time his dad dropped me off at our house fifteen minutes later, Peter had confessed that he had been in a talent scout's room at the Y having pictures taken of him in a skimpy Speedo bathing suit and in the nude. Peter's dad was choking with fury when he dropped me at home and sped off from the curb to take Peter to the police station.

With an officer in tow, Peter and his dad returned to the Y and found the man who had taken the photos. He was arrested immediately because a large number of developed photographs of young boys, pubescent girls and adolescent men in various stages of lewd behaviours and nudity were found in his room. This man was in his early thirties, married with three daughters and had just been hired by the local TV station. He admitted to the police that he was staying at the Y (as many travellers on meagre budgets did in those days) and as the police suspected, he was a pedophile there to prey on and photograph children under the age of 14. Since I had seen this man in the shower talking to Peter, I would become part of the prosecution team trying to convict him of sexual misconduct. The police knocked at our front door about 9:30 p.m. to ask if I could identify the man I had seen talking to Peter in the Y's shower room earlier that evening. After stating I could positively identify the perpetrator I was told to go back to bed while the officer remained to talk to my parents. The officer, who was a neighbour of

David R I McKinstry

ours, told my parents that I would be summoned to court to identify the man with whom Peter had been talking in the shower. My mother cried for a week and my dad couldn't get the anger out of his voice whenever this issue had to be discussed. They were concerned about the impact this experience would have on two twelve-year-old boys. My father kept mumbling something about "Shooting those queers." I heard his anger and knew I didn't ever want to be one of those queers.

Peter swore me to secrecy and asked me to promise I wouldn't tell anyone how stupid he had been. Being a good friend and committed to a teenage code of honour about squealing, I wasn't going to tell anyone. Besides we were both at an age that the word "homo" or "queer" would send shivers up our spines as it wasn't smart to be associated with anything homo or queer when you are twelve and entering into the confusing world of puberty.

Weeks later at the courthouse, I sat in the waiting room with my dad, Peter's dad, the attending police officer and Peter. We had taken the day off school to be in court. It wasn't the first case on the docket so we sat together for an hour almost shaking with fear while we waited to be called into the courtroom. The rage of our fathers was palpable. Our dad's talked about many things while Peter and I just stared at the ceiling or read from a stash of comic books. I was confused and anxious. I sensed in my subconscious that I was different from other boys. Every time I found myself thinking about being different, I blocked it out, afraid to acknowledge it to myself. At twelve, I didn't know of any nice words for what I was feeling towards men. Therefore it was important that I make a good masculine heterosexual showing in court against this man who had assaulted Peter. I will never forget the words uttered by our fathers that morning.

"They should kill those fucking homos and piss on them."

I had not heard my dad swear, ever. I knew from the tone of their voices and the gestures they made about homos that being a homosexual was the WORST thing anyone could be. It was clear to me then and there that I certainly shouldn't/couldn't/wouldn't ever be a homo! My

A Swim *Against* The Tide

father was incensed at the accused man I was to testify against and I feared the wrath I saw in his eyes that morning.

Twenty years later in a psychiatrist's office, I clearly remembered the mood of that court room when I realized I could never be a homosexual – I didn't want to incur hate and disdain from my parents or society. It took twelve sessions for me to realize Dad's vernacular about "homosexuals preying on innocent kids" was totally off base and incorrect. He should have said paedophile not homosexual when referring to the man who had accosted Peter twenty years before at the YMCA.

I thought I had become gay because of early childhood sexual abuse. The psychiatrist pointed out that homosexuality did not result from being sexually molested as a child. He mentioned the nature-versus-nurture argument and said that being gay was the result of genetic programming *not* the product of your experiences.

By high school I knew I was attracted to men but refused to acknowledge those feelings. I dated girls, concentrated on being an athlete and Mr. Popularity. I consciously developed my physique to attract women but subconsciously I was buffing up in hopes that someday men would find me attractive.

David R I McKinstry

CHAPTER FOUR

Coming of Age

I arrived in Toronto to attend university in early September 1973. My next four years were already etched in stone. I was entering the University of Toronto, would be living at the New College Residence, studying toward an Honours in Physical and Health Education and swimming Varsity for Canada's number-one ranked university team. Who could ask for more?

During my first three weeks of classes I got to know many people, mostly due to the fact that we had similar class timetables, were overtly social in class and our personalities were in sync. Marilyn Butt, the sister of an ex-girlfriend, ran into me on campus one afternoon. We went for a beer at the Tuck Shop in Hart House where she drilled me

David at U of T, 1973.

about my impressions of campus life so far. She was the President of Gamma Phi Beta sorority and began telling me about the men's fraternity system. The fraternity lifestyle sounded incredible – lots of interaction with sororities, the best parties anywhere and meeting all sorts of great people who would be lifelong friends in school and in business. Marilyn emphasized that upon graduation my fraternity brothers and their family networks could be of great advantage to me in finding a career. Having had a large diverse group of friends back in Peterpatch, I decided that joining a fraternity could be my ticket into Toronto's inner society and achieving my goal of becoming a big fish in a big pond.

My biology partner introduced himself as Richard Woods. We were exchanging some notes at the end of a class one day when he saw the name Gamma Phi Beta scribbled at the top of my binder.

"Do you know one of the Gamma Phi's?" he asked. That led to a discussion about fraternities and he invited me along to check out the Alpha Delta Phi Fraternity where he was being rushed (recruited). I agreed and later that night called Marilyn about being invited to lunch at the Alpha Delt's.

I had dated Marilyn's younger sister Nancy in Grade 13 and it was she who had influenced me the most to go away to university. Our phone call was twenty minutes long and we reminisced about Peterpatch, common friends and my first impressions of U of T. Finally we got down to the subject of me joining Alpha Delta Phi. She was full of interesting information about the history of that particular fraternity and encouraged me to do whatever I could to become part of the Rush Program. Armed with this ammunition I headed off to meet the guys of Alpha Delta Phi.

The fellows I met at the fraternity house seemed genuinely interested in what I was doing and where I came from. Prior to sitting down to lunch the fraternity's Vice-President, Michael Chow gave all the rushee's a tour of the house. It was a massive old building and housed eighteen live-in members in a series of single and double rooms. We were in the lower games room being shown the antique slate-bottom

David R I McKinstry

billiards table, when a voice from behind me asked, "David McKinstry, the swimmer from Stoney Lake?" I turned around to face Jamie Anderson. His family had a cottage near Juniper Island, just a few miles from the island my family owned. Jamie made a big fuss over my swimming reputation around Stoney Lake.

"This guy always cleans up at the summer regattas and never loses the Lech One Mile Swim. Are you swimming Varsity?" he asked.

I replied that I was on the Varsity team and from that exact moment I knew this fraternity was to be my home away from home. I was astonished that someone actually recognized me, mentioned my family's island, talked about my swimming background and made me the centre of attention. I was sold on this place. Now to convince Mum and Dad to cough up the additional money to join this fraternity – I knew their main objection would be the time it might take away from my studies and the commitment I'd made to the Varsity swim team.

I spoke to my family almost every day of my first semester in Toronto. Dad had never gone off to university and in some ways I felt he was experiencing university life vicariously through me. He loved to hear all my news each afternoon. It didn't take long to convince him that the fraternity would be good for me

I spoke to the swim coach about joining the fraternity and his reaction was mixed. He had been coaching varsity swimmers for ten years and said fraternities, their parties and too many sorority girls had been the downfall of many talented swimmers. But in the end he just said it was up to me to make the decision. So I joined.

The parties during the first five weeks of the school term at all fraternities are called Rush events, aimed at rushing new brothers into the fold. Spectacular beer-fest nights, hayrides at members' farms, honky-tonk piano parties with incredibly talented bands hired to entertain the brothers and their dates. It was everything I hoped it would be; it smacked of elitism which at that time in my life seemed crucial to my dream of "Small town boy makes good in Big City!"In early November I was inducted into the history book of Alpha Delta

A Swim *Against* The Tide

Phi, Toronto Chapter, during an elaborate Annual Initiation Banquet held in the Great Hall of Hart House. One hundred and fifty men, from all generations including many illustrious and well known Torontonian's like Christie Clarke, Robert Laidlaw, Bud Porter and Jack McClellend, dressed in black tie to witness our induction into the hallowed halls of ADPHI. I was so proud to be a member of this great society.

Annually, the Varsity Swim Team spent the Christmas holidays at a training camp. It was either in Mexico, the Caribbean or in Florida. In 1973 the team went to Fort Lauderdale, Florida to train with some of the best university swimmers from across the USA. I had worked hard to earn a berth on this team and was excited about seeing Florida, its beaches and being part of an exclusive training camp. I became best buds with a fellow Varsity swimmer named Scott. We'd both been adopted as infants and that seemed sufficient to cement our friendship. We did a mean rendition of *Rock around the Clock* and *California Dreamin'* on the bus home from swim meets, but none of the other swimmers enjoyed our singing as much as we did.

The Florida training camp was to begin only a few days after my last Christmas exam. A room in the fraternity house had become available and I was going to be moving from the New College Residence to the fraternity as of January. My first Christmas holiday spent away from family, this two-week training camp would be the source of several first-in-my-life experiences.

It was hot in Florida and we spent most of our days training with 500 other swimmers from across the continent. Early morning workouts, mid-afternoon volleyball games on the beach, weight training and back in the pool late afternoon for a two-hour fast paced workout called the Salmon Run. This was our daily routine in Fort Lauderdale. However, when the sun set and the coaches went to bed, the swimmers cavorted and danced in local night clubs along the beach strip. We had a blast day and night. There were friendly people all around, mostly university aged and wearing loose hot weather cottons. The guys on the team were preoccupied with finding new locations to cruise and pick up girls. We'd walk down the Ocean Blvd en masse, seeking out new clubs and new flocks of ladies. On each block there was usually a mooning session in front of obvious queer bars. I didn't think much of it and usually went along with the gang's silly antics. By now I had reckoned in my mind that I was going to get laid in Florida.

A few days before New Year's Eve 1973 our motel was invaded by three carloads of pretty co-eds, members of the University of Texas swim team. They were given rooms two floors above our ground floor suites. We made the usual remarks about this fabulous turn of events and after one late afternoon practice our Varsity swimmers were greeted with invitations under our doors to join the Texas babes upstairs later for a party.

We joined in with the festivities that night in the girls' rooms. They had been recruiting all sorts of swimmers and beach volleyball co-eds to their party. There had to have been a hundred people crowed into four adjoining rooms. We were unable to drink booze because of training agreements. However, the coach had agreed to lift that restriction for one night only, New Years Eve. I met Becki, a Texas swimmer, that night. She was gorgeous, tanned, and stacked. She said she was eighteen (I thought she looked barely sixteen). This was what we called a *trophy* catch. It was late in the evening and most of us were preparing to head down to our rooms to avoid a curfew violation from the coaching staff monitors. Becki sauntered over to me, in full view of Scott and a few other teammates, and asked me to stay for one last dance. I looked into her eyes and instantly knew this woman would be my ticket to manhood. We danced two fast dances followed by one slow dance. Becki made it clear that she wanted the night to go on forever, but my curfew was hanging over my head and the thought of missing the next morning's time trials wasn't an option. I told her to come and watch me at the time trials the next morning and we'd spend New Years Eve and Day together. She reached up and kissed me softly and romantically for everyone to see. I thought I'd pop my cork there and then. We parted knowing tomorrow night would be OUR night together.

Time trials were over by noon and we headed back to the motel for lunch. We now had a full 24 hours off to enjoy the New Years festivities planned on the beaches and at parties along the motel strip. Becki was lounging by the motel pool when our team arrived home from the time trials. I was really looking forward to being with her that night. We spent the afternoon together at the beach with the rest of my team and the girls many of them had picked up along the way. We played volleyball, swam in the warm surf, had piggyback fights with Scott and his date. By 5 p.m., everyone headed back to their respective motel rooms to be read the riot act by the swim coaches.

Scott and I were sharing a room with two seniors from our team, both of whom had been to previous training camps. While Scott and I were shaving in the bathroom the seniors were telling us tales of nocturnal activities we could expect to see and hopefully participate in on the vast expanse of beach across the road from our motel. Our roommates delighted in telling us about the beach being layered with couples screwing behind every mound of sand and how the cops never even take notice at New Years. They said it had been like an orgy on the beach in the Caribbean last Christmas. Neither Scott nor myself needed any more encouragement than that to decide where the BIG event would happen later that night. We plotted our evening pillage and decided that regardless of wherever we were at 12:30 a.m., we'd make a rendezvous on the beach with our dates and set a course for manhood a few sand dunes apart.

The evening was hot and the buffet dinner around the motel pool was incredible. Every type of cooked meat, fish, poultry and shellfish was stacked on the buffet tables and dessert ran the gambit from passion fruit custards to cheesecakes. Wine and beer flowed aplenty, the music, dancing and frivolity was like an aphrodisiac to every horny male on the team who had found a potential conquest for later that night.

Shortly after 10 p.m., many motel residents began to leave the pool area and head down the strip to a dance club. We all followed and spent the next two hours dancing and laughing with hundreds of other merrymakers at this club. Midnight came and went. It took only a few

David R I McKinstry

moments to finish the kiss with Becki, leave the club and head for my pre-ordained date with manhood on the beach. Scott and his date were only feet away from us as we strolled arm and arm down the beach, all of us very aware of what lay ahead of us. Although walking along the beach was very romantic with Becki hanging onto my arm and splashing water with her toes, hormones racing through my body were driving me crazy with the desire to make love to her. We walked until we found a nice mound of sand to cuddle up into and then it all happened too fast. Becki was all hands. We immediately began to undress one another with remarkable speed and dexterity for two teenagers who had consumed as much alcohol as we had. Desire was pounding in our heads as we lay curled together behind the sand dune oblivious to two cops beaming their flashlights through the hundreds of mini-sand dunes filled with co-eds doing the deed that no parents want to know about. Catching a glimpse of the approaching cops meant time was of the essence. We were lost in each other's kisses and naively whispered our undying love for one another. We accomplished what we had set out to do with barely enough time to slip our clothes back on and pretend we had only been on the beach watching the stars. The cops flashed their lights on us and told us to get off the beach and return to our motels or we'd be charged.

"Sure thing, officers," I said, and we headed back to the motel.

As we were approaching our motel, Scott and his date suddenly appeared behind us. "Did you see the cops on the beach?" he drunkenly bellowed in our ears. "We just about got arrested."

By the time we walked the girls to their motel rooms and had lavished them with drunken kisses, I was ready for bed. My head was swimming and I just wanted to close my eyes and sleep. I didn't even change my clothes; I just crawled into my cot.

Becki emerged from her room the next morning only minutes before our team headed for the pool and a gentle afternoon practice. She ran over to me and gently nudged me with a hello and a kiss. She hugged me, smiled and asked how I was feeling today. Then she told me that her carload of juniors was going to leave for Texas later that afternoon due

A Swim *Against* The Tide

to the death of her roommate's grandmother. I didn't want to part like this. I wanted more time with her and more sex on the beach. I gave her my address and told her to write me. Becki promised to write me a note once she got back to school. Scott overheard my goodbye to Becki and shook his head at me when I returned to the group walking to the mini-bus that took us to the pool.

"Why give her your address, jerk?" he whispered as we boarded the bus. "I won't give out my address. What if you knocked her up last night? She'll be sitting on your doorstep in a month and you'll be dropping out of school. Dumb move, my man." Scott was being the jerk, I said to myself.

Two months later I received a phone call at the Fraternity house. It was the assistant coach from the University of Texas swim team. Becki had asked him to call and tell me she was pregnant. We didn't talk long before he asked me to copy down her telephone number so I could call her later that night. He said very clearly to me, words I will never forget, "Did you know Becki is only seventeen? If you lived in Texas you'd be in big trouble young man."

I telephoned Becki an hour later. Becki answered the phone and we talked for thirty minutes. She wasn't going to quit school, as the baby wouldn't be born until after the summer. Being southern Baptists, her parents were furious and they didn't want her getting married at 17 and ruining her life. However, Becki's parents were insisting she carry the baby to term then give it up for adoption, which Becki concurred was the best thing to do.

"Let's face it, we just had fun. I don't love you but I am pregnant with your baby. I don't want to quit school and this way I can go back to my junior year in September. Just a minute my mother wants to talk to you." I could hear the phone being handed to someone else.

In a thick Texas drawl I heard, "David, this most regrettable situation will be looked after by us. We felt Becki should let you know what you had done." Those words stung in my ears, as if I had been the lone culprit. She continued quickly, "We don't want any more contact

David R I McKinstry

with you. This was just a courtesy call to you and hopefully you will both learn from this mistake. Sex before marriage only creates problems like this. Please don't call Becki again." Her remarks had been icy cold and then she handed the telephone receiver back to Becki.

"Becki, will you get word to me when you have the baby. I'd like to know if it's a boy or a girl and if it's healthy." Becki said she would get word to me but for me not to call her at all. Her parents were being very old fashioned about her pregnancy and she had enough problems with them without having to deal with me. We said goodbye in tandem and that was it.

I immediately felt a myriad of emotions begin to flow. I was happy to know I had it in me to make a girl pregnant, in a strange way validating my desire to be heterosexual. On the other hand I was heartsick that I had added to another generation of kids created out of wedlock. In the days that followed, I felt anger that my child wouldn't be raised by me. Quickly the realization that I couldn't raise a child alone at this stage of my life sunk in and I became at peace with Becki's plan to give the child up for adoption. I never told Scott. I couldn't tell my parents, or anyone; even Elizabeth was kept in the dark about this secret. I was ashamed and vowed I'd keep this indiscretion my secret forever.

Becki was true to her word. Her father called in mid-September to tell me Becki had given birth to a healthy boy. The phone call lasted only as long as it took for him to tell me the gender and health status of the baby.

Years later, in Vancouver I placed many ads in Texas newspapers requesting information on a baby boy born in September 1974 who had been given up for adoption. I contacted various adoption firms who helped adoptees in search of biological parents. Finally in the mid-1990s my efforts to locate the son I had created paid off.

I had a wonderful forty-five minute telephone conversation with Drew from his home in Texas. He sounded well adjusted, had finished college a year earlier and was working for a securities firm in Houston. Drew had married his high school sweetheart after graduation and within six months of becoming newly weds, she was pregnant. He told

A Swim *Against* The Tide

me his life had been privileged and he had wonderful parents, three brothers, one sister and both sets of grandparents were still alive. But he didn't want any on-going relationship with me as his parents had appeared really hurt and confused when he told them he was going to call me. I understood his reason for not wanting to complicate their lives or his own. The last half of our telephone call was filled with Drew asking me a million questions about my background, my education, had I married and did I have other children. I rambled on, intuition telling me he was writing down all I was saying. I told him I was gay, had lost a lover to AIDS and that I was HIV-. I told him I had located my own biologicals just a few years earlier and how we had formed a great bond without it confusing or threatening the relationship I had with my mother. I shared my personal history with him for his own interest. He was happy with his life the way it was and not keen on adding me to his definition of family. I could understand his desire to maintain the status quo and not bring some unknown person into his life. The telephone call ended in a mature but awkward way, both of us agitated by our feelings and left wondering if we'd ever speak again. I could feel a new emptiness begin to root deep inside me. Never knowing this child would become one of my deepest regrets.

David R I McKinstry

CHAPTER FIVE

The Truth Shall Set You Free

At the Alpha Delta Winter Formal in February 1976 my date was Maggie. We had dated off and on in high school and I'd often dreamed of marrying her. She was a highly ranked Canadian athlete, talented and articulate, compassionate and beautiful. Maggie could walk into a room and every one turned to watch her. We became the Fred and Ginger dance pair at all our high school dances and continued to see each other while I attended university. I kept telling Maggie that she would end up marrying me but she would laugh and say that we would be better friends than lovers.

My fraternity roommate Doug was getting engaged in a few weeks and I wanted desperately to get married too. Partly because a month prior, I had experienced an anonymous sexual encounter with a man. I never really thought of myself as gay; I was just one of the unlucky men of this world who have the propensity to be bisexual.

I had arrived back at the fraternity house the day after News Years and found myself alone in the house. I decided I had to try sex with a man to find out if I liked it. We all have our ideal mate in mind and I hoped I'd find someone handsome and athletic to either wow me or gross me out. I went to a gay bar in a back alley off Yonge Street and sat in a dark corner petrified, waiting for Mr. Right. The person who approached me seemed nice, friendly and talkative. I really wasn't into chitchat and just wanted to get it over with. He became my worst nightmare. I ended up running back to the fraternity house and showering for hours to get that man's cologne out of my senses. I told myself that if being gay made me feel this bad, then I obviously wasn't gay and I pursued Maggie with a passion to prove my point. I'd drive to Oakville and wine and dine her in hopes of changing her plutonic inclinations into a burgeoning furnace of romantic passion. I convinced myself that if I asked her to marry me at the formal, she just might say yes, and I'd be normal.

Maggie accepted the ring and said she'd think about it. All my fraternity brothers were excited for me and treated me like all the other guys who got engaged at that formal. But a few weeks later Maggie made it clear that it just wasn't in the stars for us to be together romantically. I was crushed and spent the remainder of 1976 concentrating on my studies.

After almost three years of swimming Varsity, my coach sensed that I was ready to hang up my trunks. He suggested I try coaching at University of Toronto Schools, a private high school for the intellectually gifted, just off campus. UTS needed a swim coach and someone to help out part-time with physical education classes.

Coaching the students became my life. In less than one year I'd built up this swim team from splashing hackers into a team about to become a dominant player at the city championships. I put heart and soul into my studies and into my part time position at UTS. It was there that I first met Matt during spring break. He was teaching the Royal Life Saving Instructor's program. I had seen him around the Hart House pool; he was a member of the Varsity water polo team.

Matt had a look about him which I found intriguing. He was handsome and fit, rugged yet he looked like he was a gentle soul. I knew I found him attractive and it scared me. Every time I found myself staring over at him or just thinking about him I'd consciously shut him out of my mind.

David R I McKinstry

During swim practice one afternoon, Matt appeared on deck and walked over to introduce himself to me. He was exceptionally pleasant, convivial and never stopped smiling. He had great teeth, a wholesome smile and I wanted us to become friends. He had recently broken off a relationship with the older sister of a student on my swim team.

Matt told me he was a second year physical education student. We exchanged extensive personal information through conversations about teaching versus further studies in human kinetics or streaming into kinesiology after graduation. Over the next few weeks I found myself looking forward to his presence around the pool deck. He would ask me to watch and correct some of his student's strokes, or fill in for him discussing lifesaving theory. Once exam time arrived neither of us seemed to be around the pool at the same time.

I didn't see Matt again until just a few weeks before the start of school. We met in the gym and he came right over to me. He had been working at a camp all summer. Now back in the city he was working out with the water polo team in preparation for team tryouts in early September. We finished our workout and headed up the stairs together. Matt asked if I lived on campus. I told him I was a member of fraternity and I lived at the house just off campus. Ironically his older sister was married to an Alpha Delt who had graduated just four years earlier. Matt asked many questions about the fraternity and he sounded ripe to be rushed during our fall recruiting season. I suggested he follow me up to the house and I'd give him a tour.

I could tell Matt loved the history and tradition of the fraternity. I told him we had a few openings for live-in brothers and if he wanted to join the fraternity he should sign up for our rush program and consider moving into the house in a few weeks. Matt said his parents wouldn't be keen on him joining a fraternity. He said his father was a stickler for good marks and the partying aspect of the fraternity would be considered counter-productive by his folks. Over the next few days Matt kept asking me about the fraternity and the Rush Program. Within a week he decided to sign up for Rush. We became inseparable from that day forward.

A Swim *Against* The Tide

Matt had reconciled with his on-again/off-again girlfriend but they were on shaky ground and he wasn't sure if it was going to last much longer. I told Matt that I had asked Maggie to marry me last winter but she'd turned me down. I told him I had lived at the fraternity all summer while working for the city's recreation program but I wasn't sure if I wanted to live in the frat-house for another year. He suggested I find an apartment for some peace and quiet in my final year. I took that suggestion to heart and within a week I'd rented an apartment at 10 Walmer Road, in the aging heart of the student ghetto.

I met Matt for lunch at the fraternity house throughout the Rush season. Every fraternity brother thought Matt was terrific. It was obvious he'd be asked to pledge to the house. He finally convinced his parents to let him join the fraternity and he began to help us recruit other prospective brothers from third year classes and from the water polo team. Matt was an enthusiastic recruiter and introduced two other guys to our Rush program within a few weeks.

Matt met me after classes several days each week and came home to my place to study between late afternoon and early evening classes. We'd cook together, talk for hours about spirituality and enjoy great meals together. I had wanted to get a pet and on a whim one day I called a Welsh Corgi breeder to inquire if any puppies were available. The breeder had one male left in a litter born seven weeks earlier.

I named my little Welsh Corgi Toby. Matt was mesmerized by Toby and told me that if I was going to be late getting home anytime, he would gladly come over and attend to Toby. I gave him a spare key and told him to use the apartment whenever he wanted.

And so our friendship grew. When I wasn't in class, coaching at UTS or attending various fraternity functions and meetings, I was in my apartment with Toby and Matt. I often came home after late practice and Matt would have chili on the stove. Three nights each week Matt had back-to-back late night classes and early morning water polo workouts. He started to stay on a cot in my bedroom on those nights. I looked forward to those hours we spent alone together, talking late into the

David R I McKinstry

night. We were young, athletic and handsome. We should have been out dating women but we preferred one another's company.

Matt and I would sit on the floor and play with Toby for hours. There were many Saturday nights we'd sit on the floor of my 12th floor apartment looking at one another smiling endlessly. Matt told me he had grown to love me like a brother and he really enjoyed my fellowship. Likewise I felt secure and comfortable enough to tell him I felt the same way.

Matt pulled his cot over beside my double bed one night as we lay talking about life. At one point he placed his arm over my arms and told me we'd be friends for life. We ended up sleeping, side by side with our arms touching every night when he stayed over. Lying in bed at night talking to Matt on the cot next to me was heaven on earth. Neither of us ever consciously touched one another sexually, nor did we ever talk about sex. However, on several occasions, lying beside one another, we were both sexually aroused and didn't bother to hide it.

My parents noticed the change in my attitude, as did several good friends at the fraternity. I just seemed very happy. Matt bought me an antique mantle piece that Christmas, refinished it and had it installed while I was writing my last exam. We put up a tree and had our own little Christmas together.

Early in the new year I was over at the fraternity house one evening and one of the few uncouth brothers whom I didn't have much interaction with, made a comment about Matt and I always being together.

"What are you, a couple of queers?" he asked loudly across a crowded room. I was embarrassed even though everyone within hearing distance just dismissed those remarks as the rantings of a jerk. But it was enough to make me question why Matt and I were spending so much time together. Without missing a beat I began to wonder if Matt was gay. The mere thought of the word gay being attached to me was enough to send me into convulsions. I thought I had better put some distance between us, at least in front of our fraternity brothers. I told Matt that maybe we shouldn't spend so much time together as people might get the wrong idea.

He knew what I meant, yet he asked, "Do you really care what people think of our good friendship?" He smiled and playfully winked at me.

I laughed, "As long as they don't think we're queer, I guess we're OK."

Matt was genuine in everything he said and did. He had a charm which made being alone with him refreshing and safe. However, Matt was becoming increasingly more clingy and wanted to spend consecutive nights sleeping over at my place. He brought over a housecoat and placed several changes of clothes in my closet. I wanted to wrap my arms around him and make love to him, that much I knew in my heart but I just couldn't let on I loved him in a physical way. After all I still wanted to believe he wasn't trying to be sexual with me. I had built up such a high fence to protect myself that the reality of my love for Matt was purposefully obscured. We had never even discussed one another's views on homosexuality and the topic never came up in conversations as we would lie on the floor beside one another with our elbows or toes touching.

Mid-winter exams were upon us and we both studied hard that spring. Once exams and spring break were finished, the ritual sorority and fraternity formals began to crowd everyone's social calendar. I had been set up with a sorority sister of a friend's girlfriend who attended the University of Western Ontario. I had dated her a few times, escorting her to other formals. She had called two weeks earlier and asked me to accompany her to her graduation formal. I told her I would. Matt asked if I really wanted to go and I told him I was looking forward to it.

"Maybe I'll get lucky?" I could tell my jesting was lost on him.

All week Matt had been out of sorts. He asked me not to go to London for that formal, as he really needed my friendship close by because he was feeling depressed and just needed time alone with Toby and me. I found this comment a bit unnerving. I knew I wouldn't risk telling Matt about my deeper feelings for him, so I began to push him away emotionally and physically. These frequent and blunt rebuffs over the next few weeks hurt him deeply and I could tell he was frustrated by the drastic and abrupt change in my behaviour.

Almost daily Matt left me poems he'd written about friendship on

David R I McKinstry

the kitchen counter. He wrote great stuff and I looked forward to being greeted with his poems at the end of a day. One Friday night we just spent the night talking about life, non-specific challenges that lay ahead for us after graduation, my desire to have a large family, and Matt's desire to just let life unfold naturally for him. We really bonded and spent the entire weekend with one another, something I'd avoided doing for several weeks. I lay in bed watching Matt sleeping on the cot beside me and it was all I could do to prevent myself from openly inviting him into my bed to make love. Finding myself so dangerously close to this precipice scared me and I consciously found myself pulling away from our magnetic attraction to one another.

The next morning over breakfast Matt asked me again to forgo my mid-April formal weekend in London in favour of staying behind and just being here with him. He said he needed me and wasn't feeling very sure of himself these days. I felt I had to tell him to buck up and get a life. He could stay at my apartment while I was away if he needed some private space.

"I'll be home by 9 p.m. on Sunday night. We can have a coffee then and talk about what's troubling you," I told him.

Matt always enjoyed staying over at the apartment pet sitting Toby but when I bid him goodbye Saturday April 16th bound for London, he wasn't very happy. He drove me down to the train station and hugged me goodbye in the car and on the platform. It was embarrassing and I couldn't get a feel for what was making Matt so upset. I waved goodbye to him on the platform and shouted, "Have fun with Toby. I'll see you tomorrow night."

The formal went well and a whole group of us went back to one of the Ivy family homes for an all night party. By late Sunday morning everyone finally became conscious. Our hosts put on a superb buffet brunch. The train was leaving late that afternoon and it would take three hours to reach Toronto.

Just after 8 p.m. on Sunday, April 17th I walked into my apartment and was greeted by Toby. Matt had left me a note on the kitchen counter.

I'd just missed him by ten minutes. He had waited until 7:50 p.m. for me. On my pillow he'd left a series of poems written over the past 36 hours. I unpacked, giving him enough time to get to his parents' house, and was just reaching for the phone to dial his number when my door buzzer sounded. A fraternity brother and his girlfriend were just dropping by to have a quick coffee and see Toby. By the time they left at 9:15 p.m. it was too late to call Matt at home. His parents went to bed by 9 p.m. and didn't appreciate their family getting phone calls after 8:45 p.m. I knew I'd see him in the morning on campus so I just took Toby out for a brisk walk around the block and then I went to bed.

As I got into bed I re-read Matt's poems. They were quite revealing about his feelings for me. I didn't feel nervous after reading his words. Maybe a bit of resignation was bubbling to the surface of my soul, realizing that I should have spoken to Matt about my deepening feelings for him, feelings of *the love that dare not speak its name*. I'd make it up to him by making his favourite chili supper the next night. I'd find out what was bothering him and hopefully find the guts to talk to him honestly about my own feelings for him.

The next morning I awoke as usual, put on the coffee and took Toby out for his morning constitutional. I fed him, reviewed some of my notes and headed off to write my last exam. I returned two hours later and was just putting my key in the latch when I heard the phone ringing inside. I grabbed the phone. It was Matt's brother-in-law, Bill.

"David," he asked, "did you notice anything odd about Matt on the weekend? Was he feeling alright?"

I told Bill I had been away in London at a formal but that Matt had stayed at my apartment for the weekend to look after the dog. Without much forethought I said that Matt had seemed a bit depressed since midterm exams.

"He's coming over for supper tonight and I'll make a point of finding out what has been upsetting him." As I said the word supper I reached for the freezer to get some frozen hamburger to make chili.

"Why the call about Matt, Bill? What's wrong?" I asked trying to

David R I McKinstry

make a joke. "Did Matt meet some floozy last night, get drunk and not show up at home?"

After a few seconds of silence, Bill told me that Matt had been discovered dead in the backseat of his car just a few hours ago by his mother. I wasn't sure if I should call his bluff and tell Bill to stop kidding around. But within seconds it hit me like a thunderbolt that this wasn't a sick joke. He was telling me that Matt was dead.

"Is this for sure?" I asked, holding back the horror building in my throat, "Matt's dead?"

Bill assured me Matt was dead and asked me to inform our fraternity brothers of his death.

Still dazed I asked, "But how did he die?"

Bill told me that the body had been taken away for an autopsy just thirty minutes earlier and it would be a day or two before they'd get the results. Matt's mother was a surgeon and even in her grief she suspected it might have been a brain aneurysm.

"Was Matt doing drugs, David? You were his best friend, do you know of anything that might have triggered his death?" Bill knew he was grabbing at straws as Matt was very vocal when it came to his stand against drugs.

Three days later, Matt's funeral was held at a Presbyterian Church in north Toronto. I was stunned that I had lost my right arm and his death was my doing. I read the notes and poems he'd left for me over and over and there was more than a hint of depression in the tone of his writing. Matt mentioned in his poems that meeting me had changed his life, how in knowing me he felt love and acceptance as never before and how insignificant life was without my love.

My mind raced with regrets. If I had only called him that Sunday night, if I had only taken an earlier train I would have seen him at the apartment and he probably would have stayed over night. The letters he left behind for me became clearer and clearer over the next 48 hours. Matt had left notes about our deepening friendship and his love for me and how he wished we could keep things like they were forever. He

A Swim *Against* The Tide

must have taken some pills! Did he commit suicide because I'd pushed him away?

After the funeral, I was the last one to leave the remote country graveyard. Alone with my thoughts, I fell to my knees and asked God why Matt had killed himself. I desperately wanted to crawl inside the coffin to keep him company.

The story circulating around after Matt's funeral was that he'd had a brain aneurysm during the night, yet suspiciously his family never released any official information from the coroner's report. I felt sure in my heart that Matt had killed himself because I'd rebuffed his love.

A few weeks later I visited with his mother in their garden. She made us tea and sat quietly as I told her I felt responsible for Matt's death. I told her I knew he'd been depressed and how he had asked me to stay behind that weekend so we could just talk. I told her about the letters he left behind for me the night before his death.

Matt's mother gently placed her hand on my shoulder, looked directly into my eyes and said, "You will cherish your notes from Matt just as I will cherish the letter he left behind for me. He shared some very personal thoughts about life, his special friendship with you and how happy he was spending time together with you at your apartment. Understand that I don't want this conversation to go out of this yard." I nodded and she continued, "Matt and you obviously shared a special kind of love. Other than me, his dad and sisters, you were the most important person in his life. I know now that Matt wasn't able to put that love into any context he could live with. My hope for you is that you'll be able to live happy and content. I don't have it in me to discuss these matters ever again, David." We cried openly for the grief we shared. She was letting me know Matt had been in love with me but he couldn't deal with it and how she hoped I wouldn't fall prey to a similar fate.

In the months after Matt's death, I graduated, isolated myself in a new job as an insurance agent with London Life, and spent weekends at the cottage alone with Toby. I talked to an imaginary Matt twenty times each day. I constantly apologized for not recognizing how emotionally

David R I McKinstry

fragile he had been. I apologized for not holding him in my arms, as I had wanted to do many times, and make love to him. I apologized for lacking the courage to tell Matt that I loved him the way he loved me. I told Matt I was too afraid to let myself say the word "gay" and I hated myself for being so gutless.

Later that summer I began to train to swim Lake Ontario. I had told Matt numerous times that I wanted to try to swim that lake at least once in my life. Matt was always encouraging me to do the swim and said he'd be there by my side as the lifeguard. I began to dedicate myself to being the fastest man to ever swim across Lake Ontario, knowing spiritually, I'd have Matt by my side cheering me on to victory.

I spent hours each day swimming in Hart House pool, developing better stroke technique and building up my endurance. By the autumn of 1977 I was mentally prepared to do whatever it took to make this swim dream a reality. I would swim up and down the pool talking to Matt every stroke of the way. It was easy to get lost in the pool and swim for hours at a time, knowing I would be conversing with Matt. He never talked back but that didn't stop me from engaging in a constant monologue with him under the water.

By Christmas 1977 I let my family and friends know why I was so obsessed with training in the pool every day without fail. Genuine support and encouragement was mixed with joking remarks about my sanity. I knew I had to rely on my own conviction and not be bothered by people's remarks.

Steadfast, I trained morning and night, seven days each week. My body was responding to the training and I became somewhat narcissistic about my ever-expanding muscular features. I had had a swimmer's body but now my features were fine tuned and chiselled. I was training four to seven hours a day by the end of April, and on alternate weekends I would do a seven to eight hour swim to pace myself and get used to long periods of straight swimming. A well-known Toronto marathon swimming coach, the man who had coached Angela Kondrak across Lake Ontario two summers before, was introduced to me and by late April he became my personal trainer. Art was an odd duck but he knew about marathon swimming and how to prepare an assault against Lady Lake.

By late June Art sent out a press release telling Toronto's media that a man was training to swim Lake Ontario in mid-July and become the fastest man to swim across that huge body of water. This announcement coincided with an announcement by the CNE administration of a proposed Pepsi Challenge Lake Swim for the middle of August. Lake Ontario swim fever hit Toronto. I was going to be the first man to swim the lake in twenty-two years. I was photographed by every newspaper and stories appeared weekly about my upcoming swim. The *Toronto Sun* printed a photo of me clad in a skimpy Speedo bathing suit as their Sunshine Boy of the Week, just a few days in advance of my swim date.

I managed to put together a good crew of friends and family to accompany me across the water for support. Three 35-foot lake cruisers (one aptly named The Fore Sure) were hired to accompany us across the lake. Finally the day came when conditions were perfect and I headed to

Swimming across Lake Ontario engulfted by heavy fog.
The ForeSure *chugging ahead of me, July 17, 1978.*

David R I McKinstry

The gang keeping me company.

David stroking 88 stokes per minute across the eerily calm
Lake Ontario, July 1978.

Niagara-on-the-Lake. I jumped into the warm 76°F waters at 3:30 a.m. Saturday, July 22, 1978.

I'd never felt faster or sleeker as I did that night making record time through the water. No one knew of my shark phobia. I effortless kept an image of Matt in my mind all the time I was in the water. I'd look down into the fathoms of black water beneath me talking to Matt, while simultaneously telling Jesus Christ not to let the teeth of some wayward shark rip me apart halfway across this lake.

I had jumped into the water a lean 159 pounds of muscle and I swam like a bat out of hell managing to set a fast pace of 88 strokes per minute. After eleven hours in the water I was only six miles from landing at Ontario Place. Art would shout to me in that, "50,000 people are lining up along the shoreline to see you swim to victory."

Unfortunately as we approached the deepest and coldest part of the lake, just a few miles from shore, the decreasing water temperatures were rapidly causing me to become hypothermic. I knew my breathing was compromised but I couldn't stop to complain or it would alert my coach that I might be in trouble. My lungs felt as though they had become blocks of ice, unable to inflate to receive the air I was trying desperately to suck in. During those last few miles as my body cooled and hypothermia gripped my chest like a steel vice, I remember talking to Matt as casually as if we were sitting in my apartment. His warm smile and calming eyes were telling me everything would be fine and that he and Christ wouldn't let anything happen to me. I didn't worry about anything except keeping my focus on those images of Christ and Matt only inches beneath my face.

Hypothermia was setting in and I didn't have an ounce of fat to ward off the inevitable internal cooling to my body's core temperature. The lead boat had become lost in the hazy fog several times that afternoon and during one of my feeding stops, I overheard someone say that we had just gone ten miles off course, down toward Oakville. I looked dismayed and from the Zodiac Art assured me that I had made up the lost time and in fact had swam about ten more miles than necessary.

David R I McKinstry

"You're doing great. Keep kicking, David." He repeated this monotonously and I put my face in the water and just rolled my eyes wishing I could at least see shore through the fog.

Within twenty minutes of my eleventh-hour feeding, I could feel my heart racing and my breathing become increasingly laboured. I knew something was up but being this close to Toronto I wasn't about to abort now. I remember telling myself just to focus on pulling my arms through the water. In my hallucinatory state, I asked Matt to swim beside me and help me make it to shore. A sense of rapturous inebriation enveloped me as I imagined Matt snuggling up beside me in the cold black water. Part of my mind understood the image of Matt beside me was a dream, yet the closer I allowed myself to be swallowed up into this dream state, the warmer and more peaceful I became.

"David's sinking, dive in and get him!" shouted my coach as I sank surreally beneath the surface during one of my strokes. According to witnesses my disappearance happened so unexpectedly and suddenly, everyone in the Zodiacs beside me were taken by surprise as I sank feet-first beneath the waves. I wasn't afraid as I slid beneath the black water. However I do remember vividly feeling warm and relaxed, Matt was beside me and Christ was hanging suspended in the darkness in front of me. I completely and willingly gave myself up to the moment and there wasn't a sense of fear as I sank beneath the surface.

I learned later I had passed out due to hypothermia. It was scary for those around me to see my near lifeless body being pulled to the surface and into a Zodiac and CPR being administered. The Fore Sure swiftly returned to the swim scene with emergency medical staff who prepared me for transfer to Toronto General Hospital's hypothermia tank.

After being revived in the hypothermia tank, I spent the next 24 hours in the hospital sleeping off the fatigue. When I awoke I expected to see Matt sitting by the bed. He wasn't. I lay there awake but not moving. What had happened? I tried to gather my thoughts. Obviously I hadn't finished the swim and the bitter reality of being a loser embraced me like a tightening straight jacket. I closed my eyes and could feel tears stinging across the skin of my sunburned face. It wasn't long afterward that my family arrived to buoy my spirits and congratulate me for being a winner in their eyes. How condescending of them, I thought. I was a loser not a winner.

Maybe I was more comfortable being a loser than a winner. All sorts of thoughts raced through my head as I spent several days recovering quietly at home. Why had I not finished the race? I questioned myself over and over. Was it easier to just let go of my dream than to fight to the finish? How much had I wanted to be a winner? Had Matt let me down? Why had Christ been with me and then abandoned me? Would being a winner not be as comfortable and familiar a state as being a loser was for me? What had I gained for all my work but to heap embarrassment upon my family? I surrendered to thinking, David the quitter, David the loser.

The press was kind and one week later I announced that I'd make a second attempt in a few weeks. Art wasn't keen on me trying so soon after having succumbed to hypothermia. He tried to convince me to wait another year before trying again. I wasn't going to spend another year training as I had the previous year, it was now or never.

Three weeks later, again becoming a feature story in all the newspapers, I made another stab at the lake. I got twelve miles out into the swells of the lake but again hypothermia ravaged my fatless body.

A good friend of mine was dying of breast cancer that summer. After my second attempt Betty said to me, "Maybe you'll be a better man for not making the lake. You have experienced a lot of humility in the past few weeks and that might end up being the essence of who you are to become in the future. You learn more from adversity than through victory."

Sage advice from a wise woman. I will always remember her advice but it was a long time before I understood the significance of her wisdom.

David R I McKinstry

CHAPTER SIX

Roadblocks and Fireworks

I deliberately chose not to interfere in the planning of Susan's wake and funeral. Her best friend Sylvia called to see how Kolwyn was handling the news and she encouraged me to keep an arm's length away from Susan's family. Sylvia had nothing good to say about Susan's elder three children and told me to watch my back. Sylvia knew Austyn had made disparaging remarks about gays and that he was royally pissed off with his mother for having made guardianship arrangements with me.

"Don't give any of them an inch or they will take a mile," she warned. "Susan made it clear to me over the last year that she only had one son, that being Kolwyn. Austyn didn't help her a bit. He wouldn't show up to help his mother and when he did he always got into arguments with her and she'd spend hours crying over the phone telling me about his cruel remarks. She had disowned him many times because she loathed the person he'd become."

I asked Sylvia if she would support me over Austyn if he took me to court over Kolwyn.

"Oh, for sure. Susan told me she wanted Kolwyn with you. She said she could die happy knowing Michael and you would be Kolwyn's father. I was Susan's best friend and she confided in me everything she was thinking about. I'd be glad to tell a judge who Kolwyn needs to be with and who his mother wanted him to be with. Susan would cause thunder in Heaven if Austyn ever gets custody of Kolwyn."

Susan's mother, Joan, had just arrived from England and was staying with her sister Molly in Scarborough. I called hoping to be able to speak with Joan. She answered the phone on the first ring and began to inquire about Kolwyn and his reaction to Susan's death. Joan wasn't keen on me bringing Kolwyn to the funeral or the wake. She felt it might be too disturbing for a four-year-old to see his mother's lifeless body laid out in an open casket. I disagreed and presented her with the argument that seeing his mother in a casket might help Kolwyn understand that Mummy's soul had gone up to Heaven and that only her body was left behind to go into the ground. Joan acquiesced.

"Well, go ahead and bring him and let's just watch his reactions. If he doesn't handle the wake, then he shouldn't come to the funeral service."

Joan said she was exhausted from her six-hour flight but that her sisters and brother had been wonderful to her, especially Molly. I told Joan that her son Michael and sister Molly had bluntly told me a few weeks earlier that they didn't like the fact that Susan had given Kolwyn to me.

"Under these circumstances don't be too harsh with them, especially Molly. As the eldest sister, she can appear bull-headed as the matriarch of our Canadian family. But I couldn't manage Susan's funeral without her. She has a great heart but sometimes she can be frightfully blunt if she feels loved ones are in jeopardy. Give her time, I think you'll like her more as the two of you get to know one another." Joan paused to gather her thoughts again. "I really don't think you should stay too long at the wake tomorrow. Two days in a row experiencing grieving family might be too much for little Kolwyn. What time do you think you'll come to the funeral parlour?" I told her we'd come early in the afternoon so Kolwyn could see Susan without too many others around. I sensed that Joan still wasn't convinced Kolwyn should see his mother's body in a casket.

"Austyn is bringing the girls to the funeral parlour around three

David R I McKinstry

o'clock. It might be best if you get there earlier and leave before he arrives. I can't stand the bugger. He was so mean to his mother. I don't know if I could ever forgive him for the way that he treated her. Kolwyn is where Susan wanted him to be and don't you pay any mind to Austyn's ranting." Joan's words were obviously deliberately chosen and for the first time I really felt her full allegiance squarely behind Michael and I.

The next afternoon Michael, Kolwyn and I arrived at the funeral parlour just a few minutes before the 2 p.m. visitation for Susan. Joan and her siblings had arrived thirty minutes earlier to view the open casket and to say prayers with the priest. Looking shell-shocked, Joan saw us enter the viewing room and came up and hugged us all. The rest of Joan's siblings, whom I'd not yet met, came over and introduced themselves one at a time to us. Courtney suddenly appeared behind us, knelt down and hugged Kolwyn. Seeing the silhouette of her dead mother in the casket across the room made her gasp. Courtney clasped her hand around Kolwyn's and headed toward the casket. I excused myself from the small congregation of Susan's family and walked quickly to catch up to Courtney and Kolwyn. I wanted to observe Kolwyn when he saw Susan's body in the casket. Courtney and Kolwyn had arrived to the side of the coffin when I caught up to them. Courtney started to cry and put her hands to her face to cover her tears. Kolwyn seemed unsure what to do.

I lifted him up into my arms and said, "Remember what we talked about last night Kolwyn, this is just Mummy's body. She isn't in there. God already took her soul up to Heaven a few days ago."

Kolwyn looked puzzled and remarked, "But it looks like Mummy. See Mummy's long fingernails," he said pointing to Susan's clasped hands exposing her trademark long nails.

"Well, this is Mummy's body but she isn't in it. Remember we talked about the turtle shell and how an empty shell looks like a real turtle except the insides have already gone up to Heaven. Well, that is what Mummy's body is like, we can see her body but all her insides have gone up to Heaven."

A Swim *Against* The Tide

I needed to choose my words carefully. I had attended the wake of a favoured great-aunt when I was only seven years old. I had been fascinated by the body lying there and watched closely to see if the chest rose to show signs of being alive. I had asked my mother if I could touch the body and she said it was fine to touch the hands. The cold feel of my deceased great-aunt's hand had given me reassurance that she wasn't in her body any longer and it felt better imagining her being warm up somewhere in Heaven's clouds.

So I said to Kolwyn, "Do you want to touch Mummy's hand? It won't be warm like when she was inside her body. She took the warmth to Heaven with her." Kolwyn, quite mesmerised with every detail of Susan's body lying before him in this casket, nodded to me that he wanted to touch his mother's hand.

"You first, Dad," he said as he almost touched her and but then pulled back. I put my hand on Susan's folded hands to show Kolwyn there was nothing to be nervous about. Without hesitation he reached out and touched Susan's hand with his fingers and held them there until the coldness of her hands registered in his little mind.

"Her hand is cold, I guess she isn't inside 'cause Mummy has warm hands," he said looking up at me for some assurance.

"That's right, Mummy went to Heaven so she could always look out after you. She is feeling good and warm up there in Heaven with God. What colour wings do you think she has on today, Kolwyn?" I asked, trying to change the mood around the casket.

Kolwyn's eyes brightened up. "Orange. I bet she has orange wings. That's my favourite colour," he stated with a smile. I prayed that this experience of touching his mother would be as positive in his memory as it had been for me when I was his age.

We stayed long enough for Kolwyn to be greeted, fawned and cried over by numerous relatives. Austyn walked into the room and I could sense the mood of Joan and her siblings change the moment they noticed his arrival. Emma walked over and gave Kolwyn a big hug, followed by Austyn. Emma leaned over and gave me a warm kiss on the

David R I McKinstry

cheek and asked how Kolwyn was doing. Austyn brushed tightly up behind Emma to avoid any eye contact with me, and lifted Kolwyn up into the air and hugged him. Kolwyn gave him a big hug back but then wanted down so he could continue to visit with one of his young cousins. Impetuously, without acknowledging my presence, Austyn proceeded up to view his mother's body in the casket with Emma in tow. Courtney joined them at the side of the casket and a hush fell over the room.

I determined that we'd get the hell out of there within a few minutes. I didn't want Kolwyn being exposed to disrespectful scenes of defiance by Austyn. I winked at Michael who caught my drift, moved close to me and said he'd get the car and wait for us out front. A few minutes passed before Susan's three older children turned around and left the casket. They dispersed around the room to talk with friends and family and to be comforted. I whispered to Joan that I thought it was time for us to leave. She hugged me and asked me to be at Molly's prior to the funeral and we'd all drive over together for the funeral mass. I whisked Kolwyn up in my arms and said it was time for his Happy Meal at McDonald's, hoping he wouldn't make a fuss about leaving just yet. Thankfully the word McDonald's did the trick and he gleefully ran ahead of me to Michael in the waiting car.

Kolwyn didn't seem too bothered by the day's events at bedtime. I talked to him about the funeral service tomorrow and how it was a time for people to think good thoughts about Mummy and to celebrate her life. I told him there would be a fun party with lots of children after the funeral service back at Aunt Molly's house. Michael couldn't get out of a meeting to attend Monday's funeral so I knew I'd be holding the fort alone.

The chapel attached to the funeral parlour was already half full when we arrived at 1:45 p.m. The priest was waiting upstairs in the viewing room with Susan's open casket for her family to have one last viewing, a prayer and to close the casket lid. As the casket lid was being lowered, Austyn, Emma and Courtney ran up the stairs. The closing of the lid was delayed five minutes to give them additional time with Susan's body. All the elder family members were quite upset with them being

A Swim *Against* The Tide

late for their mother's funeral. Courtney was inappropriately dressed in a revealing low neckline shirt and tight leather pants that showed every crease in her curvaceous teenaged body. Several of Courtney's school friends, similarly attired, met her at the bottom of the stairwell and walked with her into the chapel arm in arm. I took Kolwyn downstairs to the chapel and we sat two rows behind the front pews. Joan accompanied the priest and Susan's casket into the chapel. Within a few minutes the small chapel was three-quarters full with about eighty family and friends waiting for the priest to begin the service.

Without incident, the service began five minutes late. Joan's emotions mounted when the casket lid was closed down over her daughter's dead body. She wept openly in the front pew being comforted by Molly and Emma. With one final prayer to go, the priest suggested to this congregation that we bow our heads and have a moment of silent prayer for Susan. Suddenly Joan lurched out of her seat and stood rigidly straight to the left of Susan's casket, uttered a guttural painful cry and dropped to the floor in a faint. Once revived, she sat slouched over and wept beside Molly in the pew as the final prayers were said. Courtney and Emma had been greatly affected by Joan's fainting spell and their emotionally contorted faces caused a swell of crying from the pews all around me. Courtney and Emma came over to Kolwyn and hugged him tightly. He didn't cry. He just looked confused.

After the service, Courtney asked if Kolwyn could ride with their family in the limo. I said no because his car seat in my car and would be safer for him and we'd meet them back at Aunt Molly's for the reception.

The reception was emotionally charged, just as the funeral had been hours before. Susan's death had hit home to her 40-something year-old friends that death could come at any age. To the elders of Susan's family, her death signified a young soul being laid to rest forty years too early. Kolwyn ran around the house playing with a flock of young second cousins. I tried to get around and work the room as best I could, hoping to introduce myself to Susan's family. I wanted to give them a chance to meet face to face the man in whom Susan had entrusted Kolwyn's parenting. I noticed many eyes watching me as I walked around the room passing sandwich and cookie trays, introducing myself as I passed each one. Although Courtney and Emma were warm and hospitable toward me, Austyn refused to look at me. Joan approached me and said she thought it would be a good moment for me to leave with Kolwyn. The frolicking children running amuck in the house were loud and annoying to the seniors. I gathered Kolwyn's things and told him we had to go. He resisted and ran off to chase one of the toddlers he had been teasing. Joan grabbed him and gave him a hug as he ran past her and she said it was time for him to put on his coat and boots.

I was holding my breath hoping that we would get out of this house without Kolwyn crying or making a scene. He grabbed hold of Courtney and said he wanted to stay with Courtney, the primary caregiver he had known for most of his young life. Courtney, thankfully, told him she would visit him soon at Woodhaven. This didn't calm him down much. Courtney sat with him and put on his boots and helped to button up his coat. Kolwyn was crying that he didn't want to leave and everyone in the house seemed to have gathered in the kitchen to witness Kolwyn being torn from their midst. I imagined a million eyes, armed with daggers, looking down on me as I struggled to pick Kolwyn up. Finally I got him into my arms. Joan was standing on the top step of the stairwell leading down from the kitchen and waved to me.

She winked and said, "Just get him in the car and go. I'll phone you later tonight."

Watching me carrying Kolwyn to the car, while he cried and struggled to get out of my arms, caused many of the relatives to sob openly over Kolwyn's grief and loss. I wondered if one of his relatives might suddenly challenge my guardianship of him. I just wanted to get Kolwyn strapped into his car seat and drive away as fast as possible. Joan had grabbed her overcoat and was following me to the car. She handed Kolwyn a cookie and told him she loved him and would see him soon. As we huddled together at the car with Kolwyn choking back

A Swim *Against* The Tide

tears and eating his cookie, Joan looked at me and said, "Take good care of my grandson and don't let him forget how much I love him."

Just then Austyn ran out of the house towards us. Was this going to be the confrontation I'd anticipated? I braced myself for whatever might happen. As Austyn approached the car, he had tears in his eyes and said he just wanted to say goodbye to his little brother. I felt sorry for Austyn. Maybe he wasn't so rotten after all. Maybe the death of his mother had brought him to his senses. He kissed Kolwyn on the cheek and said goodbye.

As he passed in front of me he said, "Thanks for bringing him to the funeral today."

I didn't have an opportunity to say anything in response as he just turned and ran back to the house. I got in the car and rolled down the window to face Joan who was waiting in the cold to wave us goodbye. She leaned in the window and said, "Just get out of here David, go on, take him back to where he belongs at Woodhaven with you." She opened Kolwyn's door and leaned in and told him to give her a big hug. Kolwyn had a mouthful of cookie bits and was crying softly as he leaned in to give his nanny a hug. As we drove up to the end of the street and turned northward on Brimley Road, I looked at Kolwyn whimpering in his car seat. I couldn't begin to imagine the bewilderment and grief this four-year-old must be experiencing. I felt so helpless. A few blocks later I asked if he would like to go to McDonald's and get a Happy Meal. Instantly Kolwyn's tears stopped and he smiled brightly.

After eating half a Happy Meal we headed back to Woodhaven. I was very relieved to have survived the past four days and two hours later Kolwyn was sleeping soundly in his bed.

The first few days after Susan's funeral were busy days on the phone trying to get a flight booked to Delhi. I was in contact with Mrs. Raghunath at the orphanage by fax around the clock in an effort to make sure all my documentation was in order. I hoped and prayed that my adoption case would be heard in the Delhi courts before the judicial offices closed for six weeks starting December 5, 1998.

David R I McKinstry

The psychologist we had hired months earlier to work with Kolwyn's adjustment to his new home, suggested we double our appointments during those first few weeks after Susan's death. Kolwyn adored his sessions with Dr. Brian Nichol and he appeared to be processing and dealing well with all the transition and grief in his young life.

Swim lessons at Trent University were nightly at 6:30 p.m. and Kolwyn was becoming quite comfortable and proficient in the water, easily capable of swimming unassisted for one length of the 25 metre pool. It was a proud Kodak moment watching him smile at me from the pool indicating he was having a great time swimming on his own.

On December 2nd, Mohini called from India to tell me that the Canadian officials hadn't forwarded my documents in time for the courts to process them before they closed; this meant that I'd have to wait for the next court session which wouldn't begin until late January 1999. This meant Nicholas wouldn't be home for Christmas. I was more devastated than angry. From the moment he arrived into our home, Kolwyn was told that he had an older brother named Nicholas who would be coming home from India soon. I loathed the idea of Nicholas spending another day separated from me and I toiled over the possibility of going to India to wait alongside Nicholas until his clearances came through. I faxed Mohini about this idea. Within hours she responded with a phone call telling me not to waste my money on accommodations and food for what could be two to six months until Nicholas' paperwork was completed by the courts. I was so sick of hearing patience, patience and more patience.

Michael hadn't seen much of his mother and her husband since the day they told me I offended them because I presented myself as being "too gay" for their sensibilities. I laughed to myself as I thought about all the examples of overtly feminine gay people I'd met in my life.

We'd met them several times over the summer at a local Peterborough park to see if through discussion a reconciliation or truce was possible. They told me repeatedly that I had misunderstood their

A Swim *Against* The Tide

remarks but I knew in my guts that I hadn't misinterpreted anything. They had clearly said, "David, you never talk about anything without giving it a gay slant. We don't want to hear the word gay all the time. It makes everyone uncomfortable. We don't mind if you kiss Michael on the sofa in front of us but please just don't use the word gay all the time." No wonder Michael was feeling detached from his mother and her husband. I was too!

We hadn't introduced Kolwyn to them because Michael had insisted the misunderstanding between them and me be dealt with first.

On Sunday December 5th Michael's mother telephoned and asked if we could come over to visit and finish off any unresolved reconciliation details. When Michael presented this invitation to me I was hopeful, for his sake, that a reconciliation could be reached.

I didn't like Louise's husband, Bill. I could tell Michael was being torn between the two sides and a truce would be good for him. I suggested we take Kolwyn with us so after the terms of the peace agreement were drawn, Kolwyn could be introduced to his other grandparents. We loaded several of his favourite Disney movies into our day-trip bag and headed off to Lindsay.

Louise met us at the door and welcomed us into her large country-style kitchen. They lived in the heart of Lindsay in a century stone house tastefully decorated with fine period furnishings. She and Bill operated a psychological counselling service out of their home. I suspected Louise had told her husband to watch his remarks so he wouldn't foil this attempt at reconciliation. Bill was artificially nice to me and I mused at just how arrogantly superficial and sugary sweet he could be when it was required.

Kolwyn had been with us for almost four months but he was meeting them for the first time. I very casually introduced Louise and Bill as friends of Daddy and as soon as our coats were off, Michael suggested Kolwyn watch a video in the den.

I complimented Louise and Bill on the warmth of the paint colour they'd used in the dining room. I was struck by how unresponsive they

David R I McKinstry

were to me. Was I being ignored on purpose? Even Michael looked surprised by their mood.

We settled into chairs and sofas arranged in perfect Martha Stewart fashion around the fireplace. The four of us sat in silence for several minutes. After being rebuffed, I wasn't about to break the silence and Michael just stared at the fire.

Bill slowly unfolded a piece of paper he'd pulled from his pocket. I couldn't help myself and said, "Do we have an agenda for this meeting?" Only Michael smiled.

Bill started off recapping what we had discussed at previous meetings. Then Louise told Michael how she really wanted to build a better mother-son relationship with him. I felt sorry for Louise. She just didn't know how to change Michael's ambivalence toward her.

Bill referred to Michael's reticence to talk to Louise about his sexuality over the past ten years and how they both wanted Michael to feel at ease to discuss this matter with them in the future. He hated any sort of confrontation. Michael smiled and said he didn't want to dwell on the past, preferring to keep at arm's-length from any controversial topic. He looked over at me as if presenting me with an opportunity to speak up. I was observing their family dynamic and didn't want to interfere, so I remained quiet. Bill asked if we understood that they weren't homophobic and Michael said he'd feel more at ease if we just dropped the issue and let sleeping dogs lie.

Forty minutes had passed with strained and deliberate conversation flowing between the four of us. Louise told Michael that not having a close bond with him was a source of great concern for her. Bill sat quietly as Louise and Michael spoke back and forth. I noticed him frequently looking over at me and staring for seconds on end. I met his stares with confident smiles. Slowly a Cheshire cat-like expression spread across his face. I excused myself to check on Kolwyn.

When I returned the three of them were quietly watching the burning logs in the fireplace. Just as I sat down, Bill asked me several questions about Kolwyn's grief over the recent loss of his mother and about any progress in finalising his adoption. I had an uncanny feeling that Bill was just playing cat and mouse with me. I wanted to give him the benefit of the doubt so I gave him a full account of the previous few months. His expression didn't change for most of the five minutes I spoke.

Bill asked Michael what books he had been reading lately to hone his parenting skills.

Michael, not an avid reader, said that he felt good old common sense would help him better than reading parenting books. Bill asked me the same question. I responded by giving him a lengthy list of books, parenting journals and publications I had been reading over the past few years.

After a few more silent minutes, Louise asked if anyone had other concerns they wished to voice. No one moved. She looked directly at me and asked if they had cleared up any misconceptions I'd had about them. I was beginning to see a different side, a softer side to his mother which I'd not seen before this. I sensed her heightened optimism that our afternoon discussion might offer hope for a better relationship with Michael in the future. I told her I felt much better about us beginning to work at a better relationship. Looking very motherly, Louise smiled and said she was pleased I felt better. Then she looked over at Bill who had shuffled forward in his chair as if wanting to speak.

"Well I have something I want to say to David and Michael about the seriousness of adoption and my impression of how you are preparing yourselves to have children. I hope my comments won't be mis-interpreted by you, David." This dig was as blunt as a wet fart. I just sensed that something was coming down the sewer pipe and I braced myself for whatever was to come. Instantly the mood in the room became negatively charged, waiting for Bill to drop a bomb.

"I have deep concerns about your level of preparedness to be parents. You talk about reading some books David, but you don't have a clue about parenting. Have you considered how you'd teach your children to make good value judgements or choose right from wrong? Parenting is a serious matter and I don't think either of you has given it enough consideration. In fact," he said, pausing as if trying to choose which barrel

David R I McKinstry

of the gun to fire next, "I don't think either one of you should be parents yet. And I truly believe from what you've said David, that your sole reason for adopting children is to make a gay political statement."

Had I heard him correctly? I was sure I hadn't misconstrued what he'd just said. Michael sat motionless with his eyes downcast beside me. Across the room his mother's face looked like the colour was quickly draining away while she looked straight ahead at her husband. My body tightened with anger. My fingertips felt cold and my heart rate was accelerating in leaps and bounds. I had been playing nice long enough. My eyes met Bill's stare and locked on target, "Fuck you," then I reacted with an even louder, "FUCK YOU!" I leaned forward in my chair. "Who the hell are you to tell me I'm not prepared to be a parent? Who died and made you God?"

I wasn't about to let him pass judgement on me any more than I would listen to his unsolicited opinion on my reasons for wanting to be a parent. Who was this asshole to judge me?

"You don't know anything about me. Where do you get off talking to me about anything to do with value judgements? You had an affair with Michael's mother before she was divorced and you have the balls to talk to me about morality, values or motives! What do you know about the fight I've encountered over the past eighteen years of trying to adopt children? You've got shit for brains if you think THE MOTIVES behind me spending $50,000 US to adopt children was to make some sort of gay political statement."

Bill sat there silently, looking directly into my eyes as if challenging me to continue. He wasn't on safe ground, personally or professionally, making baseless assumptions about me.

"Why do we need a motive to adopt? Why can't it be simple, like we love children and want to raise children within the framework of our family unit, just like our straight counter-parts."

Raw emotions took over and I could feel myself seething at the bit as my nostrils flared. I stood up to tower over him.

"If I wanted to make a public gay political statement I could have

— 101 —

A Swim *Against* The Tide

found a hundred other causes less expensive and more popular than an adoption forum. It has cost Michael and me a lifetime of savings to adopt our sons! Before Michael came in to my life, Nick and I had spent $50,000 US on surrogacy and adoption firms. Michael has cashed twenty years of savings bonds just to pad our adoption account. So don't look at me and assume to know what it has cost financially and emotionally for me, for us, to adopt children. You're a pompous arrogant prick and you've just blown it for your wife to have a friendly familial relationship with us as long as you're in the picture. I'd let my children call you the arse end of a buffoon before you'd ever be called grandpa. You're one stupid prick!"

All I wanted to do was ram my fist down his throat. The only phrase that kept coming out of my mouth with rapid-fire precision was, "Fuck you!"

I turned toward Louise and said, "I apologise for my language. I have never used that language in the company of elders. Your husband knows nothing about me, so listening to him pontificate about the realities of parenthood, and his perception of my state of preparedness to be a parent is absurd. He'll never be around our children, Louise. If you want to visit us alone at our house or in the park you're welcome but your husband will never be around our boys."

I moved toward the archway of the hall and told Michael I'd meet him in the car. My feet planted themselves heavily on the wooden floors of the long hallway leading to Kolwyn in their TV room. I marched over to the VCR and pressed the stop/eject button. Kolwyn didn't say a word, which was strange for him, considering I had just turned off his favourite video. I guess he could sense the steam rising off my skin.

"We're leaving NOW. I'll take you to McDonald's if you hurry and get your boots and coat on." I didn't have to say another word. Kolwyn rushed to the kitchen door and sat down to put on his shoes. I bent down to help him. He jumped up and put on his coat and I gently but quickly ushered him out the door toward the car without saying goodbye to anyone. As I turned behind me to close the door I saw Michael entering into the kitchen with his mother. I slammed shut the

David R I McKinstry

door and walked out. Kolwyn was fumbling with the seat belt of his car seat so I helped him get secure.

Michael joined us in the car thirty seconds later and turned to Kolwyn and said, "Are we going to McDonald's, Kolwyn?" It was evident that Kolwyn was ready to tackle a burger. Michael drove, I kept my eyes forward and silence enveloped the car like mist over a Midlands moor.

After several minutes I put my hand on Michael's knee and quietly said, "I'm adamant about Bill never being around our kids. Honestly, I thought I was going to jump out of my chair and rip his head off."

"I'm surprised you sat and listened to him as long as you did," he said gripping my hand. "I could feel your blood pressure rising and you were right to say what you did. He was totally out of line making those remarks about our readiness to adopt. Even my mother told me so at the door, but he's her husband and I'm sure she felt caught in the middle." Michael paused, chuckled and asked, "Have you ever seen the arse end of a buffoon?" We both laughed and I could feel my neck muscles begin to relax.

We decided to let Kolwyn enjoy the McDonald's play area for an extra long time that afternoon. Michael and I talked about Bill's senseless comments ad nauseum. Michael agreed that our meeting with them had been going well up until that moment when Bill annihilated any possible chance of me ever reconciling with him. We gathered up Kolwyn and drove home to Woodhaven in the first big snowstorm of the season.

A few weeks later while I was wrapping gifts for the upcoming women's shelter Christmas program, a strange late-model car drove into our parking lot. The driver was Kolwyn's half-brother Austyn. My first impulse was to yell upstairs advising Kolwyn to stay there and be quiet. I had a feeling this unscheduled visit was going to be confrontational.

I greeted Austyn at the door and he asked if his girlfriend and her two young kids could come in too. I nodded yes to him and he waved out to the car to his girlfriend. Austyn asked where Kolwyn was and I told him he was playing upstairs. The girlfriend and two very small children walked into the hallway out of the cold winter wind.

A Swim *Against* The Tide

"I want to take Kolwyn home with me for a week or so. I have friends in town who want to see him again and I've got time to take him around with me," he announced cavalierly.

"That's not going to happen, Austyn. I have legal custody of him, as per your mother's instructions. Kolwyn isn't going anywhere with you unsupervised. Besides which, he is in school three full days a week and I'm not going to take him out of classes."

"Well I'm not happy with this," said Austyn. Just then Kolwyn came down the stairs, having heard the dogs barking upon Austyn's arrival. "Hi Kolwyn, I've come to visit and take you home with me," he said and tried to walk past me toward Kolwyn.

I firmly placed the flat of my hand on his chest and stopped his forward movement toward my son.

"Kolwyn please go to your bedroom now. I want to talk adult-talk with Austyn so you go to your room until I call you." I said this in a tone of voice that Kolwyn knew meant serious business. He didn't argue and an unsure torn-between-two-worlds frown spread across his little face, he walked away from us to his bedroom.

"He's coming with me, David, I'm his family." Austyn said.

I told him to get his girlfriend and children out of my house and under no circumstances was he to come up and visit Kolwyn without giving me advance notice. "I have only to call the police and they will have you arrested on the spot for trespassing. But before the police get here I'll have rearranged your face. This isn't an idyll threat; it's a promise. Now get off my property."

Austyn's girlfriend tugged at his jacket and Austyn nervously laughed. "Alright, I half-expected this from you. I got something from the sheriff for you in my car." Austyn helped his girlfriend and the two toddlers out to his car. It didn't take long before Austyn came back to the door, walked in, sneered at me and threw some papers on the floor.

"See you in court, asshole," and without waiting for an answer he walked quickly back to his car.

I grappled for a second about whether or not to call the police so

David R I McKinstry

they would have a record of this trespassing infraction on file. Instead I just looked out the library window and watched Austyn's car fade out of sight. I went down into the foyer and picked up the papers he had thrown inside. It was a legal affidavit telling me I had to appear in court on December 18th to defend my right to have Kolwyn.

A few hours later when I had calmed down, I called Susan's mother Joan, still staying at Molly's and trying to clean up Susan's estate. I told her about the surprise visit from Austyn and she cursed him for being so stupid and brash.

"He mustn't get Kolwyn … Susan would turn in her grave if you lose Kolwyn to them. You must fight this. Do you have a lawyer?" she asked. I told her I would mount a defence through a good lawyer in town but if she had any damning information on her eldest grandson that would help my case, she should put it on paper and courier it to me. Joan said Susan had written in her journal that she had denounced any claims Austyn might have to being her son. She was completely devastated by his contempt for her. I told Joan that I would be up to Toronto in a few days to collect the necessary documents for Kolwyn, such as his birth certificate, health certificates, passport, etc.

Sylvia called the following day and I told her about Austyn's visit. Immediately she offered to write a letter to the court indicating her close friendship with Susan and how in ten years of knowing Susan she had only heard Susan mention Austyn's name a few times.

"I only ever met him in person around the time Susan got sick."

Friday, December 18th. I was dreading having this case heard in Peterborough, a town not known for its liberal thinking judiciary. Our Toronto lawyer told me she would arrange for local counsel to take on this case and represent me in court. After a few hours of waiting for our case to be called, Austyn and Emma strode into the court's reception area. Twenty minutes later, Austyn began to tell the story of his little half-brother and his mother's recent death.

"The only way, your Honour," he said, "for two gays to get custody of Kolwyn was to take advantage of our dying mother. I just want what is best for him."

Before my lawyer could interject the judge looked down over his glasses at Austyn and said, "I've read and reread this case. First things first. Your mother was of sound mind when she made her choice of surrogate parents and we must honour that. Secondly, young man, don't ever try to use a gay offence in my courtroom again. This is 1998 and that just isn't going to happen here."

The judge went on to tell Austyn that he could fight me for custody but it would end up costing him a lot, which would be difficult for someone unemployed.

"Kolwyn is to remain in his custodial home and I declare this petition to cancel interim custody by Austyn denied. I further order that any visitations by Austyn, Emma or Courtney be requested in writing to David McKinstry at least 48 hours before any proposed visitation occurs. Court adjourned."

Kolwyn's first Christmas with us, 1998.

David R I McKinstry

Kolwyn had stayed with Mum that morning, just in case Austyn had tried to kidnap him from school or Woodhaven. Neither Austyn nor Emma looked at Michael or me. When the court was emptied, they walked to their car and drove off without saying a word to us.

"Hopefully that is the last we see of them," I said wistfully to Michael.

A few days later our first group of mums and tots from the women's shelter arrived for what was becoming an annual Christmas event at Woodhaven. I had just returned from taking Kolwyn to the dentist for the second of two root canals resulting from a diet of hot dogs, pop and candy the first four years of his life. We had really gone all out this year in terms of buying them presents over the last the few months and donations from Disney Canada and a host of other groups had risen five fold.

Huge snowflakes fell on Woodhaven all Christmas Day. Inside was warm and the smells of turkey and pies in the oven made it seem like paradise. Outside the falling snow made each of us feel like we were at the North Pole. Kolwyn's first Christmas at Woodhaven was spectacular. Not only did our Christmas guests and their children get hordes of gifts under the tree, so did Kolwyn. It seemed like every person we had ever met was visiting us with a gift for our new son.

We served supper to our guests and after successive rounds in the hot tub, the children were so sleepy by 8 p.m. Christmas night that there was no fuss when their mothers suggested they go to bed. Kolwyn was just as tired and I was very strict about his 7:15 p.m. bedtime. He was asleep within minutes of his head touching the pillow. Michael was going to drive him to Toronto so he could have a few hours with his half-siblings the following day. I was worried about letting them have anything to do with Kolwyn yet didn't feel good about denying them access, especially since this was their first Christmas without their mother.

Kolwyn was in an emotional turmoil after his Boxing Day visit with Austyn, Emma and Courtney. Austyn told him not to refer to me as Dad or Michael as Daddy. It took several days for Kolwyn to return to normal. We were definitely not going to allow Kolwyn to have unsupervised visitations with any of his half-siblings from that point onward. It was too disruptive for Kolwyn and he already was a little boy living with too many disturbing memories.

We arranged for Brian to have an extra session with Kolwyn a few days after New Years. The great strides Kolwyn had made were nullified after his visit to Toronto. His anger was back and he just couldn't deal with all these resurfacing feelings. At almost five years of age, Kolwyn still had not mastered potty training. Our poor little guy had been through enough in his young life and potty training was low on my priority list. I knew that once he felt love, comfort and stability in his new home that it would follow soon afterward.

What came next, however, was a shock. Brian opened Kolwyn's file, put his reading glasses down on the pages and said he had something very important to discuss with us.

"Kolwyn is sexualised far beyond his years. He presents as a little boy too aware of both male and female sex organs. I have observed him frequently putting male dolls on top of female dolls and demonstrating a humping action. This clearly indicates that he has either observed adult sexual behaviours or has been a participant. He told me about putting his hands on a female relative's genitals and touching her breasts. I will put this in a report for you to give to the judge," he said quietly.

I could feel my guts begin to knot. Thirty-nine years previously I had been forced to touch an abuser's body parts and the memory of it hung like an anchor around my neck. I could still conjure up the feelings of shame, fear and lost innocence I had felt as a helpless six-year-old. How fateful, how ironic to adopt a son who had probably experienced the same sexual abuse at the hand of a woman. I wanted to vomit. I wouldn't wish my worst enemies to have experienced what I so vividly remembered. The thought of our son having to deal with this was beginning to overwhelm me.

Brian told us to talk to Kolwyn about private body parts and how they are private.

"Reinforce in him that he must never touch another person's body parts with or without their permission nor should he allow anyone to

David R I McKinstry

touch him. Kolwyn is sexualised to about that of a ten-year-old boy."

Michael and I were dumbfounded by Brian's report. Not that we hadn't suspected something, but suspicion and confirmation had seemed poles apart. Brian told us that consistent discipline and love in the home, and a concerted effort on our part to tell Kolwyn that body parts are private, would help Kolwyn in the long run. Brian said Kolwyn was an intelligent child and he would learn quickly once boundaries and limitations were set on his behaviours.

I hadn't been feeling well and I kept getting recurrent bouts of pneumonia along with fevers and chills. When the second bout of pneumonia was diagnosed in the emergency department, the attending physician asked if it was possible for me to be HIV+. I half-smiled and told him only if by Immaculate Conception ... he wasn't amused. But neither was I. I asked, "Does being gay and having pneumonia mean you should assume I am HIV+?" He got my point. I told him there wasn't a chance in hell of me being HIV+.

As the days passed, my breathing became more compromised. Simple chores around the lodge would have me gasping for air. Paul and Clara arrived to spend one night with us a few days before Michael had to return to work after his Christmas break. They said they really enjoyed being Kolwyn's Nanna and Poppa and likewise, Kolwyn looked forward to their visits. I thought it odd that they hadn't raised the subject of Nicholas' adoption and my upcoming trip to India for at least several weeks. I gave them an unsolicited update on my travel plans over coffee that afternoon.

Clara looked at Paul, sighed and then said point blank, "Why don't you put off the adoption of Nicholas. You have a real gift in Kolwyn. You have a very happy healthy son. Aren't you better off to stop while you're ahead? Adopting another child, especially one from India who has no health records and is a different colour from Kolwyn, could spell trouble. You don't know what kinds of health problems he'll have as he grows and Nicholas will stand out in the classroom. Kids learn prejudice

A Swim *Against* The Tide

early and he'll be teased about being different. You know how mean people can be," she said. Paul echoed her sentiments.

I told myself to count to ten. The hackles on my neck stood straight up at the suggestion of me leaving Nicholas behind in India just because Kolwyn had suddenly appeared in our lives. Unfortunately several insensitive friends had recently implied that we should just accept our one-white-child status and not bother with all the hassles of adopting a racially different child. These implications were insulting and I had swiftly and angrily responded to their insensitivity.

Paul regularly made remarks and jokes about racial minorities. He did this more to get a laugh than from being mean-spirited. My cousin Elizabeth had stopped allowing jokes of any kind to be spoken in her home, stating that whenever a joke is made about someone's differences, its always mean-spirited to someone somewhere. This made good sense to me and I was trying to follow suit.

Clara thought I was being too sensitive. Paul had made some really offensive remarks about blacks and Toronto crime going hand-in-hand. As a cop, he'd had many altercations with criminals and the high recidivism of young black offenders had probably caused him, and many other good cops, to lose their perspective, become jaded and too suspicious of racial minorities.

From day one, Clara and Paul had been attentive, loving grand-parents to Kolwyn. It was important for me to give them the benefit of my doubts and have faith that they would be just as loving and wonderful to Nicholas.

"Please do not ever suggest I cancel my trip to bring Nicholas home. He isn't yet in Canada but he is my son just as Kolwyn is my son. You'd better get used to it. You will have two grandsons in this home – one white and one brown. If you were in my place right now I know you would be fiercely protective of Nicholas, just like I am. After all," I softened my tone and smiled, "your genes are in me so I come by this tenacity legitimately!"

Clara and Paul's facial expressions told me they didn't like my

David R I McKinstry

inference that they might be prejudiced. I wondered if I had been too harsh with them. I wanted to freeze this moment in time so I could find a better way to articulate my feelings on this matter. Yet I also knew Clara and Paul couldn't bring themselves to tell their friends that their shared biological son was gay. I had lots of questions on the tip of my tongue. Why would I expect them to immediately embrace having a coloured grandson being raised by their biological son and his male lover? Why would I be loyal to those who would deny my identity? For obvious reasons I preferred not to think about this too much. Michael and I had already discussed possible prejudice within our family circles. We had decided everyone would have a chance to play a role in our sons' lives as grandparent, aunt, uncle or cousin but there would be no second chance for anyone who impugned the dignity of our family portrait.

Clara assured me that she wasn't being prejudiced, just trying to be realistic.

"You live in the country and the boys will go to a rural school. Kolwyn will have enough to deal with having gay parents, imagine all the problems Nicholas could face dealing with two gay fathers *and* being the only brown boy in a country school. I just don't know if its fair to Nicholas," she said. I knew she was genuine in her concern for all the adjustments that lay ahead for our sons. However I didn't budge and the subject of me cancelling Nicholas' adoption was never raised again.

Weeks earlier Michael had touched on the issue of us not being able to fully finance Nicholas' adoption. I verbally decapitated him at the suggestion that I not return to India to bring our son home. I told Michael I loved him dearly but that my love would sour overnight if he ever hinted that financially it made better sense for me to abandon Nicholas in India. So when Clara and Paul raised the subject and said, "Be happy with what you have and forego the trip to India," my anger resurfaced unfairly with a vengeance.

I hadn't been feeling well over the Christmas holidays as my lungs felt like soggy bags of mush. I was beginning to think I had a bad case of persistent pneumonia so I made an appointment to check my lungs again on January 9th. The physician on duty suggested that the green sputum I was coughing up in large amounts was most likely from the persistent lung infection. He would do some tests and call me with the results in a day or two. He sent me for a chest X-ray and then ordered me home to bed. A few days later, my doctor called to say that I did in fact have a really bad case of a resistant pneumonia. It took a few days on heavy medication for me to begin feeling better. I laid low, doing minimal work while Kolwyn was at school, so I'd be alert and mobile when he got home. By the third week of January I was feeling much better and resumed much of my normal routines.

Toward the end of January, I became very impatient for news from India. I would fax Mohini each morning. I wanted all my bases covered. I longed to tell Mohini about Kolwyn but I knew the Ontario government wouldn't allow me to simultaneously adopt domestically and internationally. I had kept Kolwyn out of the picture to our social worker so it wouldn't require changes to our Home-study, which would cause further delays. If Mohini learned that I had custody of a Canadian boy who was in the process of being adopted by me, then her government wouldn't allow Nicholas to be placed with me for eighteen months after Kolwyn's adoption was finalized in the courts. I decided to tell Mohini that I had been named joint-custodian of a little boy whose mother was dying of cancer. I said this boy's mother was still very much alive and hopefully would live another few years. But I wanted Mohini to be able to receive photos of Kolwyn, without any whistles going off. I lied and told her Kolwyn was staying with me a few days each week, to give his mother much needed respite from parenting. I didn't want Mohini to know too much but I did want her to be aware that Nicholas would have a possible sibling down the road. Mohini was pleased to hear Nicholas would eventually have a brother and tactfully she reminded me that I couldn't be engaged in an international adoption if a paper trail existed for a domestic adoption.

In early February, I received the news that I had waited so long to hear. Mohini called and told me to book my flight.

David R I McKinstry

"Nicholas has been given clearance for the adoption by the High Court in Delhi."

Thrilled at the news, I informed her I'd be there in a week.

Mohini giggled and replied, "You have waited this long, don't be impetuous. Book your flight for early March instead. It will take me another three weeks to get his health certificates together and have the Canadian doctor check him over and do blood work. As of this moment, Nicholas is yours ... its only a matter of weeks before you may take him home now." I could tell Mohini was thrilled too. She said she would book me into a small hotel near the orphanage so I could walk from her house to my hotel in about ten minutes. I told her I had already booked my flight but that I could still extend the start date of my trip without any financial penalties. She laughed and said, "I knew you had booked your trip. This is of no surprise to me. You have lived with hope in your heart for so long and it has finally paid off for you. Congratulations David."

I left Michael a message at school to call me URGENTLY to hear some good news. I was on the phone spreading this news to our long list of interested friends and family within the hour. Then I called Mum to let her know her other grandson was finally coming home to Canada.

The tone of Michael's voice convinced me he really was thrilled to hear this good news about Nicholas. I had been worried for weeks that some last minute glitch would arise and postpone my trip again. I worried that the Indian courts would say that I hadn't filed all the right documents in the proper order, or that the Canadian officials forgot to stamp the right day of the week on the documents. Considering the screw-ups thus far with the Canadian officials and the Indian courts, nothing was beyond my imagination.

Michael would be home for March break beginning March 9th so I booked my flight out of Toronto on March 10th. Mohini had said I should only have to stay in Delhi about a week and then jet home with Nicholas.

I called my social worker to tell her the news. Barbara was happy for me and said she would inform the immigration law firm in Ottawa to expect me and Nicholas home around the 20th of March. I had not been able to tell Barbara about Michael, which bothered me terribly. Since my Home-study had been modified to reflect that I was a widower, I hadn't mentioned Michael coming into my life. Again the costs in time and money to have my Home-study updated was too great, so I kept Michael out of the equation. What a ridiculous rouse. This contrived duplicity that each level of government forced me to play, was so unnecessary. The moral blindness of dumb-ass politicians who enacted such policies did nothing to promote integrity for the adoption process.

Mohini said she would courier the court documents to my designated immigration lawyer so they could make up the necessary papers for Nicholas upon entry to Canada. I would have to take this paperwork with me but the immigration lawyer had told me that as soon as they got the court approvals from Delhi it was only a matter of a day or two until they'd have the immigration paperwork stamped and in my hands.

I was overjoyed. The end was in sight and Nicholas would soon be home in Canada. Financially I wasn't sure how I'd do it. I needed more than the $4,500 left in my account. The plane tickets for Nicholas and I alone had cost me $4,100. I needed $2,500 US to pay Mohini for the final adoption expenses. I knew I had to have incidental expenses covered and food and accommodation would cost me another $2,500 US if I was there more than a week. Bribes and transportation costs had to be factored into the equation.

My health had continued to worsen. Since Christmas I'd had two bouts of pneumonia. One night Kolwyn and I were horsing around in the living room and he jumped on my back and asked for a piggyback ride around the room. He wrapped his hands too tightly around my neck compromising my airway. That action combined with constant fatigue and shortness of breath caused me to faint on top of him. I was only unconscious for a short while before I came to and realized Kolwyn was squirming beneath me. He was frightened and asked me if I was going to die. I too was unnerved by fainting and decided to get

David R I McKinstry

some medical advice the following day. I assured my little son that I was fine and wouldn't die.

I managed to get into see the doctor and over the next few days I had a battery of X-rays, MRIs and blood taken from my veins. I had already been told I had pneumonia and thought these additional tests would just confirm a worsening case of pneumonia. It was surreal to have the doctor tell me I could have lympho-sarcoma, lung and heart cancer. Several specialists agreed with my physician's immediate concern and suggested that it was irresponsible of me to consider adopting another child if I wouldn't be around to raise it.

"You mean I could die?" I asked. The doctor told me my lung x-rays didn't look good and that if it was as they suspected, lympho-sarcoma was terminal.

My first thoughts following this bad news were of Nicholas waiting for me to bring him home. Getting to India took on a heightened urgency. I had lots of life insurance for Michael and the boys in the event I croaked. I informed this medical team that I needed enough puffers and steroids to keep me going until I got home with Nicholas. I was leaving in seven days and nothing was going to deter me from bring my son home from India. I invoked my right for doctor-patient confidentiality and told Michael that I had a manageable but deep-rooted pneumonia which was slowly getting better. I wouldn't let Michael's concern for my long-term health jeopardise bringing Nicholas home. My health, as far as Michael was aware, was a non-issue as I packed and prepared to fly to India.

My dear friend, Deb Reid, called a few days later to inquire about my pneumonia status and the adoption of Nicholas. Deb had been a single mum for most of her kids' lives. She and I had gone through high school together. She moved west, married, had two children and finally left her bad marriage and returned to Peterborough to raise her children. She and I had reunited at church a few years earlier just after Nick and I had moved to Sandy Lake. Deb had often stated that if she had been a few years younger, she would have gladly been a surrogate to give us a child.

A Swim *Against* The Tide

I told Deb that health wise I was fine but I was still $6,000 to $10,000 short of my financial goal. I joked with her saying I'd have to sell my body on the streets of Delhi to rich gay Indians to finance the remainder of this adoption. She asked how I was going to raise that kind of money and I said, "Where there is a will there is a way. God has helped me this far and he won't desert me now."

Later that afternoon Deb telephoned again. "David I have two credit cards with a combined $6,000 limit sitting in my freezer for just such an emergency. If $6,000 will help bring Nicholas home, I could get you cash tomorrow off those credit cards and you and Michael could pay off my credit card and the interest monthly until you can afford to retire the loan completely."

Like an angel come to give me good news, I was overjoyed at her offer. I told her to think about it and I'd call her the next day to let her know how my money hunt had gone. I called Michael to let him know that Deb had offered us this loan and he was greatly relieved. We had stripped all our savings for the house renovations, funding legal expenses and adoption costs. Michael was worried sick about how we'd get the cash I'd need to complete this journey.

I spoke to Mum the next morning. I had agreed to take her to her medical appointment that afternoon. I suggested we go out for lunch beforehand. Over lunch Mum asked me how my money was holding out and I told her we were really worried about having enough cash on hand for the adoption.

"I don't have much money David," she said, "but if it's a matter of needing a few more thousand dollars to get Nicholas home, I have qualified for another VISA with a $10,000 limit. In fact I have already spoken to the bank and am having a second card made up with your name on it. It should be at the bank tomorrow and you could take that along to India." I was stunned and could hardly believe my luck. Between Deb's offer and now my Mum's additional VISA, we had the cash required to bring Nicholas home.

There was no stopping me now!

David R I McKinstry

Throughout February, Woodhaven had been full up on weekends and empty during the week, just the way I liked it. Kolwyn was feeling very much at home with us. He loved to play computer games with Michael on weekends and during the week I took him for swim lessons, out for lunches, to sessions with his child psychologist and for weeks he had helped me to pack four suitcases full of children's clothing for the kids in the orphanage. I had borrowed a camcorder with which to video my first meeting with Nicholas. I had cash in hand, American money orders tucked into safe hiding spots, stashes of necessary drugs. I wasn't leaving anything to chance. I even continued to make telephone calls to Ottawa about my immigration paperwork and to Delhi inquiring about Nicholas. Kolwyn got to talk to Nicholas a few weeks before my departure for India. I called Mohini early one morning and by luck Nicholas had been brought to her office by one of the orphanage workers to attend another child's going away party. Nicholas uttered a high pitched "hi" over the phone to Kolwyn and me. I told him I would be there in a few weeks, knowing full well that he didn't understand a word I was saying.

I had enjoyed having Kolwyn to myself for the past seven months. It gave us a chance to bond well and to learn lots about each other. I had been thrust into parenthood but felt I had adjusted to it quite well. As the countdown to my departure got closer I became remarkably calm, yet saddened knowing my time alone with Kolwyn had come to an end.

Finally I was only 24 hours away from leaving for India. That night I could barely get through Kolwyn's story time without huffing and puffing. I snuggled up beside him as we said prayers. We both knew tonight would be our last night before he got a brother and Michael and I got another son. I felt sad that this chapter of our lives was about to end but my excitement over bringing Nicholas home outweighed the melancholy. Kolwyn hugged me tight. It was a very special father and son moment.

I put the dogs out for one last pee. Twenty minutes later I was in bed, propped up on pillows, reading Rohinton Mistry's novel *A Fine*

Balance. I had started it during my first trip to India and I was determined to have it finished before I returned in a few days. My health had worsened but I was singularly focused on getting Nicholas home. I believed in mind over matter and couldn't afford to shift my sights at this stage of the journey.

I read for over an hour. I glanced at the clock at 10:45 p.m. and I decided it was time for sleep. Three of the dogs were curled up on the pillows around me and I couldn't get comfortable. I put my pillow at the bottom of the bed and made myself comfortable under the duvet. The night light by the door caste a dim glow on a photo of Nick I kept on my dresser. It was a handsome photo of a robust Nick taken in 1989. I paused and stared at Nick's photograph for several moments before my eyes welled up with tears. I missed him terribly. I knew intellectually that I had to move forward with my life and emotionally I was committed to Michael, but after three years in the grave, Nick was still a constant spiritual force in my life. Tears slowly gave way to a smiles and chuckles over memories of life with Nick. His namesake would soon be home in Canada. My hazy mind took me back in time to meeting Nick DiCicco and how I had almost cancelled our first date.

David R I McKinstry

CHAPTER SEVEN

Nick

It had been one of the busiest weeks of my headhunting career. McKinstry & Company was a small player in Toronto's executive search industry but I had carved a niche for our firm recruiting high-end environmental lawyers and mid-range computer sales specialists. I had interviewed forty computer salespeople for various job assignments at three of our firm's larger clients. By Friday at 3 p.m. I'd had it with computer prima donnas who thought they were prophets from God sent to earth to stand in technological glory. Not one of my candidates had more than four years direct computer sales experience but each one gave me the impression the industry would fall apart without their input.

I went to the Y for an aerobic workout. It was a nice autumn afternoon and I decided to walk along Yonge Street for a while. Two hours later I found myself standing at Melrose and Yonge, only ten minutes from my house. The dogs were happy to see me after having been outside all day in the yard chasing squirrels and digging for moles in the back garden.

I immediately checked my calendar to see if tonight was a Fraternity film night. The Fraternity was a group of gay businessmen who got together several times each month for social and educational meetings. I was the founder of this group and after five months of meetings our membership was already at 125 men. Tonight a new Fraternity member was showing a film at his home. *The Rope*, a Hitchcock thriller starring Jimmy Stewart and Stewart Grainger, was being shown as part of a trilogy of older Hollywood films which had subtle homosexual undertones. Since I was living and breathing the Fraternity and in charge of recruiting new members, I felt I should attend the movie. It was a great evening and I was home by 11 p.m.

Saturday was spent exercising the dogs. I had a regular morning dog group in the local park just up the street. On any given morning I would meet four or five owners and their dogs, but on Saturday and Sunday mornings that number swelled to twelve or more adults and at least twenty dogs running after tennis balls. Although my pets had a doggy door available to them and could come and go from the house all day for romps in our enclosed yard, I always felt guilty when I wasn't there for them. These two pets had been lifesavers for me and now in their golden years, I wanted to be sure I provided them with frequent individual attention.

A new Fraternity recruit, Nick DiCicco, called me around noon to firm up our late afternoon date. I'd met him the week before at a Fraternity brunch. Although he was a very charming, handsome and popular fellow, I really didn't want to disrupt the relaxed solitude of my day off at home by going downtown on a Saturday afternoon. I felt awkward about breaking this date at the last minute and told him I'd meet him as arranged.

I ran up the escalator from the subway station knowing I had lots of time to walk to the hotel. I hadn't been keen earlier in the day about this date but as the hour approached, I became very conscious of my appearance and wanted to make a good impression on Nick.

We met just inside the door of Alexander's Bar and found a quiet corner table at the western end of the lounge. Conversation flowed easily and just listening to his deep sexy voice had me mellowing in no time. I found myself quite intrigued by the way he talked about his family and

David R I McKinstry

growing up in Guelph, entering the priesthood at seventeen, coming out as a gay priest within a small circle of elite Jesuits, being educated from coast to coast in North America and having studied in Rome. Nick was at a crossroads in terms of his vocation as a Jesuit. He had just started a year-long sabbatical to decide if he should return to full ministry or was it the right time for him to detach permanently from his Jesuit vocation.

One hour passed into two hours and finally after three hours of drinks and intensely satisfying conversation, Nick turned to me and said, "Well I think I have complied with all your demands. You wanted to know about my financial and emotional status and I've told you I'm poor in money but rich in heart. You've made it clear that you don't want a fly-by-night relationship, nor do I. I'm eager and willing to work toward adopting children if it's possible and you told me to bring along a health certificate from my doctor. I don't have that with me," he said half smiling.

I was mesmerized being in the company of this man, listening to him tell me about his dream to find a lover with whom he'd grow old, confessing his desire to adopt children and his love of dogs. I'd lost my aloofness within minutes of sitting down at the table with him. I knew it would be wrong to be cavalier with him about anything.

Our sometimes-intense conversation was mixed with hearty laughter and lots of dreamy smiles and eye contact exchanged across the table. This was romance at its finest. I could feel a tingling in my chest and my mind was telling I had fallen in love with Nick after only a few hours of conversation. I wasn't thinking about his body type, his cologne or his rich smooth voice; I just knew that I loved him. Nick had broad shoulders and a wonderful physique which showed through his Izod shirt. His sensitive hands gripped his cup of Irish Coffee in a special way. Nick was so handsome, kind and loveable. I knew this was it. As if out of a daze I awoke to ask him to repeat his last remark. I was embarrassed that I had become lost in the sparkle of his green eyes.

"I've told you everything there is to know about me except about my health status."

In an almost off-handed manner I asked him, "Are going to tell me you have diabetes? Don't worry I'm not as superficial as I may have let on. Go ahead, what is wrong with you?"

Nick continued to smile warmly at me. As I was melting in his gaze from across the table he leaned forward and lowered his voice.

"I became HIV+ about a year ago. My doctor informed me I was positive on my first day at Yale, then said I might have a year to live. But I'm as healthy as can be. I've been part of drug study in Buffalo for ten months testing a new drug and its working well." Without blinking he whispered across the table, "It is important for you to know this up front, David."

The scourge of AIDS in the 1980s had every gay man running scared. People were dying, not living with HIV. I knew of three men in Vancouver in the mid-1980s who died within six months of being told they had acquired the gay plague. I wasn't worried about contracting a dose of gonorrhoea or syphilis or crabs but exposure to AIDS was a death sentence no matter how one looked at it.

For a brief moment I could feel my breath being taken away as Nick told me why he was in treatment. I instinctively grabbed for his hand when I asked him if he had diabetes but his grip loosened and then pulled back. I don't know the how, when, where or why of the next few moments but I do remember reaching for his withdrawn hand and taking it back into my grasp. I knew I was in love with this man sitting across from me and I had to let him know it. We'd deal with the HIV as part of my love for him.

"Nick I am so sorry you tested positive, but you know new drugs are being discovered every month to fight AIDS and soon there will be a vaccine. Don't worry," I continued tighting my grasp on his hand, "You won't go through this alone. You now have me on your side. I know it sounds premature ... actually it sounds nuts for me to tell you I'm in love with you. But I am."

I could hardly believe what I was saying, part of me wanted to slap my face so I'd clue in to the reality of AIDS. The other half wanted to hug Nick, make love to him and tell him we'd beat this together as a

David R I McKinstry

team. I'd been sitting with him for three hours intrigued by his personality and hearing all about his life. I wasn't scared about catching the deadly virus from him as much as I was feeling fearful about what lay ahead of Nick. My mind and heart were debating my motive for loving this man. Was knowing he had AIDS intensifying my feelings of love for him because of some warped saviour complex in me? I wasn't into martyrdom so it couldn't be that. I paused for a moment for my words to sink in. I looked at his face to see tears welling up and I chuckled, "If you think tears will get you into my pants, you're nuts! The next time I make love I want it to be with the guy I'll settle down with. There is so much more for us to learn about one another. Let's just take it a day at a time. Besides I told you on the phone that it was my policy to date without any sex for at least six weeks."

This announcement brought a smile to his lips and he squeezed my hand. "Thank you David, I feel the same about you. I have since I met you at that brunch a week ago."

We had spoken about so many things in the hours since we first arrived that my head was spinning. I suggested we go for a walk along Wellesley Street to the University of Toronto grounds as it was a pleasant cool night. As we walked along dimly lit walkways throughout the historic campus, Nick asked if he could hold my hand. I was mortified at his suggestion of a public display of affection.

"Its dark David, who'll see us?"

"I'm no prude in private but in public," I said, "it is a definite NO." Nick laughed in his deep sexy voice and I could feel my heart thumping as we walked around Hart House circle before finally heading back to the subway station at Yonge and Wellesley Streets. He suggested driving me home but I preferred the subway. I told him that even though I declared my love for him, I had to be independent. The urge to kiss him goodbye at the subway entrance was almost overpowering. I knew I had to get on that train or I'd be with this wonderful new beau, racing in his car back to my place about to break my rule of NO SEX FOR SIX WEEKS.

A Swim *Against* The Tide

Surprisingly I didn't dwell on his HIV status during my ride home on the subway. I couldn't get the scent of his cologne out of my memory nor his green eyes, deep mellow voice or the glimpse he had given me into his character. I fell into bed exhausted at 10:30 p.m. with both dogs stretched out beside me. As I lay there, halfway between sleep and being awake, my heart began to pound as I thought of Nick. I knew this was it, the real thing.

Within six months of meeting one another, Nick moved in to my house on Melrose Avenue and we became a couple. Nick left the Jesuits, got his teaching certificate and my Executive Search business took on a mind of its own. We added two Golden Retrievers to our home and within two years we had added 3 puppies (from two litters) to our family. Before turning to adoption, we spent $30,000 US searching unsuccessfully for a surrogate who would carry a baby for us. It was also a time for saying goodbye to many friends; between 1988 and 1992 we attended the funerals of twenty friends who had died of AIDS-related complications.

We decided to have a Home-study prepared, just in case adoption became an option for us within North America or internationally. We moved to the suburb of Richmond Hill four years into our relationship with our five young Golden Retrievers and two aging Welsh Corgis. Living with someone HIV+ made me a pariah within my heterosexual circle of friends and I began to come out of the closet, growing more proud and militant as each year passed.

This was a period when Nick and I fought to be recognized as a couple and rigorously pursued any path that might get us into the adoption arena. We desperately wanted to adopt lots of orphaned children into our home. By a stroke of good fortune, we got a referral to a social worker who was prepared to work with us and our dream to adopt. The next three years on this long road to finding an adoption agency in California cost us another $20,000 US.

As we waited for our social worker to finish the rough draft of our Home-study, summer 1992 came to a close. Nick was excited to be

David R I McKinstry

joining a new school in Markham as head of chaplaincy and religion. We hosted 150 Fraternity members in our yard for an end of summer regatta, complete with teams of wanna-be athletes who did human chariot races, swam relays in our pool, participated in Jell-O eating contests and ran a mini-triathlon through an obstacle course mapped out around our one acre property.

Life was great so far.

Nick and David, 1988.

Nick and Jenny, (the pup).

A Swim *Against* The Tide

CHAPTER EIGHT

The Bio-Files:
Finding My Birth-Parents

Rifling through some old file cabinets during the Labour Day weekend, I came across long forgotten files on my own adoption. Nick saw me reading the notes I had made in the file and suggested I either toss the material or once and for all make some inquiries to find my biological parents. I told him I didn't need to find them to fill any huge voids in my life. He quietly made the obvious point that subconsciously I was interested, if only just to meet them and see what they looked like.

"Why else would you have kept the file this long if you didn't want to thank her for giving you up for adoption?"

"Good point," I admitted and decided to make one final effort.

The next day I called a good friend about her dad's alumnus connections with a local Peterborough high school. Jennifer told me her father was the chairperson of the upcoming 75th anniversary reunion and had access to the archives and every yearbook. I called her father and asked if he remembered a reddish-blonde haired student named Clara Samson from the early 1950s at Peterborough Collegiate and Vocational School (PCVS). He remembered her immediately and said he'd search through some old yearbooks to see if he could find her photo and he'd send it to me by courier. I told him the reason for my inquiry and the sleuth in him was excited to be of any assistance in solving my mystery.

A few days later, Jennifer arrived on our doorstep just after supper. Her parents had been visiting the night before and her dad had left behind an envelope for me. Jennifer, anxious to help me search for my biologicals, drove up after work to deliver the envelope containing a photo of my birth parent. Excitedly the three of us stood clustered around the sealed legal sized brown envelope wondering what the contents would reveal I ripped open the envelope and unravelled a folded photocopy of graduates from a 1952 year book. Smack dab in the middle of the back row was a black circle penned around the face of a woman that I immediately recognized as having my features. Jennifer and Nick looked on with mouths agape, unable to believe how similar Clara Samson's facial features were to mine. We began to read the names of other people in the photo and one popped out as being the same last name as a high school friend of mine. Wondering whether this familiar name was the aunt of a high school classmate of mine, I made a few calls to satisfy my curiosity. One name led to another and within an hour I had the name and phone number of Clara's youngest brother. Nick opened a bottle of white wine and poured three glasses and we nervously enjoyed several sips before I dialled the Peterborough number.

A man answered the phone. I had already decided to pretend to be on the alumni committee for the high school's upcoming 75th reunion. This broke the ice and soon information was freely flowing from his lips to my pen.

"Clara can be reached at home or her office," he said. Quickly I copied down her address, phone numbers and other bits of information he shared with me. "She's married and has two adult kids, Annabelle and Iain. They live in a nice neighbourhood on the Scarborough bluffs and her son Iain owns a cottage on Sandy Lake." I thanked him and said I hoped we'd see him at the reunion.

Could this be possible? I had actually just pieced together the

A Swim *Against* The Tide

puzzle of my birth mother in less than three days? What should I do now? I'd had enough excitement for one night but turned to my friends with a raised goblet, face shining with happiness and proposed a toast. It was decided that I should sleep on it and give myself a few days to come up with a game plan to meet Clara.

Nick would be spending his first day at the new school in the morning and wanted to complete some preparatory work on his computer. Jennifer left shortly afterward and I began to write a letter introducing myself as the infant Clara put up for adoption 37 years earlier. I wrote late into the night and decided to let the letter sit on my desk for a day or two and then revisit its contents in the cold light of day. It sounded good to me and Nick concurred that it was succinct and gave a good description of the person I had become and the life that surrounded me. I knew where she worked and I decided to pay a visit around lunch hour, hoping I'd see her going for lunch, strolling on the lawn, or sitting under a tree. Maybe I'd ask the receptionist to point her out as she walked in from the parking lot. Regardless, I would drop off the letter. I ended the letter to Clara writing that I'd waited a lifetime to meet her and hear the sound of her voice. We had to meet at least once for me to look her in the eyes and say thank you for having given me up so unselfishly to the perfect family who raised me.

I sat in the parking lot attached to the side of her office complex. It was 12:45 p.m. on Thursday and I was hell bent that I was going to drop off the letter to the receptionist and ask her to deliver it to Clara at her desk. Just as I was unbuckling my seatbelt and reaching for my door handle, a gray sedan slowly manoeuvred past my car and came to a dead stop as the driver waited for a space to become vacated by a departing salesman. Clara's car quickly moved into the vacant spot and she got out of the car, locked her door, took a wayward glance in my direction and began to walk toward the front door of her office building. I sat mesmerized by the sight of my birth mother thirty-seven years later. She still looked much like the high school grad photo I had seen a few days earlier. I got out of my car in a dream state and began to follow her, keeping my distance so as not to arouse suspicion.

She walked into the office building without looking behind. I gave her a one-minute head start and then I opened the door to the lobby and walked over to the receptionist. I asked if I could leave an envelope for Clara Trueman (her married name) and she said Clara had just come back from lunch and I could catch up to her just beyond the closed door if I hurried. I told the receptionist that I too was in a hurry and had just wanted to leave the information that Clara had requested. Without waiting for a reply, I turned around with my heart beating wildly, left the lobby and walked to my car. As part of my letter to Clara I suggested she call me at home later that night or the following day so we could arrange a lunch to meet one another. I drove away wondering if this woman would be happy or angry that I traced her down and was about to confront and unveil a secret from her past she had wanted to keep hidden.

I returned to my office and finished an afternoon of interviews for two sales specialists. My usual thoroughness in such interviews was lack lustre as my mind was miles away. Thoughts of my birth mother and how she might be reacting to my letter occupied my mind. I wondered if she might just call me up at the office and tell me to forget it and not to bother her again. I hoped she might call later that night and the mystery about the sound of her voice would be solved. Nick called me about 4 p.m. to ask me how the letter drop-off had gone. I told him about seeing her in the parking lot and how I had left the letter with her receptionist. I said I was going for a workout at the Y and I'd be home for supper.

After supper Nick and I sat around the fire and chatted about his first few days at the new school. He was on an emotional high and he became very romantic as we sat on the sofa. As if on cue, the telephone rang and we both looked at one another wonderingly. It was 8 p.m. and it might be Clara calling.

I picked up the receiver to hear Jennifer's voice. "Have you heard from Clara yet?"

A Swim *Against* The Tide

After a quick conversation I said, "Clear the line." She laughed and told me to call her the moment I heard from my birth mother.

Not thirty seconds later, the phone rang again. I heard a woman's voice asking, "May I speak to David McKinstry." It had to be Clara. Nick knew by the twinkle in my eye that the caller must be my birth mother and he smiled and motioned for me to bring the portable phone over to the sofa so he could listen in.

"You must be Clara," I replied.

Clara was nervous and it showed in her voice. There was a measure of caution in her tone. She said my letter had really caught her off guard and that upon reading it she began to shake and had to leave work for the rest of the day. Her husband had known about me before they got married but they hadn't discussed her giving up a child for adoption since before their marriage 34 years earlier. Grant, her husband, thought she should call and talk to me, as she owed me that much. So Clara mustered the courage, picked up her telephone and dialled to connect with her past.

I took the lead with the questions and answers. I fired questions off at her in rapid succession, perhaps too quickly. Before long she asked if my adopted dad had worked at Outboard Marine in the purchasing department. I said, "Yes, Eric was my Dad." Clara told me that she had worked in my dad's department at the time of her unplanned pregnancy. She had quit his secretarial pool and gone to Toronto to live until she gave birth to me. She asked if I had been the McKinstry who swam across Lake Ontario ten years ago? I told her that was me and she said when she saw my photo in the paper as the Sunshine Boy she had an eerie feeling about me but hadn't been able to pinpoint the origin of that feeling. Now she knew she had recognized subconsciously the features of my face which so resembled hers.

We talked for 90 minutes about her family, my half-siblings and were they aware of having a half-brother out there. Clara had not told anyone about the pregnancy except the biological father, her best girlfriend and years later, her husband. She didn't want anyone to know

David R I McKinstry

her past and most specifically her children. On that she was adamant.

I asked her questions about my biological father but she provided only non-identifying information. I could tell her husband must be listening in the same way Nick was listening with me. I suggested that we meet for lunch the following Monday. She agreed and I was delighted. Clara said she would call me Monday morning to set up a place and time for us to meet. I thanked her for her prompt response to my letter and she said that after speaking to me she was also glad she had called.

I said good-bye and hung up the phone emotionally drained. Nick hugged me and he had a smile a mile wide across his face. Had we just opened a Pandora's box? I wondered about that for many hours after I made that call. I had the weekend to think about what I'd say to Clara over lunch. I was happy, excited to attend the reunion, somewhat anxious about what might evolve, and worried that I might not be what she had expected her baby to be like as a grown man of 37 years. I wasn't about to tell her about Nick as I wanted her to get to know me better first. I then became confused about my reason for contacting her, experiencing guilt for having connected with her while Mum was alive. Would this threaten Mum and make her think I was trading her in for a newer model? How glad I was that I had the weekend to mull over the experience of having just talked to my birth mother after 37 years. I tried to imagine what it had been like for Clara to hear my voice for the first time since hearing my cries in the maternity ward of Mount Sinai Hospital.

Clara called me shortly after 9 a.m. on Monday to suggest we meet at the Silver Dragon, a Chinese restaurant, only minutes from her office. Her lunch hour was flexible and she could extend it to a couple of hours without any problem. She'd spent the weekend feeling less hesitant and was becoming more excited about meeting me with each passing hour. I too felt the same way. The timing was right, so unbelievably right.

I had a busy morning of phone calls and reference checking for an ace candidate. He would be meeting the regional director of sales later that afternoon, a fellow who had given me many job searches over the past few

A Swim *Against* The Tide

years. If he found my candidate suitable then it could mean a quick close to this deal and I would garner $13,000 for my headhunting fee.

Since we had to pay on-going advertising expenses at the California adoption/law firm, any big money I could earn would significantly underwrite our costs. Our American lawyer had placed 45 children into adoptive homes during her career. She was aggressively advertised in magazines read by female university students who might be pregnant and wishing to find a home for their babies. I had budgeted $1,000 a month for her advertising costs and this one placement fee could pay for an entire year's worth. In order to get the biggest bang for our advertising buck, we had to keep a steady flow of cash going to the United States.

Anxious about my luncheon with Clara I hopped in the car and headed to Kingston Road to talk to my birth mother face to face for the first time in my life.

I arrived at the restaurant, found my way to a quiet table near the back, ordered a cup of coffee and told the waiter I was there to meet Clara Trueman. She obviously ate at this restaurant frequently as the waiter said he knew Clara and would direct her to my table.

Five minutes later I watched her approach the table and my eyes drank in every inch of her movement toward me. She was smiling and I stood up to greet her as she closed the gap separating us. I started to hold out my hand to shake hands, thought better of it at the last second and let her walk into my waiting arms and we hugged briefly before sitting down.

She barely sat down before making a déjà vu comment, "You look so much like your biological father that it took my breath away as I walked toward you." The waiter hovered nearby and she ordered a glass of wine, squirmed briefly in her seat and then smiled as she became more comfortable. It was quite exhilarating sitting across the table from the woman who had given birth to me. Although I was happy seeing her face to face, there was also a sudden sense of finality and closure to my search. Here I was meeting her in person, being able to compare the reality of this woman's attractive features with the imaginary version of the birth parent I'd conjured up in my fantasies for decades. In a surreal

David R I McKinstry

sort of way, our luncheon meeting seemed almost anticlimatic.

I'd brought photo albums of my childhood and family. I gave her copies of *Toronto Star* articles about my three attempts to swim Lake Ontario, a photo of my ex-finance, all in an attempt to make a good first impression and to somehow validate this fine woman's decision to carry me to term and give me up for adoption.

As more coffee and wine arrived, our comfort level with one another grew. I told Clara that one of the pressing reasons for me searching for her was to tell her face to face how much I appreciated the anguish she must have gone through just to give me life.

I wasn't prepared for was her quick response. "Don't make me out to be a saint. If abortions had been legal back in 1953 I would certainly have had an abortion."

I tried to mask my shock at her response as Clara began a thirty-minute explanation about my conception.

"Your biological father was well known in Peterborough as a nationally ranked sports figure in the early 1950s. His name is Paul. He had light brown hair, was handsome with broad athletic shoulders, and a charming laugh. He was the gorgeous boy next door who every girl in town wanted for a boyfriend. I got him and he gave me you," she said matter of factly. "I came from a broken home with alcoholic parents. My dad abandoned our family early on and he died a long time ago. My mother had four children and as a single parent she found it difficult to handle us. I was sent down the street to live with my grandparents when I was a youngster. It was really hard for my mother to work and be a parent to all those children." I quietly observed Clara's eyes while carefully listening to her divulge abandonment issues from her childhood.

Questions about her family popped into my head non-stop. Clara seemed pleasantly relaxed and pleased to journey down the memory lane of her ancestry.

I was aware that Clara's sister had wanted to adopt me but the CAS talked her out of that option. I asked about her sister. Clara told me her sister Alice had married and lived only a few blocks from my house in Peterborough. I had gone to school with her son and daughter!

Now that my memory was being jostled, I remembered how the south-end gossip mongers on our street had viciously chided the mother of a grade six classmate. The talk was all about how horrible it was of this woman to abandon her children to the care of her husband and then leave town. This was really scandalous back in the 1960s and it was something I easily recalled.

"Alice was a good mother but her husband was an alcoholic and she just didn't know what to do. She had to escape to survive. She left the kids behind rather than uproot them from their home, school and neighbourhood. It wasn't fair of people to judge her as harshly as they did, as she was a trailblazer for the many women who today leave their kids with the husband and no one says boo about it. She had to get out of that marriage, move far away and at the time she felt that leaving the kids behind was her only solution. I know from personal experience how unfair judging others can be, so I have always been supportive of my sister and tried to keep in touch with her kids as best I could."

Wow, I thought. I could have been adopted into that family when I was born and that would have been my fate. Wasn't I lucky that the social worker finally convinced Clara that an inter-family adoption wouldn't be in the best interest of her baby.

Since Alice, and Clara's best girlfriend, were the only ones to know about her pregnancy besides Paul, Clara decided that leaving town before her pregnancy showed was her only option. Paul and Clara had been in a six-month courtship, fraught with ghosts from his past. Paul's ex-girlfriend kept hounding him to go back with her, making Paul frustrated but randy in his efforts to please both girlfriends. Clara and Paul had broken up just weeks before she was convinced she was pregnant. Clara was scared and went to the CAS to talk confidentially about what she should do and she was counselled to speak to the biological father as soon as possible. The CAS told her, other than marrying the biological father, she had no option but to go to a Toronto

David R I McKinstry

halfway house to live until she gave birth to the baby. An adoption would be arranged in Peterborough for her baby and the file would be sealed and no one would ever know she'd had a baby out of wedlock.

Clara approached Paul eight weeks into her pregnancy and told him she was pregnant with his child and asked what they should do about it. It crushed her emotionally to hear that Paul had reconciled with his old girlfriend and in fact they were engaged. Enraged and hurt, Clara walked away from Paul feeling abandoned and all alone once again. The CAS brought Paul in for a meeting to discuss his financial responsibility for Clara's costs at a Toronto halfway house for unwed mothers. As long as his fiancée didn't have to know about Clara's pregnancy he was very willing to pay any amount of hush money to help Clara get through this pregnancy. Paul wanted to talk to Clara but she wouldn't have anything more to do with him. She left town shortly afterward, telling everyone that she had received a job in a Toronto hospital and would be training as a nurse.

I congratulated Clara on being so courageous and I was surprised when she glared back at me as she said, "What choice did I have? Abortions weren't legal and I didn't have the money to go to Buffalo for a back alley abortion. I knew once I left Peterborough that summer of 1953, I'd never be able to return. Girls who left town and then returned ten months later were branded sluts because everyone assumed she'd been away to deliver a bastard baby." Clara spoke so matter of factly that I was somewhat stunned by the monotone of her voice.

"I couldn't even come home for Christmas because it was obvious I was very pregnant. I was so homesick and lonely. Being pregnant had ruined my otherwise carefree life. I lied to my grandparents and told them I had to work at the hospital over Christmas." Some of that long forgotten pain began to find its way to her eyes. She wiped the tears with her napkin, looked up with embarrassment and continued.

"You were born with sores on the scalp of your head, nasty looking open sores. It wasn't serious but the CAS wouldn't take you until the sores had healed. My breast milk was pumped and taken to you in the nursery while I stayed in the hospital for the week after your delivery. I remember how cold and bleak that hospital room was. I was given a private room because I was unwed and my baby was up for adoption and they wanted to sequester me from the happily married decent mothers, almost like I was diseased. There had been no happy cries from the nurses in the delivery room as they cut your cord and weighed you. No one shouted, 'It's a boy!' No one said, 'Congratulations on the arrival of a healthy baby boy.' There wasn't any counselling given to me about what to expect in the coming weeks before I handed you over to the social worker. No postpartum information that young mothers get today – absolutely nothing."

Her tears were evidence of Clara's emotional baggage and the upset over reliving the events of my bastard birth.

"Paul was my first true love and without much sex education at school or from home, I believed Paul when he told me I couldn't get pregnant the first time. Boy, was I wrong," she mused as her hand gripped the stem of her nearly empty wineglass. I decided to give her a breather and tell her what I'd been told about arriving into my parents' arms.

"I was in foster-care for three months before being placed with my parents. I suspect the hematomas took longer to heal than initially expected. I spent the first three months after my birth in a foster care facility before deemed 100% healthy and being handed over to the care of my folks. Actually I was handed over to my parents family physician who then telephoned them to say their baby boy had just arrived in town." Clara stared directly into my face as I told her the time-line of my placement into the McKinstry home in April 1954.

I wanted to know how I got from Toronto to Peterborough during those first few months of life.

"Had you been instructed to just leave me behind at the hospital?" I asked.

"I brought you to Peterborough myself. The nurses kept you near me for ten days because of your head sores. My best friend and the Peterborough social worker came to pick me up at Mount Sinai

David R I McKinstry

Hospital and I held you all the way to Peterborough. It was just after lunch when we arrived in Peterborough at the County Courthouse on Water Street. My friend Marge was so upset over seeing me hold you and knowing I had to give you up, that she was beside herself with grief as we drove up to the courthouse side entrance. I cradled you in my arms as we walked inside. Even the usually expressionless social worker was crying as she rested her hand on my shoulder. The only comfort I felt was holding the warm bundle of my baby close to my chest."

"Did you whisper anything to me during those last few hours you held me?" I inquired. It surprised me that I sounded just like a reporter.

"I was too numb and too angry to talk out loud to you. I just cradled you, embarrassed to look into your eyes. I was so ashamed. I felt like the worst person on the planet." Clara's tears cascaded down her cheeks as she recalled the specifics leading up to the moment she handed me over to the CAS. "We were led into the judges chambers within minutes of announcing our arrival to the court clerk's office." I was amazed to hear this part of the story. I had no idea Clara would have had any contact with me from the moment of my birth. Now I was hearing that I had been fed her breast milk, that she had held and comforted me during the two-hour car ride to Peterborough.

"You must have been horrified at the prospect of giving me up?" I asked and for the first time I reached over and took her hand in mine to give some comfort while she told me the rest of the story.

"I was a walking zombie. We were led into the judge's chambers. He was wearing a black court frock and was standing behind his desk as we entered his chamber. I will never forget that feeling, knowing I was about to be sentenced to life without my baby. My heart was pounding, I wanted to be sick to my stomach and part of me wanted to run away with you but the other part of me knew I just couldn't." Clara's entire body seemed to heave and shudder as tears from her memories of that day rolled down her cheeks.

Giving her a chance to compose herself and wipe her tear stained

A Swim *Against* The Tide

face, I asked, "What did the judge say to you? Was he kind and compassionate or strictly by the book?"

Clara continued to wipe her eyes. "He asked me if I understood the ramifications of relinquishing my baby for adoption. When I said yes he asked the court clerk to hold the baby while I signed several official documents he pushed toward me across the wide desk. I handed you over to the clerk just so I could sign the document and before I knew what was happening the court clerk disappeared behind me through a door. I didn't know you had been taken out of the room until I looked up from signing the forms. The social worker witnessed my signature and pushed the papers back to the judge. Then all he said was, Clara I hope you know that you have done the best thing for your child by giving him up to a good family. He will be loved and well-cared for all his life.' With that he motioned to the social worker that we were done. I asked to say goodbye to you. The judge said it was better this way rather than having an emotional goodbye and for me to leave and get on with my life now that the adoption was completed."

With that she excused herself from the table. I watched her walk in the direction of the washrooms. I suspected Clara needed time to compose herself in private. Reliving those memories had been very painful for her.

Ten minutes later she returned to the table looking less defeated after reapplying her make-up. "You must have been devastated at not being able to say goodbye to the baby," I murmured, watching her emotion-riddled face closely.

"I had been abandoned by my parents, abandoned by Paul, forfeited the life I'd known in Peterborough, and now I was losing my baby. I suppose I was just exhausted emotionally and physically by the thought of all these losses and I just crumpled into Marge's waiting arms when I came out of the judge's chambers. The social worker asked if she could drive me to the bus station so I could return to the halfway house in Toronto. I was so upset over not saying goodbye to you, I just crumpled into my best friend's arms. The social worker left me sobbing into

David R I McKinstry

Marge's shoulder in the foyer of the courthouse. After crying ourselves empty, Marge walked with me downtown to the bus terminal and I got on the bus alone and headed back to Toronto. I was allowed to stay on at the unwed mothers house for four more weeks until I got a job and found an apartment to share with some girls I'd met during my six months at that house."

Clara seemed almost rigid and stone-faced. As if by telling me the story of my birth and being put up for adoption, she had become drained of all emotion. I got up and walked around to her side of the table and threw my arms around the mother who had given me birth. I tried to give her comfort by saying I'd had a good life, despite the anguish around my birth and adoption, and that I would always love her for having mustered the courage to do what she did all alone.

Composed after the emotional roller coaster, I asked if she was ready for another glass of wine. Clara smiled and nodded her head and began to ask me a host of questions about my life. But I wasn't through with my questions. I wanted to ask her about my biological father as I didn't have much information about him and she hadn't really given me any details – I could tell she had purposely neglected to mention his last name. I could see she wanted to shift the talking over to me.

After talking for almost thirty minutes about my life, I came back to the question of my biological father. "When you first arrived you said I resembled him. What was he like? Was he tall? What is he doing now? Have you ever seen him since you left Peterborough in the summer of 1953?" I hoped she would give me some details about the man who had sired me.

Clara was reticent to disclose any identifying information as she felt it wasn't her place. Paul had been promised confidentiality by the CAS back then and she didn't want to disrupt his family today. Her girlfriend Marge had kept tabs on Paul and knew he lived north of Toronto and that he had become a police officer after a successful athletic career back in the late 1950s. Other than that she knew little else.

Clara told me she had been loving and hating him for so long that it was difficult to talk about him. She felt chronically wounded by his rejection when she told him she was pregnant and other than paying some of her bills at the halfway house, he got away unscathed.

Our luncheon had been nearly three hours of non-stop talking before Clara told me she must return to the office. She gave me her work number and said I should call her there rather than at home. Her son was still at home and she didn't want her husband to be made uncomfortable by the sound of my voice on the phone.

I smiled at the ease with which she gave me her office phone number and asked, "If you're giving me your work number am I to assume this meeting was positive for you? And does this mean we could schedule another lunch meeting at the end of this week to continue getting to know one another?"

Clara grabbed my hand and said this had been one of the best days of her life. She suggested we meet again for lunch on Friday at the Silver Dragon.

After watching her leave the parking lot, I got into my car and headed home to Richmond Hill. I couldn't wait to tell Nick about my afternoon and I wanted to go home and record in my journal all that my birth mother had shared of her life without me.

During supper by the pool, I shared with Nick the fascinating details of my luncheon with Clara. He was intensely curious and listened to every word. I was most relieved to have my first reunion behind me. We discussed the ramifications of the meeting, as life would never be the same from here onward as I now had the face of my birth mother locked in my mind. Would I tell Mum about meeting Clara? Would Mum feel threatened by Clara or sad that I had actually gone ahead without consulting her to search for my birth mother? The warm September air was conducive to us sitting and relaxing poolside with the dogs. Like it did many evenings, the warm water was an open invitation for us to skinny dip while two of our dogs, Jenny and Tyler, were playing tag with Caitlyn, the four-month-old pup we'd kept from her litter. Our older Welsh Corgis were annoyed by their raucous carrying on and burrowed

David R I McKinstry

beneath the shrubs lining the back patio to avoid being trampled by three energetic Golden Retrievers in the midst of frantic playtime.

We hung onto the side of the pool as the sun set over our yard and Nick asked me, in contrast to Clara's experience of handing me over to the court, how had I arrived in the arms of my parents. I told him that my folks, childless for the first fourteen years of marriage, had decided to adopt and stopped trying to conceive children in 1951. My mother had had numerous miscarriages and her physician suggested they try adoption, as getting pregnant didn't seem to be a healthy possibility.

In late autumn of 1953, they had been contacted by Miss Young, of the CAS in Peterborough, and told of a child who might be available early in the new year. They had been told not to get their hopes up just yet but that they would be assigned to this child once born. Mum was 39 and Dad had just turned 43. They owned their own home, had a large extended family and a five-year-old Pembrokeshire Welsh Corgi, named Chubby. They were very active in their neighbourhood United Church and at the local YMCA. I told Nick that the waiting from that moment onward was painful for them. They wanted to be parents so badly and Mum's maternal instincts, so anxious to nurture a child, had taken a beating during the course of several years of not being able to carry a baby to term. She had at one point suggested to Dad that he divorce her and find a woman who could bear him children but little did they know in the early 1950s that the cause could equally have been placed on my Dad. Back then it was the wifely thing to do for women to say it was their fault rather than cast doubt on the impregnating ability of their husbands.

While anxiously waiting for news of my birth in January 1954, my mother's father became ill with a prostrate infection. Antibiotics were still a developing medical phenomena at that time, and within a few weeks of falling ill, my 70-year-old otherwise healthy grandfather died. My parents were consumed with funeral details and adjusting to life without this family patriarch when Miss Young called to inform them that they would soon have a son to raise. Elated, they readied the house for my arrival. Neighbours and family held several baby showers and

A Swim *Against* The Tide

they were well stocked with diapers and baby clothes by the time I finally arrived in early April.

"Did the social worker just drop you off to your parent's house or did they pick you up at the foster family?" Nick asked, intrigue heightening.

"Out of the blue on a Wednesday afternoon, my parents' physician, Dr. Carlton, telephoned Mum at Outboard Marine with the news that I had arrived. She worked on the switchboard at that time. The moment she got confirmation of my arrival, she handed in her notice and after work she and Dad drove to Dr. Carlton's office to bring me home."

"Did she take a few months off for maternity leave or did she just quit?" I told him that the CAS preferred to put children in homes where the mother would stay at home fulltime and that my mother had agreed to stop work the day I arrived. It was no surprise to her employer as their entire office had been eagerly awaiting the day the baby would arrive.

My parents' experience was the sweet of Clara's bitter. Nick wondered aloud if our experience to adopt would be anything like this and we spent many, many hours that week discussing different scenarios of our future adoptions.

Three weeks later, having had five lunches with Clara, I decided to invite her for supper one night. She seemed quite eager to see my home and meet the dogs. Nick was also very anxious to meet her. Only four months earlier Mum had cornered Nick and I over supper and announced that she knew we were a gay couple and that Nick no longer had to move into the spare bedroom when she came to visit. Our new friendship had really deepened over the summer being able to tell her about the love of my life and honestly share our life with her. I figured that if my 77-year-old mother could handle the news then Clara should be able to hear it without a great deal of consternation. Besides, as Nick and I had discussed on several occasions, we wanted our relationships with people to be honest and open, which meant that those people we felt close to had to know the reality of our love for one another. If Clara couldn't handle this information then better we tell her now rather than it become known

David R I McKinstry

through someone else down the road when rejection for being gay would be more painful.

Clara took the news like a trooper. She had wondered why I hadn't mentioned any women in our conversations and when I told her I was gay it was just like another piece of the puzzle dropping into place. She told me several male relatives in her family were suspected of being gay. I told her that a lot of research was being done on the genetic predisposition of families that produce generation after generation of homosexuals. She wasn't ready to buy that explanation but nonetheless she was eager to meet Nick. I hauled him out of the office where he had been listening at the keyhole. They hit it off immediately and Nick felt a solid connection to Clara. Over supper I asked her once more to reconsider contacting someone to get Paul's phone number so I could also meet the paternal connection to my being. She said that she had been discussing it with her husband and he felt that she should go ahead and let Paul know about me. She said she was nervous to call him because they had parted on such bad terms 38 years earlier. Over dessert, Nick questioned her about her resentment toward Paul. After meeting me, Clara said she no longer felt she hated his guts, and that she was just plain mad at having been second choice to his wife when to her he was number one. She conversed easily with us about how hurt she had been after their break up, and how she really did love him more than she had ever let on. She agreed to call her friend Marge to quietly find out where Paul was living. She seemed confident that Marge would have his phone number to her within hours then she would call him about me.

Within days, Clara called my office to tell me she had spoken with Paul. She said that it took every ounce of courage to dial his number and thankfully he had answered. She introduced herself and Paul sounded thrilled to hear from her, even more thrilled when she told him, "Something we shared 38 years ago has resurfaced and he would like to meet his biological father." Clara said Paul suggested they meet for lunch as his wife would be home any moment and he'd never told her about Clara's pregnancy. They agreed to meet for supper the following

A Swim *Against* The Tide

day. Clara said she wanted to meet with him alone to discuss my contact with her. I asked Clara to call me as soon as she got back home to tell me about her reunion. She asked if she could give Paul my telephone number or did I prefer to call him? I said it didn't matter to me who made the call as long as the connection was made.

I had a YMCA Board meeting until 8:30 p.m. that fateful night of Clara's supper with Paul. By the time I got back home it was almost 9 p.m. and Nick told me Clara had called and said she'd call me in the morning from the office as her son was home and she wanted to talk with some measure of privacy. What a long night that was. I prayed for the hours to pass quickly as I was anxious to make the connection that would let me learn about the person who was my biological father.

Clara called just before Nick left for school the next morning and so he was on the extension phone to listen to her account of supper with Paul the previous evening. Paul had been a cop for 31 years and lived in Stouffville with his wife. They had three adult children, one named David, just eleven months my junior, who unbelievably was a physical education teacher in Peterborough! Clara said she was really nervous to see Paul after all those years and lied to her husband that she and some of the girls from the office were going out for a ladies night at a downtown restaurant. Clara was like a schoolgirl telling me about her first date on the other end of the phone. Her reaction to seeing Paul again was cute and I was entranced with her giddiness.

Paul wanted to meet me. He told Clara he had often wandered around malls and streets wondering if Clara had given birth to a boy or girl. Could he be seeing his child and not know who he or she was? Paul had become very emotional over lunch telling Clara how wonderful it was to see her.

"So do I call him or will he call me?" I asked.

Clara said Paul would call me in the next few days to arrange a time when we could meet. Paul told Clara that he needed a few days to digest all that she had told him about me and to get up his nerve to meet me.

David R I McKinstry

Once again I waited nightly by the phone. Three days later I got a call from a rather nervous Paul.

"Is David there?" I knew immediately who it was.

"This is David," I replied, "and this must be Paul," I said praying my guess was correct.

"Yes this is Paul, I'm your ..."

He didn't seem to be able to say the words so I said them for him, "You're my biological father."

Paul laughed and said he didn't know what he should call himself but that this was one of the happiest moments of his life speaking to me. I could feel my throat thicken and eyes start to mist. We didn't talk long as he was on a precinct desk phone and couldn't tie up a line very long with a personal call. He asked if I knew a convenient Richmond Hill coffee shop where he could meet me later that night. I suggested a coffee bar in a plaza. He agreed to meet me there on his way home from work.

Nick wanted to come along but knew this was a trip I must do solo. Besides, Clara hadn't told him about me being gay and in a relationship. Being a cop, I figured he might not take too kindly to his offspring being gay so I felt I should meet him and feel him out for his views on gays before introducing him to Nick and our wonderful life together.

From our house, it only took a few minutes to drive to the plaza. I was ten minutes early and took a coffee to a seat in the far corner. There were only a few customers scattered around the room. I wished I had suggested a restaurant or something different from this place which would afford Paul and me some privacy for our first eye to eye contact. Paul told me what type of car he would be driving. I gazed out of the coffee shop to wait for his headlights to brighten the darkness. No beams came for several minutes but then in drove a car that fitted his description. A man, about my height and build, got out of the car and walked toward the coffee shop peering in the window obviously looking for someone who might be waiting for him.

Paul entered the shop, stopped and looked about. He saw me in the corner and smiled and we both knew this was it. By the time he had

A Swim *Against* The Tide

walked ten paces across the room he had tears in his eyes as he grabbed me and hugged me real close.

"I can't believe this is happening. I'm so glad to meet you, David," he said, his emotions getting the better of him. "This should be a *60 Minutes* program with Hugh Downs and Barbara Walters."

I laughed with tears in my eyes and pushed him away from me so I could get a good look at my other blood relative. Paul took off his jacket and sat down with a sigh, then smiled as he began to chatter away to me about his reunion with Clara and how unexpected this all had been. I pummelled him with lots of questions about himself, his kids, and his sports career. Likewise, Paul asked about my life, my parents, siblings, dogs and sports I liked. We told each other of our mutual love for animals. Paul said he and his wife were very involved in the Canadian Kennel Club, owning a small kennel with ten Canadian Champion dogs. Paul asked if I was dating anyone.

"No one special at the moment," I lied.

I asked Paul what it was like getting Clara's telephone call and subsequently having supper with her. I could tell Paul was smitten with Clara immediately. I asked him how their relationship had evolved and ended so many years ago.

We kept buying cups of coffee over the span of an hour during our mutual inquisition. Then Paul glanced at his watch and said he had to get going. He said his wife had no idea that her archrival had produced a son of his. Paul said sadly their marriage had been dead for many years; even so, he didn't want her knowing about this just yet. He suggested we call Clara and arrange a lunch at the Silver Dragon for the three of us the following week. He gave me his phone number at work and told me to call anytime. Paul said he wanted us to get to know one another and not to lose anymore time.

Over the next ten weeks we arranged a lunch each week including a supper to exchange our first "family" Christmas gifts. It was early December and I had several things I wanted to discuss with them. The

David R I McKinstry

first thing I needed to do was tell Paul that I was gay and in a relationship with Nick and that Nick was HIV+.

Paul listened and as I finished telling him about Nick, he reached over the table and said, "Your mother already told me, David. I've known for a few weeks that you are gay. Through dog breeding circles, my wife and I have been best friends with a gay couple affected by AIDS. In fact I was a pallbearer for Jim who died of AIDS last spring. I'm not worried about AIDS or you being gay." Then he whispered across the table, "When do I get to meet Nick?" I couldn't have wished for a better reaction.

But I had a second request of them.

"I want to meet my half-siblings," I announced. Neither of them looked away and I knew that they had discussed this matter already. Paul didn't want his kids to know about me until he told his wife, which he planned to do within a few days. Clara suggested that we drive to Belleville to meet her daughter first and then she would tell her son about me. Paul said his kids would be fine with the news of having a gay half-brother. Likewise Clara said her son Iain might be a bit taken aback by her having had a son before she met his dad, but that the gay issue wouldn't bother him.

A few days later Paul told me he had been having lunch with Clara most days for the past six weeks. He said they had just been enjoying one another's company so much that they decided to spend as much time getting caught up on the lost events of their lives. He said he told his wife about me the night before and the air at home was even more icy. His wife had had a fierce rivalry with Clara and it was still a sore spot with her 38 years later. She wasn't keen on him making any announcements about having a child by Clara but Paul said she would have to get used to it as he intended to tell his kids about me before Christmas.

Paul kept his word and within a week he had gathered his two sons and daughter to the house for what he called an important meeting. With his wife purposefully absent from the room, he began to tell them about the circumstances of my birth and how I had resurfaced recently.

He was proud of me and Paul told them he hoped they would want to meet their half-brother as much as I wanted to meet them. The kids couldn't believe what he was saying. David said that this only happens in film or books, and he was excited to meet with me. Telling his kids that I was a physical education graduate, had taught, was an athlete, and now lived in Richmond Hill with my gay lover who was HIV+, somehow heightened the intrigue and they wanted to meet me as soon as possible. They wanted to know how their mother had reacted to this news. Paul said Kay's absence from this family meeting was a good indicator of her reaction.

I had grown up in awe of friends who had brothers. Now I had three half-brothers between their two families, and one brother in particular who shared the same name as me, had studied Physical Education at Western while I was in Physical Education at the University of Toronto so we had many things in common. Meeting them was paramount in my mind as Christmas approached. Nick and I were hosting Mum and my sister Karen in Richmond Hill over Christmas and I decided it was time to tell Mum about this recent bloodline discovery. I wanted my family to know before I began to meet my half-siblings.

Mum took the news well; in fact she said she was glad that I had finally pieced together the puzzle. Mum said she didn't believe that all adoption information should be sealed and locked away from adults searching for birth families. She seemed genuinely intrigued and asked many questions about my recent discovery.

My sister wasn't all that certain that I should be doing this, feeling it would hurt Mum. However, Mum told her that she wasn't offended at all, nor was she threatened by my birth families.

Mum said, "I AM his mother. I'm the one who held my arms to him when he hoisted himself up and walked at eight months of age. Your father and I taught him morality and we devoted our lives to the two of you."

Paul told me a few days before Christmas that his son, Dave, had been pestering him to get my phone number. Paul gave him my number

— 148 —

David R I McKinstry

but told him not to call until he had spoken with me. I said it would be great for Dave to call and I'd be very receptive.

Within an hour Dave telephoned. Our forty-minute conversation flowed easily and I felt very comfortable with the sound of his voice. We asked each other a battery of questions and each gave lengthy responses. We agreed to meet at his house on December 27th. He said his wife and two young kids were anxious to meet me, as were his brother and sister.

What a thrill it was to go into the festive season having just met my biologicals and finally being able to look into the faces that had created me. I could see how my hairline was the same as Paul's, how my hair colour was a combination of his light brown and Clara's red hair.

On Christmas Eve, Karen and Mum arrived early for supper so we sat around the fireplace and chatted. The dogs were a constant source of entertainment, especially Caitlyn, now only six months old and eager to play with the ornaments hanging from the seven-foot spruce. On Christmas morning we enjoyed one of Nick's specialty breakfasts and opened our gifts. Nick left for Guelph to spend some time with his family. He wanted to accompany me to meet my biological half-siblings but I told him I wanted to do this solo.

My sister left on Boxing Day to visit friends in Burlington. I drove Mum back to Peterborough the next morning. She was excited for me to meet my half-siblings and wished she could come along to be a fly on the wall and watch my reactions. She encouraged me to enjoy each step of this interesting process.

I called Dave from Mum's for directions to his house. He said the coffee was on and his siblings had arrived and were anxiously waiting to me. Mum kissed me goodbye and in less than ten minutes I drove into my half-brother's laneway. As I sat in the car looking toward the house, I could see the front curtains fluttering and small hands parting them to reveal two young children peering out. I approached the house, and a tall handsome man in a sweater came out the front door and waved.

"You must be David." I gave a nod and he walked over and said, "I'm Dave" then bear-hugged me. I could tell he was on the verge of his emotions getting the best of him. Dave was a wondrous sight for me to behold. He was taller than me by two inches, more broad in the shoulders, and I was immediately struck by the familial resemblance I saw in his face. This was something biological kids take for granted, but I was in awe as my eyes scanned the image of my biological brother standing in front of me.

Dave introduced me to his wife and children, then we walked into the living room where his brother and sister were waiting to meet me. What a surreal experience! I just wanted to look at them, observing every inch of them in the momentary silence that had befallen us. I felt an instant connection with Dave, whereas his sister and brother were much more reserved and cautious. Dave's wife Nancy ironically looked identical to the Nancy I had dated twenty years earlier. I looked at their children and imagined that they probably had the features of children I might have sired had Nancy and I married. It was a moment of reckoning with the past, all the what-ifs, specifically in terms of the children I had always wanted. We talked and dined for three hours, exchanging information about our youth, our relationships with parents, our families, careers, political leanings, pet peeves and highlights of our lives. Politically, Dave and I were also in sync as the only NDP party members in the room.

I told them I was gay and about Nick and his health status and made it clear that if my being gay was a problem for them, then I'd expect them to express those concerns to my face. Nick's HIV+ status didn't have to worry them about their own safety but if they had questions to ask me directly. My forthrightness and protectiveness of Nick and my relationship with him, made them smile. They said I must be one of their family because listening to me defend Nick was no different than the way they would defend their spouses.

David R I McKinstry

CHAPTER NINE

AIDS Unveiled

I was delirious with joy as I headed back to Toronto later Boxing Day afternoon. Nick wouldn't be home for another day. I was anxious to call him and give him the low-down on meeting my half-siblings. It was 10 p.m. before I could through to Nick. A large annual post-Christmas levy was happening at his parents' house and the noise of a hundred people milling around was so loud that no one had heard the phone ringing. Nick's laughter was contagious and by the sound of his voice, the party was going well. Lots of his high school classmates and neighbourhood friends were there. Nick had taken the portable phone into the attached garage so he could talk privately. I told him briefly how incredible it had been to meet my biological brother Dave and his siblings. We laughed at the odds of us both having a brother named Dave and Nick said he'd return the next day after lunch to get every detail. In the privacy of the garage he murmured softly that his love for me just kept growing month by month … and for the zillionth time asked, "Will you marry me?"

Nick arrived home around 2 p.m. looking very tired. He said he hadn't been able to sleep much the past two nights as he had been sleeping on the upper bunk of a room shared with his two-year-old niece. He told me she had chicken pox and had been awake numerous times during the nights crying and needing attention. Hearing the words "chicken pox" immediately set warning bells ringing in my head.

"Don't you realize that chicken pox is a virus and that with your compromised immune system you could easily catch it?" Nick looked sheepishly at me and said he hadn't known what to do when he discovered his niece had chicken pox. His family was still unaware of his HIV status and if he had made a big deal out of it, it probably could have compromised his secret.

I blew up. I was so mad that I could have chewed steel nails into paper clips! I berated him up and down for half an hour, lashing out at his stupidity. He wasn't only compromising **his** health but **our** life together. I was trying my best to keep him alive. Nick lay down on our bed after listening to my bout of anger and fell into a deep sleep (or pretended to). He wasn't a fighter and he hated to get into arguments, especially one with me when he knew I was right!

I hadn't told Nick much more about my luncheon and meeting my half-siblings. He just went to bed to catch up on a few hours of sleep. I had kept the HIV+ secret from his family for four years. Even Mum knew about Nick's HIV status but Nick was opposed to telling his family until such time as his health began to worsen. I decided I had to breech his confidentiality with at least one member of his family. I felt it was now necessary for me to have one ally in Guelph who could run interference for me in my absence. Someone who would call me and tell me when one of the nieces or nephews was ill with a childhood disease so I could prevent a trip to Guelph with an excuse that would keep him out of harm's way. Since his return from Yale, Nick had been building a wonderful new adult relationship with his brother Dave. It seemed logical and right that I would choose to share Nick's health status with his only brother. Dave and his wife Karen had become really close friends with us and I knew they'd be devastated but I could no longer chance Nick's health by staying silent.

I poured a glass of single malt scotch and took the portable phone

David R I McKinstry

to the recreation room. The fire was on and I settled into the wing back chair. I dialled Nick's brother and by a stroke of luck Dave answered the phone. We exchanged the usual light-hearted pleasantries and I asked him if he was alone so we could talk about something important.

Dave replied, "Karen is upstairs reading a bedtime story to the kids. Why? What's wrong?" I knew Dave's life would change forever the moment I broached the subject of his brother's HIV status. The moment of truth gripped my neck like a hangman's noose. Dave listened to my monologue for the twenty minutes it took for me tell him the story of Nick becoming HIV+, his medications and their side affects. I told him that Nick zealously guarded his privacy about being HIV+ primarily because he felt personally vulnerable and violated knowing his particular health records were public property.

"I'm just reclaiming my brotherhood with Nick after so many years of him living far away from us, and now I'm going to lose him." Dave asked many questions about how long Nick had been HIV+. Did he know who gave it to him or when he got it? Was I HIV+? Who of Nick's Guelph friends knew about his health? Dave was so upset at one point that he excused himself from the phone and his wife Karen took hold of the receiver. She had been listening beside Dave and was trying to comfort him. Karen was dumbfounded by the news and asked if Nick knew I was calling them. I told her no and that I didn't want Nick to know what I had told them. I explained the recent chicken pox scenario and how potentially lethal that could be to someone with a compromised immune system. I repeated to her that I needed to know I had someone in Guelph who wouldn't let another dangerous situation innocently occur. I made it clear that even the most insignificant communicable infection in healthy people could be fatal for Nick.Dave took the phone again and said he wanted to digest this information overnight. He said he'd call me back tomorrow to continue this conversation and that he wouldn't tell Nick what I had just disclosed.

I had no sooner put the phone down than I heard Nick upstairs letting the dogs out into the yard through our bedroom door. My

A Swim *Against* The Tide

timing had been perfect and I went upstairs content that I had done what was necessary.

I made supper and we were sitting down to eat when the phone rang. I grabbed the portable phone from the bedroom. It was Dave DiCicco calling back to tell me that he had thought about our conversation but he wanted to talk to his brother in person about the HIV. Dave felt that he owed it to his brother to hug him and tell him he loved him, HIV+ or not. Dave wanted Nick to know he would be by his side every step of the way.

I was nervous and tried to convince Dave not to discuss this matter with Nick. Dave said he almost got in his car and drove down to see Nick without calling me first. But he was determined that he was coming down tonight to be with his brother and there was nothing I could say or do to prevent it. I gave in and realized that if I had been on the receiving end of such devastating news about my brother, I would probably have done the same. I told Dave to come ahead and that I would tell Nick why he was coming to visit.

I wasn't sure how Nick would take knowing I had breached his confidence. He'd certainly understand my motivation for telling Dave, especially in light of the severity of the chicken pox scare. Nick was waiting for me to finish supper when I returned to the dining room. I didn't know how else to tell him but to give it to him straight. Surprisingly he wasn't upset; in fact he said he was glad I had spoken to Dave. He hadn't known figured out how to tell his brother so my revelation took a heavy load from his shoulders. Exhausted emotionally, Nick cried on my shoulder and we moved over to the sofa to sit and wait for Dave to arrive.

It was very emotional when Dave walked into our front hall and hugged his brother. It was a moment worthy of freeze-framing in time. They were crying into each other's shoulders. Finally they separated and still clutching each other's arm came into the dining room. I got them both a glass of wine and sat down across the room from them looking with envy at the brotherly love that held them together. They needed

David R I McKinstry

time alone so I took three of the dogs out for a long walk. An hour later I returned to find Nick packing an overnight bag on the dining room table. He and Dave were going to drive back to Guelph immediately so that in the morning Nick could visit with all his sisters and disclose his secret. With his siblings by his side, he'd then tell their parents. Nick hugged me hard and then Dave joined in our hug. I didn't want to let go of Nick but I knew he had to do this on his own.

Nick called from Guelph late the following afternoon to give me a report on how the disclosure had gone with his family.

"I got Mom alone and told her while Dad was at the office. She was really mad," Nick said. "She asked how someone so smart could be so stupid and then she went into her bedroom and slammed the door."

I asked how his dad had taken the news. Nick said he just sat looking at him for several minutes and then asked if I had given him AIDS. Nick said no.

"I think Dad wanted to hear that you had given me the virus. He said you must be special or crazy knowing about my health and still going into a relationship with me." I laughed and Nick said his dad obviously had a newfound respect for me.

Telling his sisters was difficult. Each of them was aware of AIDS. Nick's eldest sister had been married to a bisexual who ended up dying of AIDS in the mid 1980s. His sisters knew AIDS killed so his declaration had been very profoundly emotional for his two sisters in Guelph. Nick said he was driving to London to reveal his health to his sister Lori (the one whose husband had died of AIDS) in the morning and he would be back to Richmond Hill the next afternoon in time to attend our planned quiet supper New Year's Eve with two other couples.

An hour after talking to Nick, his sister Teresa called and she talked to me about AIDS and how infectious it could be and should she be worried about her newborn baby around Nick. She had many questions and I felt honoured she had called me for answers. I felt as if I had crossed over into a whole new role in the lives of his siblings and I felt sure his parents would also come around in time.

A Swim *Against* The Tide

Nick carried on with his usual frenetic pace of activity during January. We made several trips to Guelph that month to visit with his family to reassure them Nick was fine and quite able to function normally. Nick was very involved in his lecture series with several Catholic parishes. Through out the month of January Nick had been recording his lectures on tape cassettes and selling them in Catholic bookstores. Several people had approached him about setting up his own little church community, as they enjoyed his brand of preaching. It didn't take long much convincing for Nick to decide to set up a small church called Agape (Greek for brotherly love).

We worked on this together and both felt that a church in Richmond Hill for those who were gay or straight was an idea that needed to take shape. Mum arrived with her sewing machine and helped Nick put together a banner for the new church. Nick began canvassing for potential members from his list of disconnected Reform Catholics. We rented the big common room of the library across the street from us for Sunday morning services. The first service was overflowing with friends and family coming to see Nick in his priestly robes and hear his message of faith and hope.

AGAPE had a faithful following of twenty regulars every Sunday for the month of March and then it dwindled to ten regulars by the end of May. Occasionally Nick would speak to a congregation of thirty, made up of teachers and school board friends who wanted to see Nick in action. We were trying to get the message out into the gay communities north of Toronto but we didn't seem to be drawing the audience. We were steadfast in our belief that it would take time to build AGAPE into a strong congregation. But time was running out for Nick.

It had been an unusually bad winter for Nick's health. Colds, flu, and constant aches and pains plagued him all through Easter. By May Nick had had several bouts of illness that had kept him home for eleven school days. He became conscious of weekly weight loss and every few weeks he would announce that the scales showed he'd lost another six pounds. This was so upsetting for Nick that in mid-June I manipulated

David R I McKinstry

the correction knob at the back of the scales to show pounds being added rather than lost, much to Nick's delight. Yet his size 32 pants always looked baggy so I bought several new size 30 pants and Mum adjusted the waist bands without his knowledge so it wouldn't be a constant reminder he was losing weight, signalling a worrisome change in his overall health status.

In late June, the doctor reported to us that Nick's T-cell count had taken a serious drop from over 400 to 280 in the past two months. A followup visit in mid July showed another dramatic decrease in his T-cells to below 200, the marker used to determine when a patient crossed over the line from being HIV+ to full blown AIDS. Thrush (a contagious disease of small white eruptions on the tongue, mouth and throat) was a constant companion to Nick and it was painful for him to eat when his medication no longer kept the fungus at bay.

The first six months of 1993 had been very busy for Nick, AGAPE, teaching, and putting together a lecture series on discernment for audiotape distribution. It had cost Nick $3,700 to put together a six cassette series of audiotapes and within two months he had doubled his money and had unfilled orders piling up on his desk. With his failing health a constant concern, the success of his tape series was a terrific emotional boost for Nick.. So in August Nick repeated his original order of audiocassettes and once again sold 300 sets within seven weeks. Hearing that people were clamouring to buy his taped series was very good for his mental health.

Other than with my new-found half-brother Dave, I hadn't pursed a relationship with my other two paternal half-siblings. It was mutual as we really didn't have anything in common. I talked to Dave twice each week and we seemed to have an innate sense of the brotherhood within our grasp and we agreed to nurture this young relationship. I was really happy having met Dave and now having the brother I had yearned for most of my life.

I met Annabelle and Iain, Clara's two adult children that summer. Annabelle was married with three children. She was cute, wise, insightful and doing a great job of raising her children. I felt a connection with Annabelle because we were close in age and she readily gave me access to her memories growing up with Clara as a mother.

Iain presented to me as an unconventional 26 year old. He wanted to be a career downhill ski enthusiast at Whistler or a water skier in the Caribbean. He was very good at talking about his pursuits but seemed uninterested in my background. If we didn't talk about sports then we didn't talk about much. Iain had been a good hockey goalie in his youth. I couldn't find one redeeming thing to say about a game that valued thugs on the ice. Clara told me Iain was popular, incredibly kind and generous to his friends. I assumed there had to be a depth to his soul … but I just wasn't able to crack the code. I wanted to know Iain but we were poles apart and besides, there wasn't a lot of interest on his part. So I just concentrated on building relationships with two of my five half-siblings.

Iain announced that he wanted to sell his cottage on Sandy Lake and move west to work at Whistler as a ski instructor. Clara, knowing we had been looking for a cottage, suggested Nick and I drive up to see his property early in July. Sandy Lake had a limestone base and the water appeared to be turquoise blue. The cottage was high on a hill overlooking the waterfront and the look on Nick's face told me he wanted to buy it. For two years we had toyed with the idea that when Nick's health declined and he couldn't teach any longer we would buy a country place and set up a Bed and Breakfast operation. Nick fell in love with Iain's retreat on Sandy Lake and from July onward we were obsessed with finding a way to afford the $229,000 price tag.

Upon hearing how much Nick had fallen in love with the cottage which he had built from scratch, Iain's kindness and generosity shone through. He lowered the price to make it affordable for us to purchase. My business was experiencing the recession and I hadn't had much commission come into my account for months. I had stashed some cash away and we would be fine for another six months even if business continued to spiral downward. Nick's audiocassette sales had put $6,200

David R I McKinstry

into our savings account but we needed another $10,000 for a down payment to qualify for a mortgage on the Sandy Lake property.

Nick started back to school in September and we spent two weekends at Sandy Lake trying to make up our minds about purchasing it. We were convinced it would be a good investment. My business had continued to plummet and I wondered if I shouldn't close the Yorkville office and relocate. It wasn't long before I closed the downtown office and set it up at the house with only a part time secretary.

It was a difficult start to autumn and we decided to go to Vermont to visit my cousin Elizabeth for Canadian Thanksgiving. During our trip we seriously discussed the pros and cons of setting up a Bed and Breakfast business on Sandy Lake. We had to decide if we could manage to purchase the cottage. What if Nick's health continued to decline? Nick also really wanted us to get married. We had had this discussion so many times in the past and I just didn't feel it was necessary for two men to get married publicly in order to indicate their commitment to one another. However Nick got me seeing his point of view.

Nick spoke about the need to publicly make our vows to one another for several years. He felt marriage was necessary to make our families understand the depth of our commitment. That seemed to make sense. I was painfully aware of Nick's decreasing strength and stamina. Our physician explained to me that Nick could qualify for LTD (long term disability) and that he should give it some serious thought. That doctor said it made no sense to spend his last years working like a dog. Nick had lost a further twenty pounds and I slowly acknowledged that full blown AIDS was going to be far more debilitating than just being HIV+. If Nick wanted us to get married then I would do it to make him happy. We laughed several times enroute to Vermont about how Nick wanted this wedding for spiritual reasons and I wanted to have it as an excuse to invite every heterosexual to whom I'd ever given a wedding gift – now it was payback time!

During the trip I confessed to Nick that I'd spoken to his doctor about what to expect from the AIDS stage of this disease. Elizabeth and

Jonathan also felt that we should seriously consider LTD for Nick at this point in time.

Elizabeth convincingly said, "Nick you can always go back to work if things get better, but for now I think you should eliminate as much stress as possible." Nick seemed genuinely interested in being able to quit work and concentrate on making his life stress free.

When we returned from Vermont I dropped the calendar down on the dining room table, turned to Nick and said, "So when do you want to get married? Pick a date ... I'll need at least five weeks to organize it, and it will take you a week to make up your list and design an invitation on the computer." After consulting both daytimers, we agreed on Saturday, December 11th. It was also decided that we should go full speed ahead with the purchase of Iain's property on Sandy Lake.

In the next few weeks, we concentrated efforts on getting our finances together, borrowing from one account to add to the other to fatten up our down payment. We got everything arranged and began to seek out a bank for a mortgage only to discover a week later that three banks we had approached all said NO to our request – we were $10,000 short of what was needed for the down payment in order to qualify for a bank-approved mortgage.

My good friend Philip had recently been out to visit us and when he heard of our desire to leave the city to make life easier for Nick on LTD, he said he'd loan us whatever we needed to get into the house. I called Philip and asked him if his loan comment had been legit. He suggested the name of a mortgage broker who could arrange a private mortgage. He felt we should seek counsel from the mortgage broker and call him about whatever cash we were short.

Philip loaned us $10,000 in cash the next day and we distributed it into our three bank accounts. The following day we transferred those borrowed funds into our down payment account and asked the teller for a signed copy of the balance in our account. Within a day of providing this new information to a private money lender, our mortgage had been approved and we were on our way to home ownership. Philip knew

David R I McKinstry

we'd repay him within a few months but his generosity paved the way for Nick to edge his way comfortably into full time retirement.Most of the latter part of October and early November was spent preparing for our move to Sandy Lake. I was winding down the job search business and only had to collect for a $9,600 job placement made in mid-October. By the end of October I'd closed the door on McKinstry and Company, and put all my efforts into organizing the wedding. Tom Harpur, a well known religious personality, author and Toronto Star columnist, agreed to officiate over the nuptials at our wedding and Philip's cousin, an opera singer, was to sing. Over 125 invitations were mailed out and we were flooded with RSVPs by early November. Most of the people we thought would be there to support us didn't let us down. Mum wasn't sure she should come to the wedding as it could unbalance her relationship with my born-again sister who rented the basement apartment in her home. Nick's parents weren't sure they felt comfortable with this ceremony for two gay men. Nick's dad sent us a cheque to cover the wedding expenses and a gift cheque to cover several months of mortgage payments. However they didn't think they could handle being at such a public wedding for two men.

Nick's siblings were going to be there come hell or high water and both of our DAVE brothers agreed to give toasts to us at the wedding. We had to stop the services for AGAPE in October when we decided to move north but we wanted the charming library pavilion where AGAPE's services had been held to be the spot for our nuptials. It was convenient to our home and had parking for 100 cars. We couldn't have alcohol in the building so we went with non-alcoholic apple wine. Nick felt this was best regardless so that guests wouldn't leave inebriated.

Nick's health continued to be precarious at best. One day he would be fine and two days later he would spike a fever and be out of sorts. Our wedding day arrived amidst the first snow blizzard of the season. Nick's sister in London called to say the highway was closed and she wouldn't be able to be there. Thankfully the snow storm didn't deter his other siblings from driving from Guelph but several older family

Nick, David and the dogs, 1993.

members left messages throughout the afternoon that they wouldn't be attending because of the weather. I spent the afternoon at the library decorating, cleaning, and setting up the music system while Nick rested in bed. Elizabeth and Jonathan arrived from Vermont that afternoon and immediately joined me at the library to set up 125 mock champagne glasses filled with strawberries. Nick had been ill most of that week leading up to our Saturday wedding and mid-week he just fizzled. I was busy trying to make sure our wedding was going to come off without any hitches. Nick's health was really concerning me and I was more than edgy.

Friends and family and been dropping off or sending gifts all week and I had them out on display in our long dining room. As sick as Nick was he would get out of bed and come to the door to greet another gift messenger. He delighted in opening the gifts and arranging them on the dining room table for display.

Saturday's snow storm had been predicted since Thursday night and

David R I McKinstry

we were prepared for numerous cancellations. Nick got out of bed around 4 p.m. that afternoon and slowly began to shave, shower and get dressed. We had gone shopping a few weeks earlier to find co-ordinating outfits to wear, green wool blazers and turtlenecks that would be fashionable but casual enough to meet our needs.

The musicians had become stuck in the snowstorm and arrived late. We were still setting up when the first guests started to enter the library's glass sided foyer at 7 p.m.. Nick arrived with Jonathan and Elizabeth, twenty minutes late, to help fill the flute glasses with mock champagne. I was so happy to see him standing and strong enough to attend his own wedding. Whatever else he did beyond saying "I do" was a bonus to me. The flow of our guests into the chapel area revived Nick and he became the perfect host, seemingly impervious to the lethal virus attacking his immune system.

With 97 of the 125 guests in attendance, our ceremony was called to order at 8 p.m. and our vows were completed by 8:25 p.m. This was the first gay wedding most of our family and friends had attended. Although different from the norm, we got lots of comments from guests who felt they had witnessed something both spiritually enriching and socially significant.

By 9:30 p.m. our guests were leaving and we cleaned the library's kitchen, with the help of numerous hangers on. At 10 p.m. we jumped in the car and headed the two blocks home. Nick was exhausted and practically fell into bed. Jonathan and Elizabeth had to leave for Vermont early the next morning and they too were tired out. I stayed and unpacked the boxes of wedding gifts and envelopes left behind after our ceremony. Early the next morning, Nick got up and made coffee and tea and a hearty breakfast for Elizabeth and Jonathan before they headed off for their eight hour return trip. We sat for a while in front of the fire and opened some of the wedding gifts and marvelled at the stash of wonderful items we had received.

On Monday morning Nick returned to school. He was feeling much better following the wedding and he seemed to have a new zip in his

A Swim *Against* The Tide

stride. I picked him up after school to drive him to sign for the mortgage at the bank which the mortgage broker had arranged. Nick was steady on his feet that afternoon but he looked quite pale and I decided to walk with him to the bank to witness his signature and feel part of the process. Because I had been bankrupt back in 1987 our mortgage broker felt that Nick would qualify easily with his salary and my credit record should be kept out of the equation. Nick could put me on the mortgage after it was completed but for now he would be the sole mortgagee. We had to wait a few minutes for the branch mortgage officer ushered us into her office. She didn't seem to mind that we were there together and I jokingly told her I was there to be his witness. She produced the forms from a file folder and proceeded to tell Nick where to sign. A few minutes later, she got up and shook Nick's hands and congratulated him on his new home purchase. As we were turning to walk out the door, as if in an afterthought, the bank officer said, "Oh, do you want life insurance on the mortgage, Nick?"

Having been in the insurance business long ago I had told Nick that he'd need a medical to qualify for mortgage insurance and that he wouldn't get it with his HIV status. Nick responded questioningly, "Does anyone qualify for mortgage insurance? What if I had a terminal illness?"

"Don't worry, just sign here." She said pointing to a line at the bottom of a page. "The medical is just a formality and just about everyone gets mortgage insurance through the bank – just sign here. If there are any concerns from the underwriters you'll be called."

Nick looked at me and I just shrugged and said, "Go ahead if you want."

Nick signed and we left the office. As we walked to the car, Nick said, "Do you think I'll get mortgage insurance?"

I offhandedly told him that the bank would contact us and ask for the name of his physician. "When they hear you have AIDS you won't get mortgage insurance. Trust me, you won't get it, Nick," I said as we drove out of the parking lot bound for home.

Two weeks later we started to pack up our house in earnest. We were

David R I McKinstry

making daily trips to Loblaws to get packing boxes. On December 30th our second Welsh Corgi, Meaghan died of kidney failure at fourteen years of age. Nick was so traumatized by our pet's death he could barely get out of bed for the next two days.

Early in January 1994 we received notification from the bank about our mortgage approval. As we read over the document, we noticed that the mortgage had been insured. "I thought you said I wouldn't get the insurance?" Nick asked and playfully gave me an elbow in the ribs. I said it was strange that without any medical information having been taken from him that he got mortgage insurance coverage. I suggested to him that like his group policy with the school board, maybe all the risks were being pooled together. With so many people getting mortgages, perhaps it was a new perk of banks to give anyone mortgage insurance without a medical. I was really sceptical by this turn of events but being busy with the move, we just put the documents away in our file drawer and kept on packing for our new homestead which Nick named "Woodhaven Bed and Breakfast."

On January 16th, 1994 we left Richmond Hill with three vans full of furniture and belongings and headed north in a horrific snow squall to move into our new home on Sandy Lake. Nick had called in sick January 14th and we knew that the following week he would make the necessary trek into the board office and initiate the LTD. We were off to a new "stress-less" life. Little did we know that our first few months of living on the lake would be full of our dogs running off in pursuit of deer or foxes, with Nick and/or me in hot pursuit, often wearing just galoshes and a ski jacket over our housecoats. We began renovations immediately, which was just the thing for me. Friends and family arrived most weekends for the first few months after we arrived at Sandy lake to assist me to put in bathrooms, tear down walls, convert the garage into a chapel space for Nick who was thrilled to have his own chapel in the house.

My half-brother Dave gave us a hot tub he had been storing in his basement. He had no room for it so he donated it to Woodhaven Bed and Breakfast. Almost nightly Nick would sit and relax in the hot tub while looking at the silent sky full of stars. We often sat staring out the living room windows watching snow storms whirl up from the lake. What sights we'd see from our perch behind the floor to ceiling windows of our living room; deer, wolves and coyotes traversed the frozen lake in front of Woodhaven. We put up many bird feeders to attract Cardinals, Blue Jays and Yellow Finches. Jenny, our Golden Retriever, was pregnant with a second litter when we arrived at Woodhaven and by late February our family of dogs had expanded to include two more pups. Five Golden Retrievers, a new B 'n' B business, lots of hope and love in our hearts, and a ton of carpentry projects to keep me occupied. We would often comment to one another, "What more could we ask for?" And in unison we'd say, "Children to adopt."

David R I McKinstry

CHAPTER TEN

Goodbye to Nick

I had to chop and split wood twice a day in order to feed the fireplaces during the winter of 1994. I liked my new lumberjack role which helped make the multiple treks to the woodpile for wood pleasant, regardless of the cold winds. January was the coldest winter on record for more than 50 years; the day we moved into Woodhaven it was –26° C, with extremely low temperatures the norm until end of February. We loved being so removed from the city, its urban noises and hyper-stresses. Nick sat and read by the floor to ceiling windows that provided us with a picturesque panoramic view of the frozen lake, forests of green coniferous trees and abundant wildlife and birds.

Early in March my biological parents, Clara and Paul, confessed that they had been having a torrid love affair for the past year. We suggested they maintain a veil of secrecy over their tryst, as it would make their lives hell if the word got out. Nick took it upon himself to speak to Paul by phone about the implications it could have on my fraternal relationship with his son Dave. Nick foresaw Dave wanting nothing further to do with me if he discovered that I had been privy to his father's infidelity with Clara. Paul was aware, he said, of the game of jeopardy they were playing and how it could negatively impact or even destroy any future relationship with my half-siblings, maternal and paternal. But both felt, and we too agreed, that their last chance for true romantic love had to take precedence over the feelings of their adult children.

Paul and Clara were so very supportive of the love Nick and I shared and they knew they could trust us with this secret. Clara was alive with excitement as she told Nick and me about checking into a hotel under the name of Mr. and Mrs. Camden. She had become a teenager again, reliving her first love and throwing caution to the wind. Paul, equally at home in Clara's arms, was in a dead-end marriage with someone he no longer loved romantically and he ached to be with Clara full-time – he just couldn't think of a way to gently break the news to his wife about her arch rival resurfacing 40 years later and stealing his heart.

Clara, much more resolute than Paul, made the first move to separate from her spouse and move into an apartment. To maintain her dignity, Clara knew she had to end her marriage, regardless of whatever became of her rekindled love with Paul.

Over supper they asked Nick how he personally felt about divorce. Nick told them that staying in a dead marriage wasn't God's plan for anyone. Unlike the church, Nick advised them that they were very lucky to have found passionate love for a second time in a world where most people have difficulty finding it even once. I agreed that at age 60, having raised their families well, that neither Paul or Clara should live life by other people's rules. At some point we all have to take stock of our lives and sometimes that means facing difficult decisions, such as leaving a marriage that has run its course. They were thrilled to have reunited with a son they could call their own. This created an instant new family, and they said convincingly that their relationship with Nick and I had given them a familial connectedness which deepened their resolve to be together. It was becoming easier to have an adult relationship with them and share in their happiness.

By late April 1994 our kilometre-long driveway was losing its snow cover. The two neighbouring rental cottages had a flood of potential tenants driving up the road to check them out. Naturally anytime a car

David R I McKinstry

ventured close to our house, the canine burglar patrol would let out a cacophony of barking and wailing. One day they caused me to race out in the middle of the morning to check a Jeep Cherokee that was preparing to venture down the still treacherous hillside road to the cottages below us.

Our dogs were standing directly in front of the jeep and neither Nick or I could scatter them to let the jeep through. Finally the sentinel saw a squirrel in the distance and they all ran off with Nick in tow. I finally saw the reason for the dogs' intrigue; a young gray female standard poodle was cowering in the back seat having been terrorised by our canine pack.

I introduced to myself to the driver who was checking out one of the cottages for rent. Brendan, standing 6 foot 5 inches tall and striking a Marlborough Man pose, explained that his wife and new baby daughter wanted to find a place to rent for the summer that would allow dogs. Casey, his wife, had given birth to their first daughter four weeks before and they'd gone off to Florida for a week of R & R while he scouted out various rental properties. Brendan was inquisitive about Nick and me and as usual I was very forward in defining Nick as my spouse during the introductions. None of my comments startled him and he just continued on with many questions about why we had chosen to live in the country.

After seeing the rental cottage he returned to his jeep. Nick was outside raking a few leaves when Brendan stopped his jeep, rolled down his window and said he had liked the look of the cottage and hoped he would be first to call the owner about renting it. Nick suggested he use our phone to call the rental company immediately. Twenty minutes later Brendan said, "Looks like we'll be neighbours for the summer."

He bid us goodbye and told us he would introduce his family to us when he brought them to see the cottage in a few weeks.

Later that same day, another car rolled up our laneway in search of an available cabin for rent. Two wives, off to find a summer cottage for their families to share, parked their car in our lot and proceeded down the hill to check out the remaining rental cottage. Lynn and Lindalee

A Swim *Against* The Tide

loved the cottage and once again we suggested they use our phone to call the cottage landlord. We found these two ladies engaging and full of energy. After sharing some herbal tea and fresh pie, our newest neighbours headed back to Toronto. We felt quite happy about the two sets of non-rowdy neighbours with whom we'd spend our first summer on the lake.

Each week completed renovation projects were checked off a huge list we'd drawn up. An old family friend, master builder and carpenter and the father of three girls who had grown up with me on Orpington Road, was our source of carpentry expertise. He guided me every step of the way, frequently reminding me to use four nails where two would suffice. It took three weeks for us to renovate the huge attached garage into two rooms, a chapel for Nick and a library for his 2,000 books.

Nick, too tired and sick to heave sheets of dry wall would stand on the sidelines being our gopher. The rooms took shape and Nick was beyond thrilled the day I returned from town with a huge carpet remnant for his chapel. He was in his glory having a library and a chapel in his home. He spent hours every day in his chapel praying and meditating, then following a rest he would catalogue books to organize the shelves of his new library.

For most of the winter I had been trying to find a physician in Peterborough who would take Nick on as a patient. The local AIDS physician's practise was full and he wasn't accepting new patients. He already had 200 AIDS related patients. The Tory government under Mike Harris had slashed health care budgets and the physician shortage in Ontario during the 1990s was worrisome and daunting. I decided to contact a local community AIDS advocacy group for help in finding a local physician. The regular medical trips to Toronto had become exhausting for Nick.

Tony Jeffery graciously accepted Nick as a patient, agreeing that Nick needed a local physician to monitor and manage his failing health. Besides providing extraordinary medical care, Tony was quite an intellectual. Often during house calls to check on Nick he would marvel at the contents of our library. Himself a budding writer, Tony and Nick struck up a wonderful doctor-patient relationship as Tony became the key player on our health management team.

Nick's bouts with fatigue and sore back had been worrisome for me but Tony kept telling us it was probably the disease taking root in different parts of his body. He told us he wasn't going to soft-peddle Nick's test results. From our first appointment, Tony was gentle but blunt when discussing Nick's prognosis. Never keen to hear that his health was into a steady stage of decline, Nick took Tony's advice with a grain of salt, telling him that he'd gladly die when God called him home rather than when his doctor announced it was time to go.

During those first long winter months in the quietude of Sandy Lake, Nick became obsessed with native folklore and mythology. On several occasions we ventured into the Whetung's Ojibwa Art Gallery, at the Curve Lake Reserve only fifteen minutes from Sandy Lake, to purchase books on local Ojibwa legends, folk heroes and the shamans who were mediums between the visible world and the invisible spirit realm. Nick sensed we were living on sacred ground. Many times he would awaken from a deep sleep and tell me that he had been sitting across from an elderly Indian on our lawn, being told the history of this area. Nick believed that an 18th century Indian shaman would be his guide to the afterlife. Some days I just wasn't into hearing all this talk of impending death and shamans swooping down to tear Nick from my life. Through my veil of pre-grieving raw nerves, I'd laugh and say, "Don't talk nonsense. You're hallucinating again. It must be time for your meds."

At least once or twice each week Nick would read my journals. Over supper we'd discuss what I'd written about my life with him, our journey towards fatherhood and our experiences as owners of a country Bed and Breakfast. Nick encouraged me to keep writing and someday make a book out of my journals. He felt he could cope with the public scrutiny of our journey into couple-hood if it meant one person might learn from our experiences. It wasn't easy to write in my journals knowing Nick had unfettered access to them.

A Swim *Against* The Tide

My mother visited for a few days, almost weekly. She said it was heaven on earth having us close enough for her to visit regularly. Mum and Nick's relationship was genuine, warm and frank. She had no intention of letting Nick die before his time and regularly filled our freezer with home-cooked nutritious meals. Mum's concern about Nick's loss of weight and fading energy levels frustrated her terribly; but her sensibilities told her she could nothing to prevent the downward spiral which lay ahead of him.

Dr. Tony patiently listened to my inquiries about new research and drugs to abate Nick's worsening health. He told me not to expect miracles as Nick was certainly heading into the final stage of his disease. When I pushed Tony for a time-line estimate, he was reluctant to be specific.

"It could be a year or it could be as soon as six months. Nick's body has been pummelled by seven years of this disease as well as all the drug therapies. His body is tired and this is the main reason for his steadily worsening health. Don't fight to keep him alive at this point. The inevitable will come soon and you both need to concentrate your efforts on living out his remaining days with dignity. Don't expect a miracle at this stage of his disease."

I never told Nick of these private conversations and my journal entries about them were hidden from him.

With our winter and spring renovation projects completed, I finally found a place for some of our belongings. The remaining boxes were destined for a big yard sale at the end of June. I put up yard sale posters at the general store and on trees lining local county roads. I felt it would be a good way for us to meet other neighbours on the lake.

One afternoon while Nick was sleeping I decided to take a jaunt over to the Gallery on the Lake, which showcased the talents of well known local artists. The curator met me in the foyer and asked one of her assistants to give me a tour. My tour guide noticed I was wearing a wedding band. She smiled and said, "Bring your wife by for a visit next time."

I considered briefly disguising the gender of my spouse, however, I

David R I McKinstry

quickly came to my senses. I just wasn't into hiding anymore and I didn't want to start our new life in the country based on lies.

"Well thanks for the suggestion. I am married and my spouse is a man named Nick."

I was pleasantly surprised to hear her exclaim, "Oh my gosh, Betty and Bertha will be thrilled to hear that another couple have arrived in the area."

She told me Betty and Bertha, a couple for over forty years, had been local teachers who had taught generations of kids in the area. Now in their late eighties, they spent six months in Florida, and their summers near Buckhorn. She smiled as she told me how Betty took great pride in her baking skills, and for many years had baked miniature wedding cakes, as their special gift, for former students when they got married.

"The other day Betty dropped in here to give me one of those cakes for my thirty-year-old daughter who is getting married in August. I was one of Betty's pupils in a one room school house over fifty years ago. Betty is even doing those cakes for the grandchildren of her students." What an endearing story to hear from this friendly stranger.

At our yard sale I introduced Nick to our new neighbours and told them we had moved here to set up a Bed and Breakfast. No one blinked an eye upon hearing we were married and gay. Sandy Lake was the fulfilment of a wonderful dream for us. Karen and Mike Sullivan dropped by and bought a spare mattress for their cottage. We learned that Mike was an elementary school principal with the York Catholic School System, and that before going into teaching, he had worked for London Life as a sales agent just down the street from the London Life office where I had worked in 1978.

Each time we met new neighbours on the lake I'd inquire about upcoming summer events. Was there a cottagers association? Wasn't there a mile swim or summer regatta for the families on the lake? It seemed odd that Sandy Lake didn't have an annual summer regatta for cottage families. By early July we had decided to organize and host a regatta at our place on the August Long Weekend. I made up flyers and delivered them around the lake to every one of the 123 cottages. Our waterfront wasn't really ideal so I inquired about using Karen and Mike Sullivan's beachfront who were happy to participate in organizing the regatta and hosting it.

I modelled the regatta events after the Stoney Lake regattas I had attended in my youth; we even added a "Cross the Lake Swim" to mimic the Lech One Mile Swim I had participated in every summer when we had our cottage on Stoney Lake.

On the day of the Sandy Lake Regatta Nick wasn't feeling well. Mum was up for the weekend and she stayed with Nick while I led a flotilla of neighbours, all in canoes, down the shoreline to the Sullivans. The Regatta was a hit! Thirty families from around the lake joined in the festivities. When Nick arrived with Mum in tow later in the afternoon, I made a point of introducing him as my other half and without missing a beat everyone applauded and thanked him for his contributions to the regatta. Nick's smile beamed out over the crowd like the sunrise over the

Sandy Lake Regatta, August 1994.

David R I McKinstry

lake. We felt so welcomed by our neighbours and it appeared they genuinely wanted us to feel like an integral part of their community.

We hosted many impromptu cocktail parties for our neighbours that summer, the numbers of people growing each time. Cocktail discussions were interesting, spanning the gambit of topics, none the least of which was that gay people should be given the right to adopt.

Every few days one or both of us would spend time on the computer exploring adoption options, legitimate surrogacy programs, and keeping ourselves abreast of changes in government policies which would open the door for us to adopt openly as a couple. Most of these neighbours seemed to know of at least one friend or family member who was gay or lesbian. It was incredible that we had landed in the midst of such a heart-warmingly supportive cluster of summer neigh-bours. On cooler evenings our hot tub became popular with parents with young children. We insisted our neighbours utilise Woodhaven's facilities and bring themselves and their kids over anytime for a hot tub before bedtime. Immersing children in warm water was a sure bet that they would be sleepy long before their parents got them back home to their beds.

A week after the regatta, I drove Nick to Sunnybrook Hospital for his bimonthly round of blood tests. I let him off in front of the doctor's office and agreed to meet an hour later. I delivered advertising artwork to several Toronto newspapers, bought herbal remedies and tonics for flushing out Nick's system, picked up a few groceries at the Loblaws down the street from Sunnybrook, and then returned to our rendezvous spot outside the doctor's office. I waited ten minutes for him, then decided to park the car and head inside.

The office was full of gaunt looking men and women. I asked the receptionist about Nick and she said I should use the side office and the doctor would see me in a minute. I wasn't sure why I should go into the side office and I was confused that I couldn't see Nick anywhere. Within minutes Nick's doctor stormed in, and barely acknowledging me, began to berate me for not having brought Nick in sooner, intimating that I

A Swim *Against* The Tide

should have sensed that something was wrong. She said he had been admitted and was on the infectious disease floor.

"He is really sick and he may not recover this time," she said. "We're doing a series of tests but you can see him now," and left the room.

I found Nick in bed hooked up to an IV and my heart melted when I saw him looking quite distressed. He said he had been poked and prodded by just about every neophyte physician on call, and that all he wanted was to go home. He knew he wouldn't be leaving that day but he didn't want to stay more than overnight at Sunnybrook. The look on his face showed me how aware he was of the seriousness of the situation. Nick's deep green eyes told me he just wanted the two of us to return Woodhaven and our dogs.

I sought out Nick's physician at the nurses' station, informed him who I was and asked him to tell me what was happening with Nick. He briskly told me he couldn't discuss Nick with anyone but Nick's family without Nick's permission. I blew a gasket and told him he was totally out of touch with the reality of his patients. I marched angrily back to Nick's room, grabbed a piece of paper and told Nick to scribble the following:

"Let it be known that my same-sex spouse David McKinstry is also my power of attorney and all my health concerns must be shared with David upon his request of such information."

With note in hand, I stomped back to the nurses' station and loudly proclaimed so all could hear from Hamilton to Sudbury, that I wanted to speak to Nick's physician. My patience had never been above-average but today it registered zero and my militancy was coming through loud and clear.

The young upstart physician, who had declined to share Nick's health chart with me, was paged and within a ten minutes stood before me. I handed him the scribbled authorisation. He apologised for not having shared the information with me in the first place, stating that he himself was gay and secondly that he had been working over 24 hours straight and his own patience had dropped off the map hours ago. He told me Nick had pneumonia and their team wanted to do an ultra sound to determine if there were any pockets of cancerous cells floating around his organs, especially in his lungs and gastrointestinal tract. An hour later Nick was on a gurney being wheeled out of his room heading toward the X-ray department

It took four days of testing before the doctor scheduled a closed-door visit with us. Nick's AIDS specialist arrived for this meeting as well and in her familiar blunt manner informed Nick that his tests had shown cancerous shadows on his liver and heart and that they would be doing a biopsy of his lung the following day to determine the extent and type of cancer growth there. By now Nick's pneumonia was under control. As his breathing improved he got antsy about going home. Two days after the biopsy and a battery of additional tests, the doctor informed us that Nick's immune system had been caught off guard by the cancer cells and that they had taken root in his spine, lungs and most probably were heading into his brain stem. The prognosis wasn't great but they were going to keep him here for another few weeks of tests.

Nick seemed keenly aware of their unspoken message of NO HOPE.

"Why would I stay on here if you have already identified the cancer? What do you expect to find with more tests? Could you possibly find out that I am not as bad as you thought?" he asked point blank. The doctor shook his head and said that further tests wouldn't change the prognosis, which was that Nick only had a few months to live at most.

I could feel the blood drain from my legs and I felt woozy as I stood beside Nick's bed. With my hands placed squarely on Nick's shoulder I questioned the need to keep him in hospital if the prognosis was so poor. The doctor appeared to dance around the issue of Nick being a guinea pig for some upcoming studies about AIDS patients.

Nick told the doctor he was checking himself out within the hour. "There isn't anything else you can do for me and I want to be at home

A Swim *Against* The Tide

at the lake." The doctor smiled sympathetically, almost as if he too felt that Nick should just go home and enjoy what time he had left.

Nick's face looked ashen and my legs still felt wobbly. One part of me was strangely aroused by the feel of Nick's shoulders and the other part of me was in total denial of Nick not becoming the first person to beat AIDS. I laid beside Nick on the bed and we hugged one another until my bravery was overtaken and my sobs began. Tears burned my cheeks and Nick became my comforter. He didn't say a word; he just hugged me tightly and whispered, "Let's get out of here and go home."

Thankfully Nick would live another five months in reasonably good spirits but late in January 1995 his health began its final descent.

Nick and my cousin Elizabeth enjoying a good discussion.
November 1994.

David R I McKinstry

It was just after 11 a.m. Friday February 2, 1995 when the phone rang. Mum had obviously grabbed it in the kitchen as it stopped on the second ring. Elizabeth was examining Nick and I was lying beside him holding his hand. Nick's health had deteriorated quickly. Although we made the adoption inquiries a larger than life focus for us, Nick knew he wouldn't live to see our child placed in his arms. Exactly six months after leaving the hospital, Nick lay in our bed stuporous from morphine, surrounded by love, and we all knew death was close at hand.

Mum walked in with the portable phone and said it was a woman calling from the California law firm. I hadn't heard from our adoption specialist for several weeks and expected this to be just another call to update me on our file. Diane was meticulous about keeping in touch with us. I took the phone and said hello.

Diane asked, "How is Nick today?" There was detectable excitement in her voice.

Two weeks earlier I had told her that Nick wasn't doing well. She knew his health had become precarious from day to day. I told her he was nearly comatose because of the high doses of morphine. She was silent for a moment. Her silence resonated in my ears and I imagined an arpeggio of profanity trumpeting silently from behind her tightly closed mouth. Diane had lost her brother and his companion to AIDS, as well as several good friends over the last decade. She spoke in a guardedly excited tone and proceeded to tell me that she had received confirmation just an hour ago about a possible baby for us. Without taking a breath between sentences, she continued to blather on about how a young twenty-two year-old student, five months pregnant, had chosen our profile for her baby. I stopped Diane abruptly and told her to wait just a moment so I could put the phone up to Nick's ear so he could hear this news simultaneously with me. My hand was shaking I was so excited.

I shook Nick's shoulder and said, "Nick you have to hear this. Diane is on the phone and they have a baby for us. I'm putting the phone to your ear."

I positioned the portable beside his ear while I grabbed the bedside phone so I could continue to listen as well. I told Diane to go ahead.

"Hi Nick, its Diane. I have good news and I hope you can hear me." She gave a polite synopsis of what she had just said to me to bring Nick up to snuff and then she continued, "This young woman is a grad student at a mid-west college and is five months pregnant. The tests have shown that the baby is developing normally and we can expect this baby to be healthy. She read your profile and decided that regardless of Nick's worsening health, she wants the two of you to have this baby. Her brother was gay, and a Jesuit, and he died of AIDS a few years ago. She told us her brother's greatest regret was not having had children. Choosing you to have this baby is her way of fulfilling her dead brother's wish to be a parent." Then there was a pregnant pause on the other end of the line.

"David do you think Nick understood what I just said?"

I was thrilled and feeling more emotionally anchored to Nick than I had for months. We were going to have a child.

"Yes, Diane," I responded from the periphery of my dreamy state. "I am sure he understood."

I told Diane he was unresponsive so we were keeping a bedside vigil. Diane's legal veneer shattered and I could hear her crying on the other end of the phone.

"Let me know when Nick dies, David. Give him a hug goodbye from me and please keep telling him about his baby."

I hung up the phone not knowing whether to laugh, cry or make a birth announcement. Excitedly I shared this information with Mum and Elizabeth who were looking on very surprised. I could tell they suspected something was up in our search for a baby from the gist of the telephone conversation they'd overheard.

The three of us reassembled by Nick's bedside telepathically telling him to follow God's voice and go home to Heaven when the time was right. The afternoon passed uneventfully. Mary called from Guelph several times, each time relieved to hear her son was still alive. By 8 p.m.

Mum was tired and left to lie down in the next room. Elizabeth and I continued to sit quietly, every now and again she'd take his blood pressure and measure his pulse. We'd talk to Nick and tell him to let go and move on to Heaven whenever he felt ready to go. Elizabeth suggested I give Nick permission to let go and follow the light in the tunnel, so I did. It was very spiritual lying beside Nick and whispering in his ear that I was alright with his dying. I repeated over and over that he shouldn't stay behind for me as it was his appointed time to meet God and to just let go whenever he was ready.

At 8:28 p.m., I got off the bed and told Elizabeth I was just going to get a cup of hot coffee from the kitchen. I hadn't moved in two hours and my back was sore. I patted Nick's knee and jokingly said, "I'll be back in a few minutes Nick, don't go anywhere while I'm gone."

I walked to the kitchen, past Mum reading in a living room chair and poured myself a cup of coffee. I looked across the lake as I walked slowly past the floor to ceiling living room windows. Swirls of snow were eerily dancing across the frozen ice because of high winds. As I walked into the room, Elizabeth was holding his wrist. She looked up at me through tears and quietly said, "David something is happening. I think Nick's going."

The coffee mug fell to the floor and I leapt onto the bed and nestled down beside Nick. His chest wasn't rising yet I could hear air being exhaled from his mouth. Oblivious to anything but him, I held Nick close and whispered in his ear, "Breathe Nick, breathe. I lied, I'm not ready to let go. Please don't go, Nick."

Elizabeth touched my shoulder with her hand and softly murmured in my ear, "He's already in that tunnel of light and he wants to go home David. Just hug him and tell him you love him. Remember hearing is the last sense to go so keep talking to him." With that she walked out into the living room and closed the door.

For every second of the first few minutes I lay there hugging Nick I wondered if I should pound on his chest or do mouth to mouth. I couldn't fathom that he was going ... gone. Why did he wait until I left

A Swim *Against* The Tide

his bedside to take me seriously about letting go? I didn't want him to go. Ten minutes or so must have passed before Mum entered the room with Elizabeth. We cried in unison, each touching Nick's hand and silently saying a heartfelt goodbye. Jenny, Nick's favourite Golden Retriever, had been laying across the end of the bed most of the night keeping Nick's feet warm. She lifted her head and uttered a pitiful low-pitched funereal howl to tell the world her master had gone to his final rest at 8:30 p.m., February 2, 1995.

As Nick wished, his body was waked in his chapel at Woodhaven for two days before being moved to Toronto to have his Jesuit brothers conduct the funeral service. The two-day wake in his chapel had made us all feel better able to cope with Nick's funeral. I just couldn't have imagined leaving Nick behind each night in a sterile funeral home. We had been able to toast a glass of wine to his memory, sit in our housecoats sipping coffee by the coffin, have private moments of prayer in the chapel and talk to him anytime day or night as we slowly adjusted to the reality of his death.

I called the law firm to tell Diane that Nick had died only hours after she told us the good news of the baby. Diane said she would tell the young woman about Nick's death and relay his excitement upon hearing she had chosen us to have her baby. Although I was still in shock over Nick's death, I was overjoyed at the thought of a little Nicholas or Nicole being born into this world in four months time.

Nick's funeral was held at Our Lady of Lourdes Catholic Church. The church held 600 people and the pews and aisles were full of his students, associates, Jesuits from across the country, dear friends and family. It was a wonderful send off.

The first week after his death I kept myself busy cancelling subscriptions, sending out death notices to insurance companies, banks and government registry offices. I walked through our house talking to Nick as if he was standing beside me. It was comforting to think of him still at Woodhaven. I talked about missing him and verbally shared just about every thought that came into my head. The reality of the baby

David R I McKinstry

news had my head spinning. I put together a list of necessary renovations required to make the house baby-proof. Which room would best suit being converted into a nursery? What colour should I paint the walls? Would it be a boy or a girl – a Nicholas or a Nicole? Somehow walking around the house blathering on like an idiot about baby preparations, asking Nick what he thought about this or that helped me get through that first week after the funeral.

Ten days later, Diane called from her California adoption office. She had bad news. The young pregnant woman, who had chosen us to have her baby, had been in a car accident which had induced labour. At 26 weeks old the baby, a girl, had been delivered alive at the accident scene but had died enroute to the hospital. Losing Nick had ripped my guts to shreds and now, only ten days after his funeral I was losing the baby that was to be have been adopted by us. I hadn't been given a chance to parent. I had lost this baby which had become my life preserver.

I felt very close to shutting down, letting life drain away into this swamp of despair. How could fate have dealt me such a massive blow in this very vulnerable period only days after Nick's death? Was God listening to my prayers? It didn't seem to matter how well prepared I was to play the game, I just wasn't going to get a child easily. I was tired of swimming against the tide.

A Swim *Against* The Tide

CHAPTER ELEVEN

Michael

For eighteen months after Nick's death, Woodhaven was in a constant state of renovation. It grew from a three bedroom Bed and Breakfast into a thriving five suite Country Lodge. Business was brisk and money was coming in sufficiently to pay the bills and keep my finances in the black. I loved being the proprietor and spent most of my nights on the computer devising new marketing and advertising programs to reach a wider range of markets. By the end of the summer of 1996 getting me back into the dating scene became an obsession of several good friends.

Our mortgage insurance claim had been refused by the bank and I had made a very public legal defence. I outed myself on *Canada AM*. Every Toronto TV news station and newspaper had interviewed me about the greedy banks refusal to honour the mortgage insurance claim of my deceased same-sex spouse. But the bank had more lawyers and money than I did, and I had to drop the case to preserve what little financial integrity I had left.

Telephone calls to American adoption firms seemed a daily event for October 1996. Nick had been dead for twenty months and I was no further ahead in my quest to be a parent. Every day I would make calls to Toronto to speak with, or more often than not to leave messages for various officials within numerous branches of the CAS.

Nick's book had remained incomplete at the time of his death and I spent a number of weeks trying to organize his files and access data stored in his computer. For years he had wanted to finish a book on spiritual discernment and another book on the philosophy of Bernard Lonergan. I was out of my league trying to make sense of his extensive, carefully arranged notes. Finally I gave up and put his files away, wondering if Nick was supposed to have completed that book. Was starting the work just a part of his journey that was never meant to be finished? Things happen for a reason, as I'd been told so many times in the past, and maybe Nick died for a reason when he did, leaving behind unfinished projects simply because that was the way his journey was meant to be travelled. Wondering about the here and now and the why and how of life occupied my mind more often than I cared to admit to anyone.

I had cleaned out closets in preparation for winter and found old scarves of Nick's in a drawer. I placed them under my nose and sniffed in hopes of smelling his scent. Like a thunderbolt hitting me square in the face, I realized that I couldn't remember his scent. Was I getting musty old scarf smells or was it the aging scent of Nick lingering on his clothes. I panicked and scurried to pull some of his sweaters from my cupboard – there was no noticeable scent. I knew I was losing Nick's physical presence, yet as upset as I was, for the first time since his death, I knew the time had come to let go.

I had established a comfort zone around Woodhaven that allowed Nick's ghost to live in my future. He had told me not to wish him back and waste my life with regrets. I clearly remember Nick telling me before he became bedridden, that when he reached Heaven he wouldn't be sending me a sign from the other side. He had lived his life believing in Heaven and he felt that others should get to Heaven in their own way and time. Nick wasn't prepared to send me a roadmap and made it clear that once he got upstairs I was to move forward with my life.

Weeks after Nick died I had received a poem from the funeral home

A Swim *Against* The Tide

which was sent to comfort me. The poem seemed unfinished and since its author was unknown I decided to finish it my way. I felt as if my motivation to finish this poem was Nick's sign to me that he was just fine and loving the other side.

> *Death is nothing at all…I have only slipped away into the next room. I am I and you are you… Whatever we were to each other that we are still. Call me by my familiar name, speak to me in the easy way which you always used to. Put no difference into your tone; wear no forced air of solemnity or sorrow.*
>
> *Laugh as we always laughed at the little jokes we enjoyed together. Play, smile, think of me, pray for me. Let my name be ever the household word that it always was. Let it be spoken without effort, without the ghost of a shadow on it. Life means all that it ever meant. It is the same as it ever was: there is absolutely unbroken continuity.*
>
> *What is this death but a negligible accident? Why should I be out of mind because I am out of sight? I am waiting for you for an interval, somewhere very near, just around the corner. Until we are reunited, you must live, love and continue along with your own special journey.*
>
> *The adventure I am now on is the best of what is to come. Our mortal journey together is complete. You must make the rest of your mortal journey unique and filled with loving others. Do not waste time mourning. Our paths now are separate but the love we share will be the magnate to reunite us when it is your time to take the next step into this glorious eternity. All is well.*

David R I McKinstry

A few weeks into November I received a supper invitation in the mail from a gay Fraternity friend in Toronto. I'd known Frank for years and I telephoned to find out more about his dinner party.

Supper, he explained, was only a rouse to get me to meet some of his single friends. A month earlier I would have been insulted by this invitation but now I sensed the time was right for me to get away from Woodhaven and my self-imposed hermitage. I asked about the fellows I would be meeting. Frank refused to provide much information other than both his single friends were outdoor types and each was interested in meeting me. Frank had told them about the Woodhaven Widower before sending me the invitation. I graciously accepted and told him I would be pleased to start meeting his friends. Since Frank and I would both be attending a mutual friend's 80th birthday party in a few days, I suggested we sit at the same table and he could tell me more about who I'd be meeting.

Bob Grimson, 80 years old with mischief in his eyes and the soul of a teenager, was an icon in the Fraternity movement. As a retired businessman living in Rosedale, Bob was a collector of great artwork and a generous supporter of the gay business community. Since our first meeting ten years earlier, I'd always known Bob to have younger gay men around him, acting as their mentor. Bob had been an astute businessman in Toronto between the late 1940s and the end of the 1970s. Gay bars were a big business in the 1970s and one of Bob's many claims to fame had been his ownership of the first gay-owned-and-operated bar in Toronto. Straight businessmen knew there was money in gay bars, so did all the beer and liquor industries. Bob's entrepreneurial success, his kind heart and his generous benevolence made him an icon within many circles of Toronto's gay community.

Bob captivated his audiences of younger Fraternity members with stories of police raids on bars and private homes in the late 1940s to break up suspicious gay parties. Rosedale's gay and lesbian socialites in the 1950s would invite hordes of gay men and women to closed-door parties in mansions north of Bloor Street. Men and women would arrive

A Swim *Against* The Tide

in cabs together but once inside the gay blades stayed on the main floor while the lesbians, all decked out in feminine regalia, would head upstairs for their private parties. If the police arrived out front, then everyone would find their assigned opposite-sex partners and pretend that the party was STRAIGHT. Bob told me stories of entertaining Hollywood stars who would come to Toronto regularly to enjoy the gay house party circuit of the 1960s. He said he was the only person he knew in his circle of friends who had been fired from a job for being a Jew and a homosexual. At age 80 he continued to play tennis four times each week and could whip most of his younger opponents. Nick and I had thoroughly enjoyed Bob's friendship and I had remained in close contact with him since Nick's death. Bob was very encouraging of my efforts to adopt, saying often that if he was only forty years younger he would be leading the charge for gays to adopt children.

Bob's birthday party was spectacular and a virtual who's who of the gay community was there. It was a momentous evening with many well wishers and friends, and I felt honoured and grateful to have been invited. I'd had a great time at his birthday party and received a few calls early the next week from fellows to whom I'd been introduced during the party. None really grabbed my attention. I was looking forward to the singles supper at Franks' condo. I had been working out and spending loads of time on my Nordic Track exercise equipment since Nick's death. I was svelte again and went on a spending spree to buy new clothes to dazzle my two blind dates.

I had been at Frank's for only a short while when the first of the two singles rang the buzzer. It didn't take long for me to realize there was no spark between Robert and myself. "This could be a long evening," I murmured to myself. Surely Frank must have had some inkling of my tastes in men. Frank had gone overboard with preparations, with attention to every detail. I wasn't about to tell Frank that I was disappointed with Bachelor Number One. Small talk filled the room and I began to unwind with my second glass of wine. I certainly wasn't interested in the violinist/accountant and hoped the next single would be more my

David R I McKinstry

type. Although I wasn't desperate to meet someone, I was ready to move forward and ease into dating opportunities. Being a parent remained a dream that never left me. I was ready to do it alone but having a companion with whom to share that adventure was my preference.

More than anything I missed being part of a couple. I was happy with myself and who I had become. I wasn't looking for someone to make me complete. I missed having that right someone to wake up beside. I hoped I could have something similar to the great relationship I'd had with Nick. I really did enjoy my privacy and would never lose myself in someone else's identity. But I could feel parenthood nearing, and as discouraging as the adoption quest had been so far, I clung tightly to the hope that I'd meet someone who could share my vision of a future with children, dogs and country living.

Just as Frank made the rounds with a cheese tray, we heard a second knock at the door.

"That must be Michael," winked Frank as he flew past me to open the door and greet Bachelor Number Two.

He walked in with a big grin, handed Frank a bottle of red wine and removed his coat. I was out of view as he entered the room and without missing a beat, single number one said, "Hello Mike, nice to see you again."

Frank looked at the two of them, chortled loudly and asked, "And how, pray tell, do the two of you know one another?"

A flurry of explanations filled the air from both men who laughed about having dated a few weeks ago. Frank turned his attention to me and pulled Michael around the corner so he could introduce us. I had been observing Michael from the sidelines as he was being greeted by Frank and Robert. Immediately I thought he looked like the movie star Tom Selleck. Having overheard the dating saga that ensued I wasn't sure if they were continuing to date, had only dated once or whether one liked the other more than was reciprocated. Michael thrust out his hand to shake mine, smiled politely, turned back to face Robert and began talking

A Swim *Against* The Tide

about the coincidence of meeting at Franks. Red flags immediately began waving in my mind. These guys like one another, so why am I here?

As if Frank read my mind he asked if I would help him in the kitchen. I followed him into the galley kitchen and Frank opened the oven door and began making low level noises so his whispers wouldn't be heard in the living room.

"So what do you think so far? Anyone stand out?" He peered eagerly into my face to see which one I'd state was the fairest in the land. I didn't appreciate effeminate mannerisms and Frank could be a queen with a capital Q, but on him it was delightfully amusing, and somehow being the Queen suited Frank.

"Did you know they knew each other when you invited them to meet me?" I replied in a whisper.

Frank chuckled and said it served him right for telling Robert and Michael about me but neglecting to tell them about one another.

"Who would have thought that they had dated!" Frank said in mock disgust. "Anyway, that aside, who do you think is more your type – tell me quick so the hors d'oeuvres don't get cold."

I whispered that Michael was more my type and that his full moustache made him look handsome with a roguish air. That was enough for Frank. He smiled and said, "My Yenta instincts are working. I had a feeling you'd choose Michael the moment you met him."

Returning to the living room, Frank manoeuvred us to be seated so we could begin to enjoy the repartee. He announced that supper would be in half an hour so we had lots of time to sit and chat. I felt a tad awkward sitting between Michael and Robert, thanks to Frank. But the moment silence fell on the room Frank would pipe up with another quip about something or other and conversation would resume for another few minutes. Michael began to warm to me as he asked about Woodhaven. He used all types of questions to understand the workings of my lodge, about its size, was it gay-only, how far from Peterborough was Sandy Lake, and many more. I asked if he knew the area and he responded that he had grown up in Peterborough. Astonished to hear

David R I McKinstry

him say he grew up in my hometown I said I too had grown up there and asked which high school he had attended.

"I went to Kenner," he said, his eyes widening with disbelief that there was actually someone else other than himself who had grown up gay in Peterpatch. We discovered that we had attended the same high school at the same time, albeit four years apart. Conversation flowed easily between Michael and me non-stop. Questions were asked and answered about people and places we knew. Had he gone to the YMCA ... had I been a competitive swimmer ... had he been involved in musical productions at Kenner ... did I like being back in the Peterborough area?

It was Robert's turn to help Frank in the kitchen and I found myself staring into Michael's deep green eyes, observing his extraordinary long eye-lashes and the perfectly manicured moustache that covered his upper lip. No nose hair sticking out; that was a bonus! His ears haven't sprouted bushes of hair, another point in his favour. His cologne also had an appealing scent.

Frank and Robert returned to the room with plates laden with food. Robert set one plate on the table and said, "Here you are Michael," then immediately sat down beside Michael. Like an ever-watchful grandmother, Frank took note of Robert's positioning. He winked at me as he placed my plate beside him on the opposite side of the table so I was facing Michael.

The meal, conversation and wine were superb. Robert travelled a lot and spoke about the warm exotic places he'd visited. Being a teacher, Michael talked about his many March-break vacations to Mexico, Cuba and Aruba. I asked if anyone in the room liked winter and only Michael showed an interest for the snow season and cross-country skiing. In fact he had been looking to buy lakefront property up in the Kawarthas for several years, hoping someday to build a weekend cottage he could access year round.

Frank inquired about my dogs as I had often joked with him when he'd call that I had been out scouring the woods for my runaways.

"Who is looking after the Goldens tonight?" he asked hoping to keep Michael's attentions on me.

Before I could reply Michael asked, "Are your dogs Golden Retrievers?"

I said I had five auburn coloured American Goldens and he sat back in his chair, folded his arms, looked directly into my eyes and said, "I grew up with American Goldens. They're wonderful dogs."

I smiled back looking quite amazed.

"There aren't many around who know about the reddish coloured variety. Do you own a dog presently?"

Michael said his ex-lover had a Sheltie named Kip and since he continued to share an apartment with him, it was almost like having a dog.

Robert asked Michael if he enjoyed being a teacher and the conversation switched to Ontario's education reform being tackled by the dreaded Tories. None of us, regardless of our common gay link, were in professions that liked the Tories or the arrogance of Mike Harris.

I could feel my blood pressure rising at the mere mention of the word Tory and Frank, in his wisdom, changed the course of conversation again to the Bed and Breakfast business. He asked how Woodhaven was shaping up. I presented an overview of my marketing strategy and described how I hoped radio advertising would give me a greater market share of dog-friendly people who wanted to enjoy a country retreat.

"I'm sure you'd get many people who live in city apartments, yet can't have pets, who would enjoy coming to that type of lodge as well," said Michael.

As conversation flowed easily, I had been observing Michael for almost two hours. I still hadn't been able to figure out how he and Robert were connected. Every time I spoke, Robert had to one up me with a story about himself. I wasn't going to play one-up-manship so after dessert I excused myself from the table and said I had to get back on the road to Woodhaven.

As Frank saw me to the door I said, "Earlier you asked if anyone was looking after the dogs, Frank. The truth is it's impossible to find dog-sitting services out in the boonies. So I have to start back now as it will take me two hours."

David R I McKinstry

I thanked him for the wonderful evening and in turn I shook hands with both Robert and Michael. I had no indication from Michael whether he was more interested in Robert or me, but I figured since they both lived in Toronto they'd continue to date. I felt like an odd man out at this singles' supper and just wanted to get back to the comfort of my slippers, the dogs, my home and the lake.

Out of the blue, I got a phone call from Michael on a Sunday night two weeks after Frank's dinner party. I hadn't thought I'd hear from him so I sceptically asked if he had tired of Bachelor Number One and was now calling the consolation prize. He laughed nervously and said he'd had one date with Robert two weeks prior to supper at Frank's and wasn't interested in having a second date. Michael told me he was shy and it had taken him two weeks to get up the nerve to make this call to me.

I softened my approach upon hearing he was interested in me rather than in Robert and I decided to try and break the ice with humour.

"So you think you want to date me. Are you sure you're up to the challenge Michael? I'm not some easy, sleazy ghetto tart who puts out on the first date." We laughed in unison and I was glad he'd found it amusing too.

Michael said he would like to drive up and go for a long walk with me and the dogs around Sandy Lake. We spent 30 minutes on the phone discussing country life versus city life and he asked lots of questions about my life as a Bed and Breakfast owner. He was engaging and sincere and I felt eager to have a face to face date.

Michael telephoned me Tuesday evening, just minutes after I'd spent an hour on the phone with Elizabeth and Jonathan about plans for visiting them early in January. We'd spoken about my loneliness and missing romance in my life. Elizabeth, herself a survivor of two divorces, knew love was out there and could be found – if I was open with myself and available to dating.

"The next man of your dreams isn't going to drive up your mile-long laneway some Sunday afternoon," she'd said. "You've got to get out there and let people know you're ready to meet someone special again." I had yet to tell them about Michael's call a few days earlier asking me on a date, so I took hold of that moment to tell Elizabeth that the man of my future dreams might just be driving up my mile-long laneway within five days.

Elizabeth and Jonathan had been vigilant about calling twice weekly, visiting every other month and sending me books on grieving, coping with loss and recovery from the death of a spouse. I promised I'd call her after my date with Michael and give them the full scoop. Jonathan was surprised at the coincidence that I had attended the same high school as Michael and yet our paths had never crossed. Naively, Jonathan seemed to think that all gay men must know one another somehow, as if by radar (which gay men refer to as *gaydar*).

Michael called to firm up a time when he should arrive on Sunday afternoon. I joked and said that he was calling because the sound of my voice was such a turn on to him. He laughed and confessed that he was really very excited to spend some quiet country time with me in my Woodhaven world. Michael asked if we could take the dogs for a walk around the property at some point, as he really enjoyed being outdoors and watching dogs run through the bush. He reminded me he had been looking for almost two years for property in the Kawarthas just so he could have a weekend place to call his own.

My weekend guests departed Sunday around noon and I'd just finished cleaning the guestrooms when the dogs started barking. A quick glance in the mirror, a finger brush of my hair, a quick gargle of mouthwash and I was as ready as I could be at the moment to welcome Michael to Woodhaven.

I let the dogs out and they bounded excitedly to his car. Michael wasn't phased in the least by five very excited large dogs, each whimpering and jostling one another out of the way to be first to jump up and give him a wet lick; a very good sign. It had rained the night before leaving puddles on the gravel driveway but there was a hint of winter in the air. I didn't want to get my Birkenstocks wet so I just waited in the open

David R I McKinstry

doorway for him to walk to the house. I called the dogs but they refused to listen to me, instead they just kept surrounding Michael forcing him to walk slowly as he divided his time patting each of them as he came towards me. Holding a covered plate high above his head in one hand, he finally reached the door smiling, his food and himself having managed to survive the gauntlet of excited canines. Michael looked even more ruggedly handsome, like Hollywood's Tom Selleck, in a country backdrop than he had over supper in Toronto. I began to fantasize about a sudden snowstorm forcing him to stay over tonight and me lustfully devouring his moustache between my lips. I hoped I would get the chance to try it out during his visit. I hadn't realized my heart was pounding until Michael and the dogs came inside and the barking noises subsided. It felt almost *too* good to be in his company.

During supper in Toronto Michael said he had been raised in Peterborough yet he never spent any time on Sandy Lake. He said the drive up was refreshing, just being out of the city and into the country made him relax and come alive. I was impressed with the homemade apple cake he'd brought along.

"After a weekend of looking after guests I thought you might appreciate someone else's cooking." What a neat thing for him to have made me a cake. Smart, too!

I gave him the grand tour and told him I had just finished cleaning guestrooms minutes before his car pulled into the parking lot. Nick's Suite was given a bit of background on how it had been built as a chapel but was now a much preferred guest room. I told him I was bored with the arrangement of its furniture and was interested in spiffing it up. Michael threw out a few suggestions that I thought were great. We spent the first hour of our date rearranging furniture and attaching a patchwork quilt to the wall behind the bed. Words and ideas flowed easily and I found myself frequently looking at him and checking out his physique.

The dogs were anxious for a walk by the time we emerged from rearranging and sprucing up Nick's Suite. I asked Michael if he'd like something to drink before we took the dogs out for a romp and he said tea would be fine, in fact he'd retrieve his empty travel mug from the car and take fresh tea along on our walk.

The entire property was visited as I blabbed on about my Sandy Lake neighbours and what a great community I had landed in. I asked Michael many questions about himself, and he asked me many more.The sky became quite dark, the air chilled noticeably and we retreated to the house. As we neared Woodhaven large flakes of snow began to blow around us. I had been waiting for snow since November 1st, traditionally the day I usually start decorating for Christmas.

With a snowstorm outside, the dogs nestled in a circle by the fireplace, some twitching in their dreams, others fast asleep. Michael wandered around the house investigating various rooms while I made a batch of hot apple cider. Two hours after he arrived, we joined each other on the sofa. What a busy afternoon it had been of impetuous decorating, walking and talking. The next few hours flew by as we continued to learn about our families, career and personal goals. I was asked about Nick and his family, life post-Nick, The Fraternity and about adoption roadblocks I was encountering.

"It isn't in my nature to give a quick verbal overview about any-thing. Are you sure you want to hear about my adoption struggles?" I asked. Michael nodded and said he was very interested in hearing it all.

We had two pieces of his apple cake each and three more cups of cider before I finally stopped talking. It was 6:30 p.m. before I realized Michael had been trapped on the sofa listening to me for hours. After a bathroom break, Michael returned to the sofa and sat closer to me than he had previously. A bit unnerved yet very excited by his closeness, I smiled and nervously nudged him saying, "Sniff some catnip while you were in the bathroom?"

Michael smiled and with the mounting sexual tension of the moment broken, he suddenly launched into a very serious topic.

"I would love to be a parent. I went into education because I enjoy teaching children new concepts and ways of looking at the world. I couldn't begin to imagine how great fatherhood must be. I also can't

David R I McKinstry

imagine being a single parent in today's world but I'm sure the rewards are worth the time and effort."

I sensed some yet unspoken conflicts about his own sexuality, his family, and about the direction of his life. He explained that his parents had divorced out of the blue when he was seventeen and that his mother's departure from the house was much more of a relief for him than an upset. Michael said his childhood years had been confusing and frustrating, always knowing he was different. He knew he was gay from his earliest childhood recollections. His mother had constantly pushed him into being more sociable but Michael had resisted for fear of people discovering he was gay. His relationship with his dad got better once his mother left the family home. Michael described his mother as not being particularly warm and their relationship was quite arms-length and formal. However, the relationship with his father was much more open, interactive and friendly. He said that both parents had remarried and that family get-togethers, infrequent as they were, always involved both parents and their new spouses.

I asked questions about his family and was immediately struck by how emotionally vague remarks about his family seemed to be. There was not much of relationship with anyone, in part from his reaction to having hidden his sexuality from them for so long. He'd found it easier to remove himself emotionally than confront them with the news that he was gay. There was a palpable suffering, a loneliness in his eyes as I listened to him talk about his family. His suffering seemed to stem from the absence of deep friendships in and out of his family unit; there was no mention of good friends, couples or singles, gay or straight. As open as he was, Michael probably wasn't aware of how lonely and alone he sounded. I wanted to take him in my arms to protect him and explain how he was missing so much of the world.

His life in Toronto seemed totally devoid of excitement when talking about teaching, coaching sports teams of his students, going to movies and taking trips to the Caribbean. Very little mention was made

A Swim *Against* The Tide

about friendships accumulated along the way. I could sense a sleeping giant within, and a soul ready for an awakening.

Michael asked me about my relationship with my family. I told him my mother was almost 82, an integral part of my life as both a parent and a friend, supportive of anything I desired to do with my life. I told him that she was excited about the prospect of becoming a grandmother, however, her enthusiasm had waned somewhat over the years as more and more adoption roadblocks cropped up against me. I openly admitted that I felt she had resigned herself to being the mother of two childless adult children and that grandparenting probably wasn't in the cards for her.

My only sibling, Karen, was a different limb on the family tree. She had become involved with a man five years her senior when she was just eighteen. He was a leftover hippie from the 1970s who just never seemed to be able to fit in. A dope head, he had hair hanging down to his butt – and he had turned away from his Bahai roots to become a reborn Christian in the Pentecostal movement. My sister embraced Pentecostalism and she'd distanced herself from me because of my Mormon theology, her conservatism and my lack of being born-again, as defined by Pentecostal doctrine. When I finally told her I was gay she ranted on that she knew the devil himself had wrapped his arms around me and swallowed my soul. Karen was angry at the world. We were the antithesis of one another. She married him much to my disappointment at the time but over the years he mellowed and proved to be more likeable than her and I grew to love him like a brother. Her husband had grown in his view of the world and life, but Karen hadn't budged one inch from her church doctrine.

Feeling strangled and suppressed, her husband eventually walked away from his Pentecostal ways and my sister just six months after our dad died in 1988. He had been the provider and Karen the homemaker. She ended up having little or no career skills, so she'd moved in with my mother and went to university to become a teacher. Her bitterness had a lot to do with her feelings of psychological abandonment by her birth

David R I McKinstry

mother, her husband, our father's death and then by me when I announced I was gay. I told Michael that my sister had provided no support to me when Nick was dying of AIDS.

There was a wonderfully warm look of understanding that crossed Michael's face indicating he understood how saddened I was by the loss of Karen in my life, especially considering we had been very close siblings growing up. Discord and contempt seemed to be the heart and soul of our present relationship which kept most of our interactions superficial at best.

"That must be quite a difficult and agonising juggling act for your mother," Michael noted intuitively.

"She's been a great supporter of us both, and she's fiercely loyal to our family. I'm sure it would be painful for any 82-year-old mother to have her only two adult children at such odds with one another."

There was a silence as he digested what I'd been saying. I reached forward to take a sip from my cup of cider. When I settled back into the sofa I garnered all my courage, looked over at Michael and asked, "May I kiss you, Michael?" I surprised myself at being so forward but regardless I was glad I'd taken the initiative. We kissed gently then continued baring our souls for another half-hour. The sound of the whirling wind hurling wet snowflakes at the picture window indicated the early evening storm was worsening. I suggested that Michael really should consider getting back to Toronto before the storm forced him to call in sick tomorrow. In spite of having my wish of a snowstorm come true, I now was concerned for his safety.

Michael left shortly afterward. The storm seemed to be getting worse by the minute making our goodbye quick but meaningful. Two and a half hours later he called to let me know he had returned safely to Toronto. We agreed that there was a strong mutual attraction. He asked if he could visit the following weekend but I told him I was hosting the mums and their children who'd be arriving for Christmas on Saturday, December 23rd. Unfortunately, I had to tell him, only men having had a recent police check were allowed to enter my place while the shelter

A Swim *Against* The Tide

residents were visiting. We could see one another the following Friday but by noon this Saturday I would be out of commission, and he would have to out of the lodge until after Boxing Day. I suggested he look at his schedule and give me a call in a few days and we'd try to plan our second date before Christmas. Twice that week I received his calls. Each time we spoke I could feel myself wanting to know him better. I could tell he was a kind-hearted loyal man, and his charm and handsome good looks were very appealing.

He arrived for a late supper on Friday night and I knew in my heart that he was about to become a permanent fixture in my life. He'd brought along a present to give me. I was a bit embarrassed that I hadn't spent any time buying a gift for him and explained that all my Christmas budget was going toward providing gifts and food for the mums and their children. I had told Michael that I usually drank eight to nine cups of coffee per day and that the seat of my jeep had coffee stains from me driving with flimsy recycled paper cups. My first gift from Michael was a much-appreciated Eddie Bauer deluxe travel coffee mug.

That clinched it, I said to myself, this guy's a keeper.

David R I McKinstry

CHAPTER TWELVE

The Commitment

I t had been an emotionally charged week preparing to host six mothers and seventeen children from a Toronto area women's shelter. Meeting Michael had been a significant landmark in the weeks leading up to Christmas 1996. Like my romance with Nick, I became committed. Deciding to host Christmas for strangers again this year gave the season a philanthropic focus and allowed me to tell friends this effort was part of Nick's legacy. Twenty-three months after his death and I still wasn't ready to let go of Nick all the way.

I was very much aware of that warm and fuzzy feeling deep in my soul each time I over-extended my budget in order to see wider smiles across the faces of the moms and tots on Christmas morning. I had spent much of the late fall and weeks preceding Christmas buying up colour, age and gender-specific presents for the children who'd be sharing Christmas at Woodhaven.

Friends came out of everywhere to help me make this project a huge success. Neighbours introduced me to someone who worked with Walt Disney Canada. He sent seven huge boxes crammed full of Disney gift items, ranging from new release and classic children videos to clothing and books. It must have been worth $2,000. A group of women from

Battered Mums and children
celebrate Christmas 1998 at Woodhaven.

Mum's church put together an envelope of cash to be used to cover food expenses for the ladies. Another neighbour showed up one afternoon with $200 to be split among the women. She knew from her own experience of leaving an abusive relationship 20 years before just how destitute an abused woman with kids could feel. A lesbian couple, frequent visitors to Woodhaven, bought size-specific clothing for all the families, Barbie dolls, train sets, lots of high-end toys for every child plus $50 Hudson Bay gift certificates for each of the mothers and an assortment of smaller gift items to put in the mother's stockings. This must have easily topped $1,500. I estimated I'd spent about $700 of my own money, double my original budget for this event. The extra cash and assortment of gifts went a long way to helping these mums and their children have a memorable, safe and happy Christmas.

The ladies and children were to arrive at the bus terminal in Peterborough on December 23 and stay for four days. Michael wanted

David R I McKinstry

to spend Christmas with me but unfortunately I had agreed not to have any other men at Woodhaven during the women's Christmas holiday. Had there been sufficient time for Michael to get police clearance it might have been possible for him to stay at the lodge and help me out, but as it was, he couldn't. Michael looked lost upon hearing we wouldn't be celebrating Christmas together. I told him we'd have our own special Christmas after the ladies and children left.

A member of Mum's church had a connection with a tour bus company who arranged for a 48 passenger deluxe coach, complete with TVs, to pick up the families at the bus station and bring them to Woodhaven. What a sight to see a huge tour bus rambling up my lane. A few inches of fresh snow lay on the ground which provided an enchanted and magical first impression for these guests.

Each family was given a bedroom of their own and I had cots set up to accommodate everyone. The children were excited about playing in the hot tub. The mothers loved having a bathroom of their own. Vivian Heinmiller, Wendy Smith and Deb Reid had brought out friends and family to help wrap gifts and bake ginger bread cookies the week before the families arrived. Two eight-foot Christmas trees were bulging from the enormous number of gifts tucked under, up and over the branches. It looked like each child and mother would get seven presents each; so many gifts and treats, this would be a Christmas they'd always remember!

Getting the children fed and supper on the table for the ladies was quite a chore. A few women friends had agreed to help out around meal times. The children were out of the hot tub only long enough to eat supper and then rush back into the warm waters. I told each of the children that they had to go to the bathroom before going into the hot tub. They were told a chemical was in the water that would turn it to Jell-O if anyone peed in the hot tub, in hopes of preventing an accident. After an hour of hot tubbing, the children were told they had to leave their mothers alone for two hours. I put on a video upstairs on the big screen TV and told the kids they could go wild up there but couldn't come down to the dining room while their mothers were eating.

A Swim *Against* The Tide

A gourmet meal was presented to the ladies, compliments of several neighbours who had wanted to cook supper. Wine and good cheer surrounded the table. These ladies had been cooped up together in cramped living quarters in the women's shelter. They were so happy to be out of the shelter on this country holiday that a meal of hot dogs would have been fine with them.

We dove into great discussions over supper. A bit of wine and the women began to talk openly about their abusive husbands. One woman's husband, a high school principal, had been beating her for years. For two months she planned her escape with their three children. Four weeks ago she landed at the shelter with her kids. She hoped to be out and into temporary housing soon. Her husband wasn't co-operating with her in terms of his financial responsibilities and she had never seen a dime of her own money in fifteen years as a married at-home mother.

Another woman had emigrated from Hungary with her son a year ago to marry a wealthy businessman but after they were married he practically made her a slave in and out of the bedroom. He told her she would be deported if he divorced her. As long as he didn't hurt her eleven-year-old son she stayed. One night her husband flew into a rage, punched and broke her nose while driving in the car. At the hospital the attending doctor asked if her husband had abused her and she broke down and admitted his abuse. The police were called and she was escorted home to get her son and sufficient clothes before being taken to a shelter. She had no money, worried about deportation around the clock, and never left the shelter for fear of meeting her husband on the street.

Jenny, 29, mother of three small children, made us all gasp over her story of abuse. She told this story which I copied down verbatim in the notepad I always carry in my pocket.

Jenny married her high school sweetheart at age nineteen. She'd come from a home with an abusive father and subservient mother. Jenny's father had forced her to give him oral sex between the time she was eleven to seventeen years of age. She had escaped a rotten home life into the arms of a great guy. Unfortunately, her husband ended up being

— 204 —

David R I McKinstry

manic-depressive and he was institutionalized several times in the first few years of their marriage. Jenny gave birth to three children, all one year apart. Her husband couldn't keep a job and began to get verbally abusive with her. Soon after the violence turned physical and by year seven of their marriage he was raping and sodomizing her regularly. They had no romantic sex life, just a forced sexual encounter whenever her husband felt the need for coital relations. One afternoon in front of the kids, he threw a tantrum over something and they scuffled in the kitchen. When she fell to the floor he grabbed her by the legs and dragged her into the bathroom. She thought he would just rape her but instead he tried to jam her head into the toilet bowl. Her eldest, a boy, had come to her rescue, hitting his dad on the head with a broom. He let go of her and began to throttle his son. Shortly afterward the police arrived, having been called by a concerned elderly neighbour she had befriended in their housing complex.

Jenny, escorted by police, went to a shelter that night with the kids. After ten weeks at the shelter she was set up in a townhouse and enrolled in a skills program through the government. On welfare Jenny was getting $1,250 month which was just enough for her to drive her car to classes, pay the rent and buy food. There were no extras and her husband had long since disappeared and wasn't paying support payments. The Harris Tories began slashing Ontario welfare payments and Jenny's monthly income soon dropped to $950 per month. She didn't have enough money to pay her rent and buy food or gas for her car to get to classes.

Somehow the CAS were contacted because her daughter said to her kindergarten teacher, "Mummy doesn't have any food for supper." The social worker assessed her situation and said the children should be put into temporary foster care until her finances improved. Jenny pleaded with the caseworker to give her a week to get the extra money she needed to keep the kids and pay her expenses.

From the moment she got married, Jenny stopped having anything to do with her abusive father. Her mother had died two years before

A Swim *Against* The Tide

leaving her father living alone but she hadn't seen him since the funeral. Jenny paid him a visit. She explained what had happened in the last six months and how she was only a few months away from graduating and getting a job. She asked him for a short-term loan to increase her monthly income for another few months until graduation. He refused. She increased the offer by saying she'd give him fifteen percent interest on the loan. Again, he flatly refused. Jenny said she knew it was now a do or die situation, so she suggested she give him oral sex twice weekly if he'd extend her a loan. He agreed. The deal was signed, so to speak, with oral sex then and there. She left with a letter from him to the social worker stating he would cover the deficit in her monthly expenses. Jenny was able to stay in her rented townhouse and keep her kids. She graduated two months later and a local hospital hired her for a $27,000 computer position through the school's placement program. Jenny never set foot again in her father's house once she got her first pay cheque. She proudly stood before us, a poster girl for getting out and moving on. Her pay cheque was enough to cover her family's needs and she was refusing to take any more welfare subsidies.

Everyone around the table was stunned into silence, not just by the details of her plight but by the sheer monotone of a voice resigned to do whatever was necessary to become independent. I had never heard anything so diabolical, cruel and barbaric from a father in my life.

Everyone sat glued to their seats, shell-shocked by what they'd heard.

I asked, "Why wouldn't he just give you the money, considering he had already abused you during your teenage years, you'd think he would feel he owed you this loan with no strings attached?"

Jenny said her father had been a bastard all his life and he'd die a bastard. I thought to myself that he should be locked up and the key thrown away.

Later that night I wrote Mike Harris a letter about the heartache his welfare cuts had thrust upon Jenny. How she exchanged sex for a loan from her father to make up the welfare deficit so her kids wouldn't be thrust into foster care. I filled the pages with expletives I felt appropriate

David R I McKinstry

for that arrogant Leader of the Conservative Party who was extinguishing the once proud spirit of so many of the down-trodden in this province. I mailed it the next morning. Four weeks later I got a response from one of the Harris government lieutenants telling me about all the wonderful programs they had initiated to get people off welfare. No one had read my letter.

This Woodhaven Christmas was an answer to the prayers of several women. Having been forced out of the family home, leaving pets and toys behind, these ladies had such limited financial resources that this Christmas would have been disastrous for their children. After four days of gourmet coffee, wine or eggnog by the fire, watching their carefree kids eating hearty meals, cross-country ski, hot tub and watch videos, these ladies were sad to leave. All too soon volunteers arrived to ferry the families back to the Peterborough bus terminal. It was time for them to return to their sparse apartments or to the crowded shelter. I have never felt so good about anything as I felt about having provided, with the help of so many others, a special memory for these sweet souls through the shelter program.

Michael had volunteered to be one of the drivers to take a family to the bus station. I was glad to see him pull up to the house. I had so much to share with him about this Christmas experience. I wanted a few days of downtime alone with Michael in front of the fireplace.

My six-week rule went out the window. Waking up and seeing Michael sleeping beside me brought back a flood of memories about Nick. I wondered if my feelings for Michael were happening too soon? Was I ready to let someone take over where Nick had left off? Michael was the first to say the words I love you. I knew I was falling in love yet the word caution kept flashing like a neon sign in front of my eyes. I didn't want to commit, yet I tried to reason with myself that falling in love couldn't happen this fast. Then all of a sudden it hit me. Why did I think it was impossible to be in love with Michael after knowing him for only four weeks? I'd fallen in love with Nick after only three hours of conversation at the Sutton Place Hotel, hadn't I? Question answered.

A Swim *Against* The Tide

I awoke one morning in late January knowing I was in love with Michael. Elizabeth told me to follow my gut feeling and if love was in the air to grab hold if it. I wondered how Nick's side of my family would react to the news that I was dating, let alone in love again. I wouldn't let them disappear from my life. They were family and losing them wasn't an option for me.

We spent a wonderful day together enjoying the outdoors. Alone over supper, I shared more about my vision for Woodhaven in the future. I told him I wanted to increase the number of mums and tots visits during the year as helping them had impacted me immensely. Michael just sat and listened to me rambling on, occasionally adding a few suggestions of his own about helping out the various charities.

While we were cleaning up the kitchen, Michael said he was really in love with me and wanted to spend every weekend with me. I too was feeling good about letting myself love Michael. He was as handsome on the inside as he was on the outside, kind and he wanted to share my life and be part of the adoption equation. Having dogs on the bed at night didn't bother him either. Who wouldn't love Michael?

Mum was thrilled that I had finally met someone and she liked Michael from the moment she was introduced to him. Michael introduced me to his father and it was easy to see he loved Michael and wanted his son to be happy.

By the end of February 1997, Michael and I were considering what we could do to upgrade Woodhaven. I didn't have much cash and told him we would have to pare down his big ideas to fit my meagre budget. Michael said he had been saving all his life to buy a country home like Woodhaven and he'd waited a lifetime to have a lover like me. Confidence oozed from Michael as he talked about wanting to buy into Woodhaven. Michael said if we were going to be together, which we both admitted was right for us both, then he would put up the cash to do a major addition.

I told him what was lacking from a functional perspective and that a new cooking space and separate dining room at the front of the house

David R I McKinstry

overlooking the lake would be the best use of our money. Five days later we compared our drawing of what a new addition to Woodhaven would look like and what features should be included to upgrade the facilities.

I called in a contractor to estimate the costs for us from our sketches for the addition. Two days later, we agreed on his price and with the stroke of a pen, the renovations would begin the first week of March when Michael started his spring break.

So much so fast. We had only known one another for three months and he was about to provide thousands of dollars for the Woodhaven renovation project. My gosh, a new lover and a renovated house all within five months! The more I thought about it the more at ease and comfortable I felt. I had always made up my mind quickly and knew my commitment to Michael was equally as strong as Michael's was to me.

We gutted our bedroom and the adjacent rooms to create a master bedroom with a large ensuite bathroom. Beside it we designed a large self-contained nursery with its own bathroom and playroom. An antique solid pine door separated the nursery from the master bedroom. It would allow us to enter the nursery directly from our bedroom. Including a nursery into our renovation plans really appealed to me and legitimised Michael's claim that he really wanted to adopt children.

A Swim *Against* The Tide

CHAPTER THIRTEEN

Surviving In-laws

ichael and I spoke everyday about our relationship and about the renovation project. I cancelled bookings at Woodhaven from the March break through to the last week in April, the estimated time it would take the builders to complete their work.

The first weekend of the construction was hectic. We dismantled shelves, moved furniture and pulled up carpeting to make way for the builders. Other than Michael's father and brother Dave (imagine the luck of me having two lovers each with a brother named Dave!), I hadn't met anyone else from Michael's family. I encouraged Michael to invite his mother and her husband on Sunday. It would give us an opportunity to meet and for them to walk around and get a feel for Woodhaven and what Michael was buying into and perhaps give us some feedback on our design for the renovations.

Louise, Michael's mother, and her husband Bill operated a family counselling service in Lindsay, a small town 45 minutes west of Sandy Lake. Michael's sister, Peggy, lived in Kingston, was single and worked as a psychologist. Coincidentally Peggy was visiting her mother when Michael called to invite them over for a visit. I was going to meet three psychologists at one time. I told Michael that having three psychologists in one room with me could be fatal.

He laughed and said, "Fatal for whom?" Little did I know how prophetic that comment would be.

We cleaned the house thoroughly so his family would see it as neat as it could get. It was a mild day and the snow had been melting in the parking lot and slippery ice was exposed under an inch of water. Michael dashed to help his mother walk across the 90 feet of slippery parking lot leading to the main entrance. His sister and stepfather stepped cautiously behind them. As they walked into the foyer I heard Michael explaining that because of pets we don't put down salt as it burns their feet and the snow plough hadn't yet been by to spread sand on the icy patches.

As Michael began a house tour, I walked around the corner and introduced myself to them. They were reserved and it caught me off guard. First impressions are usually lasting ones for me and I wondered if they would warm up over the afternoon. I let Michael give them the tour while I prepared tea and spread plates of hot apple crumble around the dining room table.

It didn't take long for an interrogation to begin. I was up to it as I felt they had the right to ask me certain questions about my background, my business, Nick's death from AIDS and my love for Michael. From the pained expressions on their faces, I wondered if I was providing too much information in my answers.

Michael's sister asked me what events led me to live at Sandy Lake and run a Bed and Breakfast. My explanation about how I'd come to live at Sandy Lake with Nick and Nick's death must have been too detailed for their liking. Peggy squirmed in her chair and said she had a question for me.

"Are you aware how much you talk about Nick, you and Nick, how Nick's family visits you regularly up here. Including his name repeatedly in conversation makes me pause and wonder if you're really over him yet? And more to the point, are you emotionally ready for a new relationship?"

A Swim *Against* The Tide

I felt this question was probably reasonable considering I did talk about Nick a lot. But there was a tone in her voice that irked me. They still hadn't warmed up to me. What was my body language saying to make them cooler than ice toward me? I hoped I could crack their icy shell.

"I was with Nick for eight years of my life. We grew into mature adults more during our life together than in the years before we met. We became one another's best friend, lover and confidant. Even our two families intertwined and became support networks for one another throughout his life and now after his death. Nick was a crucial part of Woodhaven that I won't let be forgotten. I probably do talk about him too much for those who didn't know him or understand the depth of our love."

I looked around the room to the faces of Michael's family and their expressions hadn't changed. The more I explained myself the more testy I felt myself becoming as I emphasized Nick's legacy to them.

"I'm *adjusting* to his loss every day but I'll never be *over* Nick. He and his family will always be a part of my life. Michael is well aware of the role the DiCicco family will play in *our* lives, and it doesn't appear to be an issue for him. In fact Michael told me he is excited to meet them and feels quite honoured that the DiCiccos are eager to put a face to the name they've been hearing about for months. Michael will be warmly welcomed into my large extended family, not as a replacement for Nick but as the man with whom I'll share my future." I hoped they would appreciate how incredibly unusual and neat it was for a gay man to have his deceased lovers family ready to embrace their ex-son-in-laws new lover.

Peggy and Louise both spoke of their need to explore my readiness to be in a new relationship so soon after Nick's death. I told them I was not going to spend my future in mourning and avoiding life. I told them my marriage to Nick had shown me just how much I loved being part of a pair, sharing all the highs and lows, making plans for a future of adopting children.

Peggy said, "Our concern has been about Michael and him getting involved with someone who could be on the rebound. You've known each other for four months and already you have him financing

David R I McKinstry

renovations from his savings. We wish you would both just slow down and give your new relationship time to develop before spending his money on your renovations." So this was the crux of their concern! They thought I was bilking Michael of his life savings. I felt my cheeks tighten at my anger over her insinuation. My fuse had been lit and I was seconds away from a rebuttal when Michael interjected in my defence.

"You could have addressed those concerns with me privately," said Michael quietly looking around the room. "My financial involvement is none of your business. If I was insulted by that comment Peggy, I'm sure David was too. He owns this place and he has already signed over half-ownership to me. I'm putting in $80,000 of savings and becoming half owner of a $400,000 business. I offered to make this investment, David didn't ask me for money." I was so proud of Michael at that moment that I wanted to kiss him. The wide smile growing across my face caused Michael to blush when he looked at me. This was the first time he'd felt the need to come to my defence and I beamed with pride.

"My relationship with David is about more than just him and me. I have baggage from my childhood and teenage years plus all those missed years between 20 and 30 when I lived in the closet afraid to let anyone see me as a gay man. All those years when the psychologists in my family suspected I was gay but refused to offer me help or give me any hint of their suspicions. We all have baggage, but I know what I want and even though it has only been a short time since I met David and knew he was what I wanted. I know all about his baggage and Nick's legacy in this building. My involvement financially with David is a private matter between the two of us and I don't feel it is your place to question me about that. I've always wanted a country place like this to call home. Just be happy for me."

Michael's mother, stepfather and sister all began to back peddle about their concern over him getting involved too quickly. They didn't talk to me and I felt invisible. It was if I was an observer watching a family therapy session. Michael didn't back off and I could tell he was upset. I too was upset by them but he was doing a great job of handling the situation.

Thankfully his family left shortly afterward. I let Michael say goodbye on his own in the foyer while I let the dogs out at the front of the house for a much needed bathroom break. Michael joined me outside to watch the dogs chase the snowballs I was tossing to them. He apologised for their conduct and reiterated that he had no reservations about my love for him. I knew we'd be a good team.

Over supper that evening I updated Michael on my recent efforts to get the necessary paperwork and visas for a future trip to India to adopt children. I told Michael that friends of mine had adopted two children from India and how they had convinced me to go to there in search of adoptable children. India was also the only country I'd investigated that would allow me, as a single man, to adopt children. Michael was thrilled to hear that my quest to adopt children was going full steam ahead. We had spent long hours discussing all my failed attempts to adopt, changing political and social climates that were opening doors to gays and lesbians wanting to adopt children, domestic adoption versus international adoption, costs and our mutual desire to see this quest end with us becoming parents. So many hours of those initial months of getting to know one another were spent talking about parenthood and how our parenting skills complimented one another. We'd laugh and look lovingly into each other's eyes and agree that life couldn't get much better than this for us. I was sure God had had a hand in bringing Michael into my life, and likewise I knew I would be his best choice for a mate, someone who would accentuate Michael's charms and his wonderful attributes. Most of all, I knew he would be a fantastic co-parent for the children in our future.

As the weeks of renovations continued along, I busied myself with day trips to an Oshawa clinic to get the mandatory inoculations required for my visit to India. Calls back and forth to various people at Canadian Immigration had my head spinning. Every time I felt I was about to enter the homestretch a new set of affidavits or forms, each

David R I McKinstry

needing notarisation, would be forwarded to me by mail. I became increasingly more incensed by the poor quality of Federal and Provincial inter-departmental communication, constant delays and screw-ups, mismanaged files and the inability of highly-paid federal employees to return messages within twenty-one days. Between the CAS offices in Toronto and the federal immigration's Case Processing Centre in Mississauga and Ottawa, I was made to feel like one holy pest. Even Barbara, my social worker, was stymied by the official run-around I was getting from the various arms of the adoption process.

The renovations were finally completed on Woodhaven and it was time to reopen for business. I knew that when a builder says it will take six weeks to complete, that meant ten weeks or more due to unforeseen delays. We were thrilled with the look of our dining room and its panoramic view across the lake. The new kitchen was mammoth in contrast to the cramped size of the old one. Guests who had been regulars were booked in for the re-opening weekend and expressed how thrilled they were with the changes. Woodhaven had grown by 2,000 square feet into a complex of 6,800 square feet.

Michael was so proud of his kitchen. He had a penchant for cooking and I gladly let him take over that department. Being Type A behaviour and inept in the kitchen, I had been buying *Master Choice* frozen meals and serving them to guests in my own crockery. Michael cringed at the thought of us serving frozen dinners to our guests, so he happily and lovingly prepared fancy Thai, Italian and French gourmet meals to the delight of our guests.

Our pack of dogs was happy with the additional indoor space in which they could chase after tennis balls, tea towels or shoes. Jenny was a bit out of sorts and limping quite a bit. Within days of discovering a small sore on the pad of her left front paw I took her to the local veterinarian to be examined. I thought this visit would be routine, expecting that Jenny might have a stone or small piece of wood imbedded in her foot and once removed she'd be back to her old self. Her life was never to return to normal after that fateful day.

A Swim *Against* The Tide

The veterinarian was concerned immediately upon examining Jenny. Vials of blood, numerous x-rays and ten days later, the results came back that Jenny had Blastomycosis, a rare but deadly fungal infection affecting only a handful of dogs in Ontario each year. She explained that Jenny probably breathed in fungal spores which had settled in her lungs. The fungal spores shooting out of the fungus at the exact moment Jenny had bent down to sniff the ground was a million to one chance. Poor Jenny.

The prognosis wasn't good. Blastomycosis was fatal and once it was detected in the lungs Jenny's chances of surviving a few months were less than one in a hundred. Seeing the frantic look grow in my eyes after she announced the results of Jenny's tests our veterinarian said there had to be some sort of new research being done. I wasn't about to let Jenny go without exhausting every avenue of hope. I had lost Nick only two years before a prospective daughter, and I wasn't about to face the death of another loved one just yet.

After many calls to veterinary experts around Ontario, Dr. Deb, our veterinarian, finally told me we could treat Jenny like an AIDS patient with fluconozol, an anti-fungal. I knew about this drug as Nick had used it and several other anti-fungals for years.

Jenny's health took many winding turns over the course of the next few weeks. It was a daily struggle trying to find the right balance of medication to give her at meal times so she wouldn't be sick or become disinterested in food and lose weight. I hated to force feed her and push pills down her throat but after a few weeks her body responded and the pads of her foot began to heal. Jenny's brown eyes had some life back in them and she regained enough strength to daily take two kilometre walks up and down the lane with me.

David R I McKinstry

CHAPTER FOURTEEN

Canada's Test Case

Uring the latter part of our first summer together at Wood-haven I had received a call from Immigration Canada asking me to consider being Canada's first openly gay man approved for an international adoption. I told them I didn't feel there was any connection between being gay and my parenting skills, but they intimated that my paperwork might be expedited if I agreed to be their test case.

My documents from the Adoption Unit arrived by mid-September and, as I'd been told, my gayness had become a focal point of my Home-study. Having this document in my hands meant I could now investigate adoption agencies in any country of the world from which Canadians were allowed to adopt orphans. I was encouraged by several sources to send my paperwork out to many different countries to widen my efforts. By mid-October, just after Thanksgiving 1997, I began receiving responses from those countries. I'd sent nine adoption inquiries, along with a copy of my Home-study, to each country on the list. Not one country responded positively to my inquiry, making it very clear homosexuals couldn't adopt their orphans. I was glad that I'd not sent a copy of this new Home-study letter to the Indian officials as it would most likely have nixed my search for a child in India as well.

I called the Adoption Unit and told them my success rate had been zero; not one country allowed gays to adopt their children. In the back of my mind was the nagging question, "Why would Canadian Immigration officials want to change my Home-study without first investigating the possibility of a Canadian gay man adopting from one of those countries on their list?"

It didn't take long for me to clue in that the Federal government really had no desire to open the door for gay adoptions domestically or internationally. Why were politicians just posturing themselves to look progressive? Couldn't they see how benign their efforts appeared? How cruel it was to prevent adoptable children everywhere in the country from having a wonderful home with a parent who just happened to be gay? Why sit on the sidelines of this debate knowing most Canadians favoured changing the laws to allow homosexuals to adopt? I was seething at the bit as I barrelled down the hallways of the various departments which had screwed around with my future adoption plans. No one would answer the simple question: "Why hadn't the government done its own homework first before suggesting I become its guinea pig?"

Every one of my telephone calls to adoption and immigration offices got me the same answer, "We had no idea that gays couldn't adopt internationally – well, sorry, but there really isn't much we can do about it now." I was furious and not about to be jerked around. I threatened to call the media across North America about this unbelievable screw-up with my paperwork. None of my ranting seemed to be taken seriously and finally I called a backbencher in the provincial Liberal Party and asked if she would help me. Liberals hated Tories and I thought this might give some sympathetic Ontario Liberal Party member ammunition during question period. It didn't take long for Susan Pupatello's office to get me a speedy reply. I was told to resubmit my paperwork, pay a new processing fee and my old documentation would be cancelled therefore negating any chance of India receiving documents identifying me as a homosexual. Unfortunately, she told me sadly, these changes would take many months to complete. I knew this meant more

David R I McKinstry

travel postponements and increased anxiety on my part as I waited and wondered when I'd get a break. The worst part of all was feeling lost somewhere in the unnecessary red-tape bureaucracy, no one ever able to provide a week by week account of the status of my paperwork.

Once more I postponed my flight to India. I decided to ride out this travesty and wait for new paperwork to be issued sometime between then and spring 1998. I was devastated. I went to bed thinking about children in India that I might be able to adopt, children who could die of malnutrition before I'd ever have an opportunity to show them a better life. I began to shut down emotionally and could feel myself slipping into a depressed psychological state. Michael was my right arm through each disaster and I found myself leaning on him more with each passing month. However there lingered a nagging doubt in my mind that Michael really didn't think I'd get to adopt a child. As much as I thought I was leaning on him I was building an emotional wall around my emotions to keep his perceived negativity out of sight. Michael had jokingly confessed several times that he did love children and although he told me on our first date that he would love to adopt, he never truly thought it would go this far. Not that he wasn't up for the challenges of parenthood, he just hadn't fully embraced the possible reality of us having children in our future.

Somehow in the face of one disaster after another, I kept going through the adoption process with eternal optimism. I had been telling people for years that I would have children under the Christmas tree this year, the next year, the year after that; it was such an old story line that I imagined no one gave my quest much chance of success. My perception of friends began to change. I became suspicious over perceived doubts they might have about any success I'd have in the adoption department.

Woodhaven continued to attract new guests. Radio advertising became the focus for 60% of our advertising budget. "David and his five Golden Retrievers welcome you to Woodhaven," became our trademark. Upon hearing the ad, people called to ask if I was the David

A Swim *Against* The Tide

with the five Golden Retrievers. In early November 1997 I received a call from a woman who wanted to visit Woodhaven with her husband. They were retired, lived in Whitby and had lost their Golden a few years earlier. They were delighted to know that a lodge existed where they could visit and be swarmed by five friendly Goldens. Barbara and Ralph decided they would come during the week when the lodge wouldn't be too crowded. They arrived for their first visit a few days after calling me. Ralph, a retired dentist, had a delightfully warm smile, an engaging manner about him and he reminded me of my dad in many uncanny ways. His skin tone was similar to the dark olive tone of my black Irish father.

Barbara was a beautiful woman, short in stature, with an infectious giggle. They loved the dogs and Ralph would encourage our Goldens to sit on the sofa beside him. During supper I watched him out of the corner of my eye handing food to waiting canine mouths resting in his lap. They had been at Woodhaven almost 48 hours when I was told that Ralph was of Black descent. He and Barbara were a mixed race couple who had been married happily for forty years. What a surprise for me to learn that Ralph was Black ... my own father had had darker skin! This led us into great conversations about race relations in the 1960s, public and family reaction to their mixed race marriage during an era when some US states still outlawed inter-racial marriage. Ralph had served in the Second World War and he entered university upon his return to Canada. He applied to the Faculty of Dentistry at the University of Toronto in 1946. Having a Scottish sounding last name, Ralph said the Dean's office probably had no idea he was Black. In those days students didn't have a face to face interview to get into the dentistry program. It wasn't until he started in the fall that his faculty advisors realized Ralph Stewart was Black.

Ralph told me he was the only Black student in the faculty. He said he was summoned to the Dean's office a few weeks after classes began. The Dean suggested that Ralph probably wasn't going to enjoy the course and that he might want to look elsewhere for a different program of study. Ralph said he knew by then he was the first Black man in the

David R I McKinstry

U of T Dentistry program and imagined that the Dean was trying to get rid of him. Ralph told the Dean he was a war vet and that he hoped to get his dentistry degree and return to Africa to help "his people" in remote villages. The Dean, according to Ralph, bought this line and never did question him again about leaving the program. Ralph finished his studies as the first Black dentist to graduate from U of T and began to practice dentistry at the corner of Spadina and College, where he stayed for the first twenty-five years of his career. Barbara had been a special education teacher during her working life and they were an awesome couple with immense charm and caustic humour.

Ralph and Barbara, from first hand experience, could understand my bitterness over adoption and immigration department's apparent prejudice against a gay man wanting to adopt. If Ralph could be U of T's first black dental graduate, then I could become the first gay man to adopt from overseas!

The following weekend, a military fellow, his wife and three children arrived at Woodhaven in need of some R & R. Ironically Blair had been stationed in New Delhi with the Canadian Consulate staff. During his three-year posting, they had adopted a young Indian daughter from an orphanage. They were excited to give us some useful tricks of the adoption trade in Delhi which would inevitably increase our chances of getting a child.

During the course of the weekend they spent hours talking to us about how to deal with people in India. Blair said that under no circumstances should I show anger in front of an Indian. Many Indians enjoy having even the slightest perceived power over British Caucasians and any altercation with an Indian dealing with our adoption could result in months of delay and further expenses.

I told Blair that I was ready to go to India once my paperwork was finished. He suggested I stop making the completed paperwork my benchmark.

"Just go to India and do your own looking and listening," he advised. Blair felt that I would score big points with Indian officials and

A Swim *Against* The Tide

those Canadians at the High Commission in Delhi if I just showed up and said I was there to check out the various orphanages, even if my paperwork wasn't 100% completed by the CPC in Mississauga. Blair's infectious enthusiasm seemed to excite Michael that weekend and we finally seemed congruent in terms of what we had to do to get the job done.

I booked a flight for January 8, 1998. Confident I had to take this maverick approach, I knew that come hell or high water, I'd be in Delhi for my 44th birthday.

Two days later the board members of the organization EGALE (Equality for Gays And Lesbians Everywhere) arrived for a three-day mid-week retreat. Twelve representatives from across Canada came for a meeting with John Fischer the national executive director. EGALE had been in the news regularly since its inception, fighting for equal human dignities for gays and lesbians, especially in the fight for recognition of same-sex marriage, pension and health benefits for partners in same-sex relationships, gay adoption rights and federal government pension rights for gays and lesbians.

The EGALE retreat brought an interesting mix of same-sex marriage advocates, gay left and right wing extremists and strategists from every corner of Canada. During one of their sessions I told them about my upcoming trip to India and my eighteen-year fight for the right to adopt children. Most of the members had heard of my fight against the bank to recover Nick's mortgage insurance but few had any idea just how arduous my adoption journey had been. It left us all thinking that if I had been mistreated, how many other gays and lesbians across Canada had had similar dealings with provincially run adoption agencies? I was encouraged by the genuine concern of this group and they promised to work on changing adoption laws.

The DiCicco clan arrived for our fourth annual pre-Christmas get together weekend. I excitedly shared with everyone that I was booked on a flight to India in early January. Although Michael was already a familiar new member of the DiCicco-McKinstry-Woodhaven clan, this was Michael's first Christmas celebration with the group. Everyone

David R I McKinstry

came, Mum, Nick's parents, siblings and spouses and all the children. Michael had been preparing food for days prior to their arrival hoping to please his new extended family by providing all sorts of seasonal treats and dishes. He became affectionately known as Uncle Michael to my nieces and nephews that Christmas. I longed for the day Michael and I would have kids of our own. I wanted our kids to grow up knowing the DiCiccos; besides being in-laws, they were also terrific people and had become really good friends to us.

Christmas was only a few weeks away. I hadn't taken any guest reservations after the DiCicco weekend so I could get caught up on all the preparations for the three groups of shelter women and children who would start arriving for three-day holidays December 20th. I had had to increase the number of allotted days for the women's Christmas program because the demand had doubled since the previous year. Many different organizations were involved in providing food, treats, and presents for the children and specialty gifts for the mums. The *Toronto Star* and the *Globe and Mail* had done special interest stories on our Woodhaven Christmas program. The response from citizens across Ontario had been incredible: little old ladies knitting scarves and mittens; retirees sending me $5 from meagre pensions to help with the program; church groups donating money for the mums; Joyce, a local Bridgenorth hairstylist, put together hundreds of dollars worth of hair products in beautifully wrapped gift bags for the teenage girls and the mums. I was absolutely stunned by the outpouring of people's generosity.

Woodhaven hosted 17 Mums and 28 children from the women's shelters that Christmas. The ladies were so relaxed knowing their children were in seventh heaven. Once again late night gab sessions around the fireplace added horror stories to my growing list of men's abuse against women. The last group of families left Woodhaven on the morning of December 29th and we sighed with relief. Michael was ready to sit back and enjoy his holiday time without the noise of many unruly children running through our house.

We had started to strip beds when we received a call from a woman

A Swim *Against* The Tide

at the Ontario adoption office to say that my paperwork had just arrived. The package didn't contain the important Letter of No Objection, but she said I had enough paperwork with APPROVED stamped across it to be credible with orphanages in Delhi. She suggested I find myself an Immigration lawyer and wished me luck on my trip.

My sister drove Mum to Woodhaven the next afternoon so she could spend a few days with us over New Years. Karen and I rarely spoke to one another and this Christmas had been too busy for me to think about her absence in our Christmas festivities. When she learned that we were hosting women and children from shelters over Christmas she commented, "Those women must all be lesbians if they are coming to your place." Karen carried Mum's bag in from her car and stood in the hallway. Michael greeted them at the door while I was off doing chores. Karen and Michael were talking light-hearted with Mum in the foyer when I came down the stairs. Being in the same room with my sister was very difficult for me and everyone could sense how perfunctory our interactions had become. Michael had mentioned to Karen that I was packing for my trip and she played dumb as if she hadn't known about my impending journey to India. I knew Mum had told her about my travel plans.

Karen asked, "Why are you going to India?" I told her I was going to find some children to adopt and bring home to Canada.

Karen shot me a look of disgust, "Why waste your money, nobody is going to give a homosexual a child to adopt." For an instant I considered pitching her out of my house and into a snowbank head first. Instead I just turned and walked away without acknowledging her last comment. Poor Michael was left alone to bid her goodbye.

David R I McKinstry

CHAPTER FIFTEEN

★≈⊕€≈★

Nicholas Comes Home

I met with JC Charette, a local college student from the hospitality program, at 3 p.m. on New Year's Day 1998. I needed to find someone who could keep Woodhaven running during my absence. JC was the Dean's first choice and he became mine too. He moved into Henri's Suite (named after my dear friend and theologian Henri Nouwen) within a few days and I showed him the routine around Woodhaven: how to make up the beds and take reservations; tips on how to save time when cleaning a room; and who to call if the water system shut-down.

I made it clear to JC that during my absence it was equally important for me to know the business and our pets would be well cared for. Michael would be up on weekends to look after the place and JC would be able to return to his girlfriend's apartment on weekends.

I took JC on a road trip to Bobcaygeon to meet Dr. Deb, our veterinarian. I had become increasingly interested in setting up this single pretty veterinarian with Michael's younger brother. I had joked with her that if I found her a boyfriend and it ended up in marriage that she would have to give me free veterinary care for the rest of my dogs' lives. Deb was pleased to meet JC and told him the signs and symptoms of Blastomycosis to watch for in Jenny. I was really uptight about

— 225 —

A Swim *Against* The Tide

leaving Jenny behind in her sickly state without me there to supervise her medications and assess her health daily.

All the necessary adoption documents were neatly stuffed into my money belt. I had purchased my ticket from an Indian travel agency which specialized in Southeast Asian travel. When I picked up my airline tickets she asked to see my passport and medical documentation. I asked her if I needed any other documentation and she said no. Finally I had my ticket in hand and my departure date was only a few days away.

I was to fly across Canada to Vancouver and would stay overnight with my good friends and their two-year-old twins. After an overnight visit, I would fly out on Cathay Pacific to Hong Kong, board a Thai Air jet to Bangkok and rendezvous with my Air India flight to Delhi. After leaving Vancouver, this leg of my flight would be across three time zones and exceed twenty-five hours of travel.

Michael was excited about my journey yet paranoid about our finances. Would I have sufficient cash to find a child, pay the bribes I'd been told to expect from some Indian officials, pay for travelling around India, food and lodgings? I had been saving like mad for this trip. Every time I siphoned off $500 from guest payments I'd go to the local Buckhorn tourist office and buy American dollars at a rate much lower than I'd get at the bank. I had been doing this secretly for six months. I had just over $17,000 in US traveller cheques in my money belt. I knew Michael would flip out if he knew that I hadn't been paying certain bills on time so I could pad our adoption account. Therefore this had become my dark little secret. Michael was becoming increasingly worried about our finances to the extent that I shut down every time he brought up the subject.

The pursuit to find adoptable children had been long and difficult but I was now closer to my goal than ever before – nothing or no one would interfere in my plan. In the weeks leading up to my departure I was made aware of the varying attitudes of friends and family. Some felt I should give up on this quest, some said very little, others were elated I was finally on my way. I deliberately put people into two categories – either bridges or walls. Walls were people who outwardly didn't express enthusiasm or give me much encouragement and bridges were those who were as excited as I was for me to be finally on my way to search for orphaned children in India. The competitive side of me was up for the fight of my life. I'd prove that all the naysayers were wrong by bringing home one or two children with me in a few months.

JC waved, the dogs watched me, their noses pressed up against the library window as we drove out the laneway. Poor Jenny. I hoped Tyler and Dylan wouldn't fight in front of JC. Regardless of the fact that all the dogs had been neutered, Tyler was challenged once or twice a year by his son for the title of Alpha dog in the pack. We hadn't had such a power struggle since last summer and were certainly due for another of their arguments to get out of hand. My mind was racing as we drove to the airport. Michael handed me a big surprise, an additional $7,000 American money as we unloaded my bags at the airport. He said he had sold a diamond he'd bought years earlier as an investment. I looked at him and knew he was with me. Regardless of his distress about our on-the-brink-of-disaster finances, he would be my right arm in good times and bad. In that moment I broke my rule of no public displays of affection and embraced him tightly receiving zero attention from all the thousands of travellers milling around us occupied only with their concerns for finding a porter. What a moment of freedom it was for me.

The flight to Vancouver was uneventful as I slept most of the way. My friends were at the airport to greet me and I was whisked off to their delightful home in New Westminster. Their children, Ryan and Rachel, were adorable. Watching this family made me even more determined to complete the task ahead.

The next morning my friends took me on a tour of Vancouver to show me how the city had grown and changed since my departure twelve years earlier. I told them I wanted to be alone for a few hours in Vancouver, just to walk around and collect my thoughts before boarding my flight to Hong Kong. I walked the old haunts of my younger days in the city. Older store fronts along Davie Street had received facelifts and had been upgraded into lavish high-end shoe

A Swim *Against* The Tide

stores, restaurants, cafes, ski shops, etc. I walked through the west end district of Vancouver and down toward Stanley Park. The urge to visit the waterfront was overwhelming. I sat on the beach looking out at Point Grey and UBC in the distance, reflecting on the memories of the years I'd spent here.

I took a shuttle bus to the Vancouver Airport about 8 p.m. At the check-in counter I was informed my departure would be delayed until 3 a.m. I spent the next six hours just walking around the airport until Cathay Pacific announced over the intercom that my flight would begin boarding at 2:20 a.m. The lounge was full of passengers, old Chinese couples, young Chinese couples with children, Caucasian businessmen and women anxious to get into Business Class and First Class reclining seats. It was a full flight to Hong Kong and the next seventeen hours would be tedious and exhausting, sitting cramped into a window seat near the back of the plane. The flight was too long and uncomfortable for all of us sitting in the Economy section. Halfway through this flight I vowed I'd never travel to the orient except in First Class seats.

Hong Kong was shrouded in fog and rain as we descended to meet the runway. I had slept very little. Two young children had been screaming most of the last three hours and their parents hadn't done anything to shut them up. Everyone around me was showing signs of anger at the utter unruliness of those children and their non-disciplining parents.

Within two hours I was back in the air heading to Bangkok. The Thai Air staff was warmly attentive and kind and never stopped smiling. Immediately upon deplaning I headed to the Air India counter to check my bags for the flight that was to leave in three hours. It took forever to find my way to the Air India desk and the lineup was 200 deep. It took an hour for me to reach the check-in counter. I placed my bags on the weigh station and handed my ticket, inoculation certificate and passport to the ticket agent. She looked at my documents and stamped my ticket and asked what type of seating I would prefer. Then she asked me for my Visitor's Visa. I told her I was going to India to adopt a child. I was puzzled by her request and said I only had my passport and ticket.

David R I McKinstry

She turned to the other agent handling the baggage and told her subordinate to put my bags back on the weigh station.

"You must have Visitor's Visa to enter India. You can't get into the country without it. Where did you come from?" She said glancing down at my ticket to see my origin. "The Canadians should have told you to get Visitor's Visa before leaving Canada."

I was in disbelief. This plane would be leaving in an hour and I needed a Visitor's Visa. "No one told me about needing a Visitor's Visa before I left Canada," I exclaimed. I felt foolish for not having this document and my face felt flushed with embarrassment.

"Well you won't be going on this flight today so just move to the side please." The agent off-handedly motioned me away so she could process the next passenger.

"Wait, I have to get to India. I am adopting a child. I have to be on this flight," I said cementing myself to the spot in front of the agent. "How do I get a Visitor's Visa in time to make this flight?" I tried to control the increasing edge to my voice. I remembered Blair Hart's advice, "Don't piss off an Indian with an ounce of power or you'll be toast."

"Sir, you will have to go to your embassy in Bangkok and apply for a visa. Call them at the pay phones and make an appointment. It will take a day to process and you can leave tomorrow. Now please move to the right so we can do our job."

I grabbed my bags and walked away from the Air India counter. I was physically tired from lack of sleep and changed time zones, the humid air of Bangkok had me in a lather of sweat and emotionally I was bent out of shape. Why hadn't the travel agent back in Toronto told me to get a Visitor's Visa? Had the officials at the India Consulate in Toronto assumed I would have known of the need for a Visitor's Visa? I thought I'd crossed all the T's and dotted all the I's long before I boarded the flight to China. If only I had known about this Visa before leaving Toronto.

I found a vacant phone and searched in the Bangkok telephone directory for the number of the Canadian High Commission. I dialled the number and was greeted with a non-accented voice softly speaking,

A Swim *Against* The Tide

"Hello, Canadian High Commission. How may I direct your call?"

I explained to the receptionist that I needed to talk to someone who could get me a Visitor's Visa to India as quick as possible. I told her I was enroute to India to adopt a child and that I just had to get on a flight today. She directed my call to one of the commission staff who told me to come directly to her downtown Bangkok office and we would work out the problem from there. She told me to forget about trying to make today's flight as it wasn't possible for me to get a visa that fast. She gave me the address of the Canadian High Commission and told me to change some money into Thai currency with which to pay the taxi.

I found the baggage lockers on the main level and threw my two bigger bags into the small interior. I stepped outside and received the full brunt of the hot steamy Bangkok midday sun and could feel myself melting fast. I waited ten minutes for an air-conditioned cab and directed the driver to the address of the Canadian High Commission. The cab got caught in traffic jams at every turn. It had taken twenty-five minutes to get into the downtown core from the airport and double that time to go the last fifteen blocks.

I got out of the cab and proceeded into the lobby of the office building which housed the High Commission. Canada's High Commission was on the sixth floor. The cab had been cooler than the building and I could feel streams of sweat begin to flood down my back as the elevator door opened into the commission's foyer. I was so glad to see a Canadian flag as I walked over to the receptionist and said I was the one stranded without a Visitor's Visa to India. This didn't twig with her so I told her I had an appointment with Denise.

"Denise is out lunch presently, but she will be back in thirty minutes."

What could I do but sit down, pull myself together and wait patiently. Denise finally returned from lunch and motioned for me to follow her into an office behind a security door. She told me I would have to go the India High Commission and apply for a visa and that the Indian's didn't take kindly to foreigners asking favours from them, such as faster processing of a Visitor's Visa. "It could actually work against

David R I McKinstry

you if our office asked their staff for a favour," she said.

Denise gave me directions to the India High Commission and suggested I be as calm and polite as possible under these strained circumstances. I asked her how long such processing would take and if I'd be out of Bangkok by tomorrow. She told me that today being Wednesday, it would probably be Friday before I was enroute to India. I then asked her for a recommendation of a downtown hotel where I could stay while waiting for my visa. We were standing by the receptionist and a young Canadian couple piped up that they were staying at the Tawana Ramada Hotel just five minutes from the High Commission's office and it was safe and luxurious for about $30 US per night, breakfast included. I thanked them for this information and they got into the elevator with me as I bid Denise goodbye.

On the way to the lobby I told them what had happened and they told me they had already been to India and said that if I wanted to get my visa faster I should pass some American money through the wicket to officials at the India High Commission.

"Bribes are a way of life in India and ditto at all their foreign offices. When you pass your documents to the visa officer tuck $200 US into the middle of the documents and he'll know you want him to process it faster. He might even ask you for more but it won't be over another $100, but it will get you your visa faster. Better to spend $200 US than $500 US staying in Bangkok for two weeks."

"Two weeks!" I exclaimed in disbelief, "I'm going to be out of here by the weekend if it kills me." They smiled at me and said that if I wanted to join them for supper at the hotel they'd be glad to have my company. I left them and grabbed a taxi bound for the India High Commission. Denise had told me it was shameful that no one had told me to get a Visitor's Visa back in Toronto as it would have only taken a matter of hours to process.

The taxi ride to the India High Commission took ten minutes. I walked into the foyer and was amazed at the number of backpackers standing or sitting around the walls. I grabbed a number and waited my

A Swim *Against* The Tide

turn. I spoke to several people during my hour-long wait. Finally my number was called and I approached the wicket. The expressionless face that greeted me was a bit intimidating leaving me unsure how to start. Should I be forceful by just passing him money then ask how long it would take to get a Visitor's Visa, or what? I decided to take it slow and explain quietly my predicament. This fellow didn't wink, smile, hold out his hand or give me any indication that he understood me. I repeated my story and he motioned for me to pass my documents through to him. I had put two $100 US bills in the crease of my passport and handed it to him. He looked up at me and smiled. I immediately thought I had luck on my side and this wouldn't be a long ordeal. The fellow said something to his contemporary in the back part of the office and grabbed some papers and began to write. Ten seconds later he handed me a slip of paper and told me to come back in one week to get my Visitor's Visa.

I was stunned. I had waited so long for this trip and every day I had visions of sad children waiting in orphanages waiting for me to swoop down and adopt them. I felt like I had bloody knuckles from rapping on the door of parenthood and no one would answer. I felt a rush of sadness overcome me hearing there would be a seven day delay. Remembering what people had told me about bribes being a way of life for Indians, I leaned closer to the wicket dividing us and said quietly, "What would it cost to get it done by Thursday?"

He looked at me and in perfect English said, "Come back in a week and we will have your Visitor's Visa ready. This is as fast as I will process your application."

His sinister smile was the same as if he had just given me the finger! Without so much as blinking his eye, he pulled down the shutter and put up a sign that read CLOSED. I stood there unsure of what my next move should be. I wanted to yell out loud, You lousy thief! Give me my money back! But I reminded myself not to upset Indian officials.

I headed back to the Canadian High Commission. I desperately hoped they could intervene on my behalf. Waiting a week for a Visitor's Visa would cost me time and money I didn't have. Images of poor destitute orphans sitting in the dust with their arms outstretched toward me had my guts in knots. Did nobody care that I just wanted to help these kids and delays meant anguish for some child I might meet to adopt?

Denise had left again when I returned. I gave in and decided to take the advice of the couple I'd met earlier and check out the Tawana Ramada Hotel. I got directions from the receptionist, who added that it was a favourite of Canadian officials and a nice place to stay.

The walk to the hotel took only a few minutes. The afternoon heat was oppressive which did little to improve my poor humour. The Tawana Ramada Hotel was as nice as any four star hotel I'd ever seen. The front desk staff was smiling as I approached to inquire if they had a room for seven nights, possibly longer. I was in luck. A convention had just finished at the hotel that morning and they told me a room would be available within the hour. I asked where I could get an air-conditioned cab back to the airport to retrieve my luggage and I was informed that for less money than a cab I could hire the hotel's private driver and his air-conditioned Benz to take me to the airport for my luggage. Three hours later I returned to the hotel with my luggage and checked into a room overlooking the almond shaped pool down in the hotel's private courtyard. Looking in the bathroom mirror I looked as exhausted as I felt. I smelled like diesel fumes so I jumped into the shower to scrub off the dirt and grime I'd collected.

Later I had a relaxed meal. I wanted to call Michael but thought it would be less expensive for me to send an email. The front desk clerk, Ning, told me I could use the hotel's back office computer to type my own email after 10 p.m. She said she would ring my room when the computer was available. The Thai staff was charming and really gave me the feeling they wanted to do everything possible to make guests comfortable.

The next morning, on my way to breakfast, I passed the front desk. It was 7 a.m. and Ning was still on duty. She smiled and hailed me over to her. "Khun David, you have email waiting for you in our office," she said.

A Swim *Against* The Tide

CHAPTER SIXTEEN

Stuck in Bangkok

D ay two in Bangkok began with me receiving an uplifting email from Michael. I had only been gone a few days but I desperately needed to speak with him. The disruption of my schedule had caused me to reflect on events that had led me to this point. I'd had eight wonderful years with Nick, his high energy and spirituality and then his death from AIDS. I had come out publicly as a gay man in Toronto's press over the mortgage issue and my desire to be a parent was stronger than ever. I had committed my love to Michael – I loved him 100% and knew what he was sacrificing for me to make my dream of us having children a reality. I knew we would become the loving parents of children from India, bringing us ever closer together.

My Canadian hotel-mates were leaving the next morning for Chiang Mia, a city in northern Thailand. I had bid them goodbye after a wonderful supper at a small back alley Thai restaurant that they had discovered soon after arriving in Bangkok. Before heading to the elevator I poked my head into the hotel's administration office behind the front desk. Nun Ning was sitting at the computer station and immediately got up and bowed. I found this custom archaic and out of sync with my North American exposure to women's liberation. She smiled and handed me three pages of emails. Returning to my suite I anxiously read Michael's long email, had a quick cool shower and cranked on my air conditioning to the coldest setting. The humidity associated with 38°C was taking its toll on me. I lay on the bed and opened my travel book on India. Within minutes I lay dozing.

Even though the drapes were drawn to keep the sunrise out of my bedroom, I awoke and intuitively knew it was hot and muggy outside on the streets of Bangkok. Today was Friday, January 16, my 44th birthday. As I walked to the bathroom I saw a note under my door. It was from Nun Ning informing me that two fax transmissions awaited me in the administration office of the hotel. I showered and dressed in casual shorts and a T-shirt anxious to read my birthday faxes. Nun Ning was smiling as I walked into the administration office. "Happy birthday, Khun David. Me wishing you much happiness today." Her broken English was wonderfully sweet to hear. It was obvious that at least one of my faxes was a birthday wish.

Without stopping to read my enveloped messages, I went to the dining room for breakfast. My stomach was a bit upset but the fresh fruit table looked irresistible, as was the strong coffee. I opened the fax envelope and read a large bold print birthday greeting from my Vancouver friends. The second fax was from Michael and it immediately grabbed my undivided attention. With guts twisting and my blood pressure elevated, I reread Michael's fax condemning me for my inept financial records. He wrote that Woodhaven was on the brink of bankruptcy because I had siphoned money from our bill-paying account to fund this trip to India. In bold letters he had typed at the bottom of the email, "I'm not used to dealing with this kind of pressure. I've never been irresponsible with money matters. My stomach is upset all the time and I'm feeling very negative about you and our relationship." No Happy Birthday greeting from my beloved partner, just a three page dissertation on my financial mismanagement and how I had saddled him with a mountain of personal debt.

Michael was justified in feeling that I lulled him into assuming that

A Swim *Against* The Tide

all our accounts were padded with sufficient funds to honour financial obligations as they came due. My reality and his needs for accountability had moved miles apart. It was my fault that Michael had sunk to such an emotional low and I had to apologise and ask forgiveness. Suddenly it became a high priority to send Michael an apology. He had to be given the option to cancel this trip now and cut our losses or for me to continue on to India. I had been so headstrong about the need for this trip and impatient for us to adopt a child. The forces driving me to do whatever I had to do to get to India had compromised my integrity and had caused Michael so much grief. Regardless of how right my motives had been, my game plan had made Michael feel out of the loop. It was necessary to give back some form of control to Michael, to give him the power to make the decision that would impact us for the rest of our lives.

I poured out my heart and soul to Michael in a two-page fax and by 1 p.m. Bangkok time I had sent it through to the Woodhaven fax machine. I knew Michael was at school in Toronto and in my cover letter I had boldly printed:

"JC, PLEASE CALL MICHAEL AT HIS SCHOOL AND TELL HIM YOU HAVE A FAX TO SEND HIM. IT'S URGENT."

Before even receiving my apology, Michael had sent another email telling me he had overreacted. We weren't broke. I had a shoebox fund with just less than $12,000 in it for Woodhaven emergencies hidden in the basement. He hadn't remembered this secret stash of cash until after he'd sent his angry fax on my birthday. Michael expressed how sorry he was for calling me duplicitous on my birthday. He wanted me to go on to India and get us a child to bring home. He'd had second thoughts about the stern-ness of his words and although he felt we were in murky waters financially, one good summer season would remedy that. It felt great having his unbridled support again. I sent him an email later telling him about the Thai economy being in rough shape. The Thai currency, the Bhat, was worth sixty times less today than a year ago. The currency exchange rate was 54 Bhat for one US dollar. American businessmen

David R I McKinstry

were turning in their round trip tickets for refunds in Bangkok and then upgrading themselves to First Class seats at 1/50th the cost and pocketing the difference.

Early in the morning of my fourth day, Michael emailed and suggested I give myself a belated birthday gift from him. He had been talking to some staff at school about me being stuck in Bangkok and they had told him I should take an inexpensive flight to Chiang Mai, in northern Thailand. I asked Ning at the hotel about a trip to Chiang Mai and she told me the one-hour flight and an all day personally guided tour was $68 US. Sitting around in Bangkok was boring and it made sense to take advantage of this opportunity to see more of Thailand than just the diesel-fume polluted downtown core of Bangkok. I booked a flight for the next day.

I spent the remainder of that morning making telephone calls to Thai adoption groups. By noon I had arranged three appointments to meet with orphanage directors. I wasn't sure what to expect when I arrived at an old Church of England orphanage residences. The woman at the reception desk was British and she was very interested in my plans to adopt children from India. I told her I had been waiting for a Visitor's Visa so I could continue on but felt I should explore a few Thai orphanages before leaving on Wednesday. I could see a schoolyard full of children through a window immediately behind her desk and she turned to see what I was watching.

"It's play time for the children. We just received a new set of playground swings donated by a family in America who adopted a child last year," she said.

After several minutes of interesting chitchat, the orphanage director entered the lobby and greeted me. A matronly woman, perhaps sixty years old, carried a fan in her left hand that constantly fanned her face. She told me she had been in Bangkok for fourteen years and still wasn't accustomed to the humidity. We walked through the schoolyard behind the church to reach her office.

Once inside she told me the history of her orphanage and exactly

A Swim *Against* The Tide

how many children they housed in the attached residence each year. She also said this orphanage was the first in Thailand to run an AIDS health program for its children, since 70% of their ninety children were HIV+ and for the most part, unacceptable candidates for international adoptions. She explained that most of her wards wouldn't live long enough to graduate from school. This wonderful woman spoke with such affection. I admired her ability to love, knowing she was going to lose these children, and the faith it took to keep herself motivated to work on in this environment. After a quick tour of the hospice unit attached to the school she walked me to the gates of the churchyard and bid me good luck in India. I told her I was meeting with one more Thai adoption facility and she smiled at me in a very kind way. She knew that I'd run into the same scenario at the next orphanage; children who weren't 100% healthy would never be considered adoptable options by Immigration Canada.

By the time I returned to the hotel at 4 p.m. the heat had become unbearable. I had visited three orphanages which left my emotions raw. The local English newspaper said the temperature for tomorrow would top 39° C. I went for a swim in the hotel pool to cool off and to digest what I'd seen at the orphanages of Bangkok. The sex trade of Bangkok seemed oblivious to AIDS. Everywhere I went taxi drivers would nudge me with their elbow and ask if I wanted to have a fun time in Bangkok? They would brazenly unravel handheld photo albums containing photos of nude men, women, boys and girls and then ask which was my pleasure. When I'd rebuff their solicitations they would switch gear without batting an eye and ask where I wanted to go. It became a tedious routine of telling them my destination then haggling over the cost of the taxi ride. I really thought Bangkok was hell on earth; the people were nice yet slyly schooled in how to deal selfishly with foreigners. The weather and pollution, especially the air quality would be unacceptable to anyone with a respiratory ailment. I wondered how asthmatics coped in the open air around the city of Bangkok. I thought I had pretty good lungs yet the pollution stung my air passages and

David R I McKinstry

made me nauseous if I walked around the Bangkok streets for more than fifteen minutes. Most people I passed on the streets carried handkerchiefs pressed close to their mouth and noses.

Chiang Mai was heaven compared to Bangkok. The flight was just 90 minutes aboard Thai Air and I met dozens of Australian and Canadian tourists on the tour. The morning visit to a remote mountainside village was like a step back in time with its hrines and temples, and colourful vegetation that grew profuse and lush.

After numerous side trips to fine jewelry stores and finally purchasing $100 US strand of pearls (for our future daughter), our tour returned to the airport and the short flight back to Bangkok. I'd only been out of Bangkok for 11 hours, start to finish, but I felt revived spiritually.

The next two days passed uneventfully. I sent several faxes to Janice McCann at the Canadian High Commission in Delhi indicating that I had been delayed in Bangkok but that I would arriving in Delhi by week's end and hoped she could spare some time to meet with me and review my list of Canadian approved orphanages over coffee. Janice faxed me back and told me to call on her private line or at home when I arrived in India. She also wished me luck in my dealings with the India High Commission in Bangkok and emphasized that she wished she could help me out but really couldn't do much to expedite the Visitor's Visa process.

Finally Wednesday morning arrived and I headed off to claim my Visitor's Visa at the India High Commission. The line up for Visitor's Visas was long and the foyer of the reception area was packed with foreign business people, Indian nationals and backpackers from everywhere. Considering that a Visitor's Visa was just a simple piece of paper with a stamp on it, I was pissed off that it had taken so long to complete. Within an hour I was back at the hotel and on the phone about available flights for the day. Air India couldn't get me on a flight for 5 days but Aeroflot had a 10 p.m. flight tonight with one available Economy seat. I quickly said I'd take that seat. The reservation agent told me my ticket could be picked up two hours before flight time at the Aeroflot check-in counter.

A Swim *Against* The Tide

I asked the hotel receptionist if I could pay for a half-day rate so I could stay in the hotel until I left for the airport after supper. The front desk staff smiled and told me I could stay for free all day and they wished me best of luck getting a child in India. I had become quite chummy with these hotel employees during my eight days in Bangkok, I'd shown them photos of Woodhaven Country Lodge and told them I was a widower hoping to adopt two or three orphans from India. My widower story always touched people's heartstrings – this story of being a widower was substantiated in my Home-study and I had to maintain this story line outside of Canada.

Aeroflot's check-in desk at the Bangkok International Airport should have been an indication of what lay ahead of me. The staff were smoking in designated NO SMOKING areas, the women behind the counter must have been Olympic wrestlers in a previous lifetime and the throng of passengers looked like they had just arrived from filming a 1932 version of Aladdin and his band of forty thieves. The plane was a 727 and packed to capacity. Men were dressed like Arab sheikhs on either side of me, and they bent forward and across me non-stop. Soon after sitting in my seat I asked them if they would like to trade seats so they could sit beside one another to talk but they didn't seem interested in giving up their seats. I had seven hours of flying time from Bangkok to Delhi and the ever-present foul stench on this plane was a result of travellers with poor hygiene and men who chain-smoked Russian cigarettes. I thought I had left hell back in Bangkok.

My lungs ached from the second-hand cigarette smoke I'd been inhaling for most of the trip. The approach to Delhi was bumpy because of air turbulence and each time the plane swayed so did my row mates who always seemed to fall into me. They hadn't shut up the entire trip except to sloppily fill their mouths when food trays were dropped in front of them. I had lost my appetite shortly after take-off, as all I wanted was fresh air.

It was around midnight Delhi time when the aeroplane touched down. There was nothing friendly about this airport. No one smiled.

David R I McKinstry

Maybe it was because of the hour of the night. I waited at the baggage claim area with other passengers for almost an hour before bags started to tumble down the carousal. Another hour passed and still my luggage hadn't banged down the chute. I went to the baggage office to inquire about my suitcases and was told that my Aeroflot plane had already departed and that if my suitcases weren't on the carousel then they were enroute to Moscow.

"Call tomorrow to Aeroflot office in Delhi." the baggage officer told me as he waved me off. "Aeroflot will send your bags back on next flight to Delhi."

I had my carry-on bag with a fresh shirt, change of underwear, books, glasses and all my documents. I could still smell my travel companions wretched BO and cigarette smoke in my nostrils and assumed others could smell it on my shirt. I wanted to get to a hotel and just get myself clean. The Canadian High Commission in Bangkok had given me suggestions of places to stay in Delhi and I called the first hotel on my list and asked if they had an available room. It was 40 minutes from the airport and the rate was $160 US for the night. I was incensed at this yet too exhausted to fight and felt that after a good night's sleep I could scout out a lower priced hotel. I needed to exchange some money into rupees so I could pay the taxi driver. The only exchange wicket open at 1:45 a.m. in the entire airport had a mile long line up of people waiting to do the same thing. It took another hour for me to get to the wicket which left me practically asleep on my feet. The man behind the counter was curt and asked me something in broken English. I didn't understand him so I asked him to repeat what he'd asked. He practically jumped through the wicket window at me and began to chatter on in a dialect that I couldn't begin to name. I handed him a $20 American bill and glared back at him and just as curtly retorted, "Give me some rupees."

He immediately smiled, took my bribe and asked how many rupees I wanted. I told him to give me whatever $300 American dollars would buy in rupees. Ten minutes later I was in a non-air-conditioned taxi heading to the hotel. The driver pulled up in front just as I was nodding off. I asked the driver how much was the fare and was told 1,000 rupees. That sounded fine to me. I had 25,000 rupees in my wallet so I didn't even challenge the amount, figuring it was probably a good rate. Little did I know that 1,000 rupees was ten times the going flat rate from the airport. I exited the taxi feeling sick from exhaustion. The reception area wasn't very fancy, in fact I immediately thought it must be a two-star hotel. It was 2:40 a.m., January 22, 1998.

My room was muggy and hot when I opened the door. I found the air-conditioning button and immediately I turned it on to the high position before I jumped into the shower and soaped myself thoroughly. By the time I'd towelled off, the room had cooled considerably and I could feel myself fading on my feet. I crawled into the bed and within seconds left the conscious world behind. Little did I know as I fell asleep that I'd experience real-life nightmares during my first visit to this city, too many highs and lows to count before I'd finally connect with Mohini Raghunath, the orphanage director who believed in me and would make my adoption dreams a reality a year later.

I had only been back in Canada ten weeks when the Delhi orphanage called about a possible son for me to adopt. On April 1st Mohini Raghunath, the orphanage director, had called to discuss a little boy who had just come into their care.

"David, he is darker skinned but not too dark, he is in good health, tall and lean and he is circumsized. Would you want a circumsized boy?"

I told her it wasn't an issue either way for me, I just wanted a son. She informed me that being circumsized meant he was most likely Muslim and that no Hindu couples would want to adopt a Muslim son. He would go on the international list for adoption and I was next on that list.

"So if you want him, he is yours," she said.

In March 1999, exactly eleven months after receiving that momentous phone call, the Canadian government could no longer delay the inevitable. I had all my paperwork in order. I had my Visitor's Visa in hand this time and triplicate copies of all my documentation divided

David R I McKinstry

between three suitcases (just in case one or more pieces of my luggage got sent to Moscow by mistake). The previous seven months had been difficult in terms of managing all the business affairs of Woodhaven, becoming a new parent, growing into parenthood with Michael and maintaining a constant flow of paperwork between Canadian government offices and officials in India.

Finally the hour arrived for me to pack and get ready for my flight back to India. Kolwyn and Michael packed my bag while I checked and re-checked all my documentation. I was really pleased that my departure started the day of Michael's March-Break so he and Kolwyn could be alone to bond for two weeks while I was away getting Nicholas. Michael had been Daddy mostly on weekends and this two week school break would be a perfect time for them to spend quality time together before our second son arrived.

Kolwyn hugged me goodbye. He knew I would be bringing Nicholas home soon but had no adult conception of the difference Nicholas would make to our home, and the extent of the adjustment we would all have to make to integrate a little boy from the streets of India into our family. I was confident we were all up for the challenges ahead. I just wanted to get there, meet Nicholas and bring him home as soon as possible. Mohini had told me that once the paperwork was signed, she didn't want me lingering in India for a month or so. She made it clear that once Nicholas was introduced to me and the paperwork completed we should fly home to Canada immediately. She said the pain of detachment for the children, leaving the orphanage family and India, was going to be difficult regardless of when we left, so the sooner the better. I thought it would take at least three weeks for all his paperwork to be completed so I'd purchased open-ended tickets for us.

Michael dropped me off at the limousine office. I brazenly kissed him in plain view of anyone nearby, then turned to kiss Kolwyn who flung his arms around my neck and said, "I love you Dad. Say hi to Nicholas for me."

A Swim *Against* The Tide

Michael and Kolwyn were heading to Grandma McKinstry's for supper after dropping me off. I waved goodbye from the window of the limousine. Watching them drive away brought a rush of thoughts into my head. I tried to imagine how different things would be with two sons racing around the house. I knew we were prepared for Nicholas. I had read articles about behaviour problems to watch out for when a second child is introduced to a family. Kolwyn would probably need lots of individual attention during the adjustment phase. Nicholas will need lots of remedial help to develop his fluency in English. These thoughts and a thousand more kept me occupied during the 90 minutes drive to Toronto's Pearson International Airport for my evening flight to Frankfurt and then onto Delhi.

David R I McKinstry

CHAPTER SEVENTEEN

What a Difference a Year Makes

A s the plane jetted into the sky, I sat quietly thinking about my first few months as a dad. Kolwyn's adjustment to life with us on Sandy Lake away from his mother and older half-siblings provided me with a doctorate in quick study parenting. Kolwyn had so many issues, especially his anger over our enforcement of the rules and regulations of our home versus the no-rules policy he was used to, and adjusting to having two men in his life where he had not had male role models previously. He seemed to make a fast study of us as well and resigned himself, albeit happily so, to the fact that this place was going to be his permanent home. From day one, we told him he had a brother, Nicholas, who was anxiously waiting in India to come to Canada to complete our family.

We told him what adoption was all about. How God knew his mummy wasn't going to stay on earth for a long time so he had us waiting in the wings to take over when Mummy got sick and returned home to Heaven to be with God full time. I'd told Kolwyn that we had all lived together as children in Heaven before coming down to earth to live life. I told him we knew one another up in Heaven a long time ago but when we get born, a cloud of forgetfulness falls over us and we don't

A Swim *Against* The Tide

remember Heaven and how wonderful a place it is. I explained in story form how God wanted Mummy, Daddy and I to raise him but since Mummy would only be down here on earth for a few years, God decided to let her have him all to herself until she got really sick then his two fathers would take over for Mummy when she went back up to Heaven. We provided him with simple explanations about what was happening in his life and Kolwyn responded better than I ever expected. He com-pletely trusted my explanation of what was happening to his mother, life before his earth life, and Michael and I being parents-in-waiting appealed to his simple view of the complicated world he'd been thrust into by fate. He felt comforted by our words. Kolwyn understood that his mother was in pain and when she got to Heaven she wouldn't have any pain. "She will watch down over you for the rest of your life, just like she does from your picture of her at the head of your bed," I'd tell him.

Most days of the week we'd end up drawing pictures of Mummy dressed as an angel in Heaven. He enjoyed this drawing game as he got to choose the colour of Mummy's wings and depending on the weather he'd draw her wings blue, pink, orange or green. We tacked up pictures of Mummy with wings all over his room, the refrigerator door and the bathroom mirror. Ever so surely, there was a noticeable peace enveloping Kolwyn whenever Mummy's name arose in conversation.

Kolwyn could spend hours being challenged by puzzles; without using the instructions or being guided by us, he could put together puzzles far advanced for his age. It was obvious from an early age that Kolwyn had inherited his biological father's mechanical engineering genes. We bought him lots of paints, crayons, art paper and Lego with which he'd amuse himself for hours. I would watch him in total awe and wonder as he occupied his time, lost in his own artistry. I wanted desperately to reach inside his mind to find out how he was feeling about all the life altering changes and adjustments he been through.

We'd designed our new kitchen with a huge laundry tub built into the counter beside the double stainless steel sink. A duo-purpose tub,

David R I McKinstry

we could use it as a soaker sink for dirty pots and pans or use it as a bathing tub when we were busy in the kitchen and Kolwyn decided it was bath time. I had grown up having baths in a kitchen sink and I figured it was good forethought to add a big white laundry tub to our counter design when we built the new addition. Kolwyn loved bubble baths in his private kitchen sink. For his sake we used to make a big deal out of bedtime baths and he enjoyed bathing in the safety of this tub while I worked at the counter beside him.

Kolwyn also enjoyed his playtime in the large six-person hot tub; a place he knew his mother had enjoyed during her short visits to Woodhaven. He attended junior kindergarten two full days per week at Buckhorn Public School. We would walk down our long lane to catch the bus each morning and I'd be there to meet him at 3:40 p.m. Being an

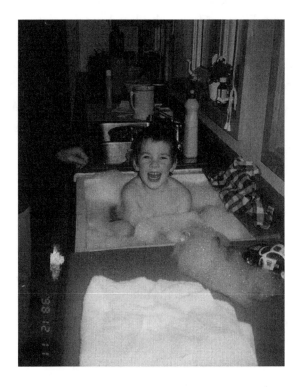

Kolwyn bathing in the tub sink in Woodhaven Kitchen.

A Swim *Against* The Tide

outgoing and very friendly child, Kolwyn adored school and his teacher. Having no immediate neighbours, it was crucial I import children for him to play with. Calling classmates' parents I'd introduce myself and suggest they bring their son over to play with Kolwyn one afternoon each week. It was an easy trade off for parents to drop their kids at our house as long as Kolwyn had friends to play with during his non-school days of the week.

Kolwyn loved to show off the big hot tub. Invariably when he'd have friends over for an afternoon, I'd let them all go in and splash around. As a child, I had grown up around the YMCA with its many kids' programs. In those days boys never wore bathing suits and swimming nude was the norm. So it didn't phase me if a child arrived for an afternoon of playtime with Kolwyn but had forgotten his bathing suit. I would tell him he could wear a spare bathing suit, his underwear or go in the hot tub naked. It wasn't a big deal to any of the parents who regularly sent their children to play with Kolwyn for an afternoon.

A few months after Kolwyn arrived, a social worker from his school called to introduce herself. She wanted to make herself available to me, as a new parent, should I need any help or suggestions during my first few months of adjusting to parenthood. We had a long chat over the phone, during which I told her about Kolwyn and his four-year-old friends having just streaked through the kitchen and into the hot tub. She asked why they were naked. I said I wasn't particular about them wearing bathing suits and most the time they took off their suits anyway while in the hot tub.

"It's no big deal for us or them," I said.

"I'd rethink your position on the wearing of bathing suits," she suggested. "Although I'm sure you have no paedophilic motives for allowing your son and his friends to splash around naked, the last thing you want now, as a gay man who has just adopted a son, is for someone in your community to start gossiping about the gay guys at Woodhaven who invite little boys over to swim naked in the hot tub with their son."

It stunned me to think anyone could twist something so innocent

David R I McKinstry

into something so vile. I wasn't happy to hear these words of warning but quickly realized she was just doing her job and most probably was right to caution me. However I wondered if she would have cautioned someone heterosexual under the same circumstances? Regardless, from that point onward, I enforced the wearing of bathing suits, just in case an over-zealous religious right-winger might want to make an issue where there wasn't any to be made. This was a real awakening for me to be ultra-vigilant about letting other people's issues become headaches for us. Forewarned is to be forearmed, as the saying goes.

It was important for me to read or subscribe to every new parenting magazine I could find. I searched for any information that would help me to better parent Kolwyn and Nicholas. I would discover an article Monday about a new child-rearing technique only to have discarded the advice by Friday in favour of something better or newer. Kolwyn would be given a time-out one day, the next time that offence occurred a totally different punishment would occur.

I remember with a smile feeling duped, many times, by Kolwyn during those first few months into his first school year. Because he had arrived to our home with no sense of actions having consequences, he was very angry when rebuked. Kolwyn was an angry little boy and he had good reason to be angry. Twenty-one days after meeting us for the first time this four-year-old boy had been wrenched out of his familiar environment and transplanted to Woodhaven with two fathers and six dogs. I marvelled at the ease with which Kolwyn moved in, immediately referred to us as Dad and Daddy, called my mother Grandma and adjusted to Buckhorn Public School.

Kolwyn was volatile and could become out-of-control angry when I'd reprimand him for naughty behaviour, to the point that several times I had to give him a controlling bear hug to stop him from trying to hurt me, himself or attempt to tear apart his room. One morning just before school he had a fit of rage after being told to get dressed quickly or we would miss the school bus. Out of the blue he threw a tantrum, the sight of which made me really nervous. I didn't want another thirty-minute session bear-hugging him on the floor. Instead, I walked briskly into his bathroom and turned on the cold water shower. It ran through my head that if I cooled him off and diffused this situation in thirty seconds, he might regain composure and we'd be able to get to the bus in time, without the usual 20 minutes of crying, wailing and flailing. He was shocked into silence by me carrying him into the cold shower. I hugged him tightly while we stood under the cold water soaking every inch of us. Within twenty seconds his body relaxed and he sobbed in my arms. For the first time since he'd arrived, he said the words, "I'm sorry Dad, I'm sorry."

I told Michael about this incident later that day and he was concerned that the cold shower technique bordered on child abuse. Shocked by this reaction I immediately called Brian Nichol, the child psychologist we took Kolwyn to see twice each week, to inquire about my cold shower method of diffusing his anger fits.

Brian calmly listened to me recall that morning's incident in the shower. Being both a father of grown children and a child psychologist, his advice was always appreciated. Brian recapped what we already knew. Kolwyn came to us with anger management issues and he had only known rules and regulations since moving in with us. Because this had been a major shift in his young life, Brian felt he was simply testing our boundaries. Although Brian didn't think cold showers should be the norm, the fact that I had gone into the shower with him and Kolwyn saw that it wasn't just him getting wet and cold made my actions non-abusive. Pleased the cold shower acted to diffuse the tantrum, Brian said it was better to cool him off that way than to have let him possibly hurt himself or the dogs. He felt Kolwyn saying he was sorry was a major breakthrough about his level of trust and love for me as his dad.

"This morning you saw him respond to you like a parent, he just wanted to be consoled by you after he admitted he had misbehaved. Just keep telling him how much you love him every hour of the day and you'll be fine."

Thankfully this became a learning lesson for Kolwyn about control-

David R I McKinstry

ling anger impulses. Slowly, as he came to believe in our love, Kolwyn's rage diminished and his angry outbursts fell into the normal range. In total, Kolwyn and I went into the shower four more times over the first three years of his life in our home.

Another lesson I learned early was maintaining my own composure while addressing or redressing Kolwyn. Aware that Kolwyn would yell at me when he tried to talk his way out of a naughty situation, one day I'd had enough and told him not to yell at me as it was disrespectful and unnecessary. Kolwyn pursed his lips together, put his hands on his hips and stood his ground looking up into my face and said

"Why can't I yell? You yell at me!" What a revelation this was to me. I did in fact raise my voice and get louder the madder I got with him. What a lesson to learn from a four-year-old boy! I became ultra cautious about listening to the pitch and tone of my voice whenever I admonished Kolwyn, and low and behold, Kolwyn stopped yelling back at me.

Out of the mouths of babes comes forth wisdom! Being a parent required a doctorate in common sense. I quickly discovered how to gauge my own effectiveness and growth as a parent through the eyes of my child.

Kolwyn enjoyed Sunday school at Grace United Church. My parents had been members of the original congregation of Peterborough residents who had built the church 50 years earlier. Kolwyn became a bit of a celebrity at church, most of the older congregation had watched me grow up and were happy to see their friend Dorothy McKinstry finally becoming a grandmother. Kolwyn was quick to introduce himself as Kolwyn McKinstry and it was heart-warming to see him connecting to his new family name. A huge oil canvass of Christ in Gesthemane had been painted by a long-time friend of Dad's and was donated to the church in honour of their friendship. One Sunday just before the processional began, Kolwyn whispered into my ear, "Since that's Grandpa's painting, why can't I take it home?"

Giving Kolwyn a spiritual grounding, similar to the one I'd had growing up in a faith-practising home, was a high priority with me. Michael had occasionally attended the Unitarian Church with his parents

A Swim *Against* The Tide

during his formative years but he wasn't into organised church or Christianity. However, we discussed it, and he agreed, that our children would be raised in a Christian home. I would be responsible for the effort, take the lead in their instruction and Michael would support us 100%.

Patsy, a 14 year old English Setter with the huge brown eyes of a doe, came along with Kolwyn when he left his mother's house for the last time. Since Susan was no longer capable of looking after children or pets at this stage of her disease, Patsy came along with Kolwyn. This delicate sweet-natured canine had the eyes of a kind grandmother. Kolwyn and Patsy were inseparable and she helped him to acclimate to his new life with us. Patsy got along well with Mylo and our Goldens. There was something spiritual in her doe-like eyes, an omniscient wisdom that made me wish she would live forever. Ten months later, in the middle of the afternoon while Kolwyn was at school, Patsy slipped away to be with Susan. We buried her body under a flowering shrub next to the Maple tree under which Nick's ashes had been laid to rest. Burying Patsy beside Nick seemed to give Kolwyn a sense of greater belonging, anchoring him to our Woodhaven family.

Kolwyn's sibling's fought us in court for permanent custody. They lost their first bid at custody but kept us in the court system unable to finalize Kolwyn's adoption for thirty months. They tried to get alternate weekend access and after that attempt failed, they took us to court for joint custody. In each case the judge deemed them naive to promote themselves as stable adults, not one with a fulltime career or the financial ability to look after the needs and demands of a little boy. We cut out most communication with his siblings, other than his eldest half-sister who occasionally wrote letters to Kolwyn. Once Kolwyn's maternal grandmother in England learned that homosexuality wasn't a learned behaviour through osmosis, she quickly became our most ardent supporter.

The daily drive to and from Toronto wasn't feasible so during the school year Michael stayed in Toronto at the apartment Monday through Thursday nights. During the week I was alone with Kolwyn and it gave us plenty of time to bond. Kolwyn found my childhood

David R I McKinstry

picture Bible, given to me by my grandmother, and quickly decided he liked Bible stories at bedtime the best. Curled up beside me on the sofa, I'd read to him every night before prayers, then lights out. Kolwyn was a good sleeper but occasionally he had bouts of insomnia and around 2 a.m. he would awaken, start singing softly, progressively getting louder until I awoke and I went to inquire why he was awake. It only took a few minutes of quiet talking to lull him back to sleep but then I'd be awake the rest of the night!

By Friday afternoon Kolwyn would often sit by the library window doing a puzzle but watchful for any sign of Michael's headlights coming down the lane way. Before the dogs heard the car, he would have spotted the headlights and begin jumping up and down at the window yelling, "Daddy's home, Daddy's home!"

We tried to make his mother's death a celebration of her life and talked about how happy she was up in Heaven with all her relatives playing on the clouds and watching over us at Woodhaven. Kolwyn liked this explanation of where his mother was and although he had been incredibly stoic during the weeks prior to and just after her funeral, within a few months he began to experience emotional setback. During this period I parented using the time-out method of discipline for naughty behaviour. I'd stand quietly outside his closed bedroom door to monitor his time out. Sometimes during these time outs I'd hear Kolwyn crying under his blanket for his mummy to come and comfort him. It broke my heart to hear him crying for Susan and I would go in and lie down beside him to comfort him. He learned early about apologising for wrong doings, and he would hug me back tightly and whimper that he was sorry for being naughty. Those moments were priceless and the gems that I had waited a lifetime to experience as a parent. It was impossible for me to stay upset with Kolwyn. His big smile would expose white teeth and through his grin he'd look up at me and say, "You're not cross with me ... are you!"

Frequent weekly trips to Peterborough for groceries, to pick up lumber or paint or visit Grandma McKinstry, gave us ample oppor-

A Swim *Against* The Tide

tunity to laugh and talk together frequently. I taught Kolwyn songs I had learned in my early youth, songs that no one but seasoned campers would know, songs that couldn't be written down but were phonetically passed along from generation to generation. I'd sing them to Kolwyn, as I had done to all of Nick's nieces and nephews over the years, and he learned every word within a matter of weeks. Merrily we'd sing these songs together as we travelled in the car, after supper or during his bath time.

Kolwyn continued to see his child psychologist on a weekly basis. Brian wanted to monitor his anger management and discover the triggers that launched his naughty behaviours. The absence of his half-sister Courtney, a primary caregiver for most of Kolwyn's early years, was a difficult adjustment for Kolwyn. Unfortunately due to her serious bouts of teenaged rebelliousness it was recommended that we not maintain any direct contact with her. I had mixed emotions about cutting off

Grandma McKinstry

David R I McKinstry

contact with his half-sisters but Michael and Brian felt it was imperative Kolwyn not feel divided between two worlds.

By Christmas, after only four months with us, it was obvious that Kolwyn felt loved and quite secure in his new life. We often joked with him that he was the King of Woodhaven. Forever curious about who owned what, Kolwyn felt very comfortable asking me, "Do I own the dogs if you die? Do I own the hot tub?"

This was a turning point in his psychological development and adjustment to us. According to Dr. Brian this was a sign that Kolwyn had adjusted to his new life and all the things that went hand in hand with his new identity. It was easy to see that Kolwyn really felt he had hit the jackpot coming to live at our house! Considering the fact that guests and friends who met Kolwyn for the first often brought him a gift, much to his delight. His bedroom looked like an advertisement for The Gap, Toys 'R' Us, and OshKosh.

I was two hours into the flight to India when a stewardess jolted me back to the present. She asked what I'd like for supper. After a quick meal I leaned back in my seat and again my thoughts were of Kolwyn. Had we prepared him well enough for the changes that were about to happen to our little family?

Kolwyn had been very clingy and wanted all my attention. Even at his tender age, he understood that my leaving meant things would never be quite the same around our home. I regularly made a point of sitting down with Kolwyn to talk about how neat it would be when I returned with Nicholas. I'd say that Nicholas would love to play hide and seek with him when Dad and Daddy were busy with guests. I explained gently that Nicholas would need lots of patience and understanding from us when he came home because he wouldn't know how to speak English. I'd ask Kolwyn if he thought it would be hard to learn a new language and we'd discuss how he could help his brother learn English. I wasn't sure Kolwyn was old enough to understand how Dad and Daddy's attentions would be divided equally between he and his new

A Swim *Against* The Tide

brother from this point onward. There would be challenges to overcome but nothing was insurmountable.

Fourteen months ago, my first encounter with India had not been positive; other than meeting Mohini at Children of the World, that trip had been mired in unpleasantries from the beginning.

Thoughts of Nicholas energized me. I hoped I would be able to capture on film the precise moments when I'd meet face to face with our son. I wanted to chronicle those special moments for Michael and Kolwyn, and also as a memory for Nicholas to review in years to come.

There was a sleeping giant of rage just below the surface of my extreme happiness. I was angry that the adoption process had taken eleven months to procure the necessary paperwork to bring Nicholas home, a year of happiness denied to him. Why was the present Canadian child welfare system draconian and out of touch with the fundamentals of placing a child into a loving family as quickly as possible? Why was it steeped in bureaucratic indifference, senseless repetitive paperwork, unbelievable checks and balances – everything but a speedy resolution?

Most of my anger stemmed from knowing that Nicholas had been subjected to living in an orphanage, watching others be adopted into new families for the past year while waiting his turn. For eleven months Nicholas had been assigned to me and he had been lost in a deliberate paper shuffle between one office and another. I could never make up for that lost time with my son. He sat in an orphanage a world away knowing about me but unable to reach out and feel the love of his new family. I'd had nightmares about Nicholas being upset and crying, lying alone in his bed unsure of what the future held for him and me being unable to reach out and comfort him. In 24 hours my reward for playing by the rules would be Nicholas running into my arms, officially together at last.

I wanted to share the truth of my life with Mohini. I knew it wasn't feasible yet for me to tell her that Nicholas would have a brother and a Daddy greeting us upon our return to Canada. This deception weighed heavily on my heart. It was necessary to maintain a veil of secrecy to

David R I McKinstry

ensure the successful outcome of this final leg of my journey. I was prepared to do whatever it took to get my son home.

The doctors provided me with every medication and puffer available to counter the effects of extreme heat on my lungs. I dreaded arriving in Delhi and sucking into my heat-sensitive lungs those first few breaths of hot humid air. I had to be thankful for small mercies, at least I wasn't stopping off in Bangkok. The smog and oppressive heat of that city would have done me in this time.

My health hadn't been good all winter, and the most recent test results sang of doom and gloom. Michael was concerned over my worsening health. I kept telling him it was just a nasty bit of pneumonia deeply imbedded in my lungs. One afternoon as we sat talking on the sofa watching Kolwyn put together a puzzle, he became serious and said that if my health was really bad then maybe we shouldn't go ahead with a second adoption because of the strain on me. Half-joking he added that if I was going to die he felt one son would be enough to raise as a single parent.

I had witnessed Michael's incredible parenting skills in action with Kolwyn. I had no apprehensions about him raising two little boys and being Father of the Year. So I kept him in the dark about the initial test results indicating lympho-sarcoma and the possibility of the angel of death coming to get me. I knew he had inner hidden emotional strength which he hadn't tapped into yet. I felt that whatever the outcome of my health, he'd handle parenthood like a professional.

There was still so much to do before I returned home with Nicholas that I didn't want to focus on what could lay ahead of me with my health. It wasn't denial; in order to get Nicholas home to Canada I just had to prioritise what little energy I had left. For the sake of our two sons, as well as Michael, I had to do everything possible to surmount the seemingly impossible.

As the plane touched down on the tarmac of the Delhi International Airport I wondered if my luggage and all the clothes I'd brought for the

A Swim *Against* The Tide

orphanage children would be lost, stolen or redirected to another port. It was just after 1:15 a.m. Walking off the plane I sensed a growing apprehension about having to deal with Indian officials, airport personnel, taxi drivers and anyone else who might have it in for me because of the fair colour of my skin.

My luggage arrived intact. I changed two thousand US dollars for rupees and hailed a cab and gave him the address of the small hotel where Mohini had suggested I stay. After getting lost multiple times, the taxi driver finally found the hotel. I checked in at 3:45 a.m. and was shown to my room by a very sleepy front desk clerk. The room was clean but very warm. The clerk turned on the air-conditioner immed-iately but it took several minutes to make a dent in the temper-ature of this windowless room. I was so tired. I threw off my clothes, laid diagonally across the short double bed and fell asleep instantly.

I awoke to someone knocking at my door. I could barely open my eyes from the sleepy stupor I was in. I looked at my watch and it read 8:15 a.m. The knocking continued. I opened the door and looked out to see the clerk.

"Your ride from orphanage will be here in fifteen minutes. You meet him outside or he come here?" he asked. Suddenly it dawned on me where I was and what time it was. The orphanage was sending a car for me to come and meet Nicholas.

"Fifteen minutes! OK, tell them I'll be waiting outside," I managed to say before closing the door and looking around my darkened room for a light switch. I needed to shower and shave. My hair felt like a greasy mess. What would I wear to meet Nicholas? I scolded myself for not having thought about the clothes I'd wear the first time my son laid eyes on me. Was the video camera ready? My mind was racing and I had only fourteen minutes before my ride arrived.

I scrambled through my luggage to find my clothes hidden beneath piles of children's clothing I'd brought along for the orphanage. I knew from my first trip to India that wearing shorts wasn't a sign of class, so I had to wear long pants in the 37° C heat of March. Then the phone rang.

David R I McKinstry

"David, this is Raghu, Mohini's husband. I am out front and will wait for you. We will walk together to meet Nicholas at the office." I thanked him for coming to meet me and said I'd be just a few more minutes.

Raghu was a distinguished light-skinned man of 70. He was very supportive of his wife's fervent desire to place Indian orphans into good homes domestically and internationally. There was a truly remarkable sense of kindness which emanated from him the moment I looked into his eyes and shook his hand. He said it was a nice day and we'd walk the short distance to their home.

I told Raghu that I was nervous. I hoped my first face-to-face meeting with Nicholas would be memorable.

"I'm sure my eyes must look like I've been awake for two days. Poor Nicholas will wonder what he's getting into if he sees me like this. I arrived in the middle of last night and I haven't even had one cup of coffee yet. Do you have coffee at the orphanage?" I asked, half joking. Raghu assured me that if I liked strong coffee then I'd enjoy the coffee he would make before we met Nicholas.

We walked for about ten minutes through streets lined with cows chewing grasses and leaves off vines attached to the walled enclosures of Delhi's rich and famous. Raghu had been an executive with the Indian railroad and he and Mohini lived in a very secure and lovely area of Delhi, referred to as Vasant Vihar. Mohini had transformed the top floor of their home into offices for her orphanage. Raghu pushed open the tall iron gates leading into his yard and I followed him along the familiar path I'd walked just a year ago. The thick walled house was cool inside and it took a few seconds for my lungs to register the refreshing cool air streaming into them.

As we passed the stairwell leading up to the third floor offices, I asked Raghu if Nicholas was already here.

"Oh, yes. He was brought over an hour ago to meet his new father. He is waiting upstairs with Mohini," he replied.

"Never mind the coffee, Raghu, I've waited a lifetime for this moment. I want to meet my son." I began to fumble in my bag for the

A Swim *Against* The Tide

video camera. "I want to capture on film my first meeting with Nicholas. Do you know how to operate a video camera?"

Raghu said he was a semi-professional videographer since it was most often him who stood back and filmed the introductions of children to parents. I handed him the camera and we headed upstairs. I wanted to race ahead of him and call out Nicholas at the top of my lungs. I was in India and had to behave, so I only took the stairs two at a time, trying to be discreet about my enthusiasm. Raghu smiled over my excitement as I turned and waited for him to join me at the top of the stairs.

I could hear Mohini's voice around the corner and I opened the door to the hallway leading to her office. Several people were milling about. Raghu walked in behind the two office assistants and they bowed their heads in respect as he passed.

"Mohini, David's here," he said as we neared her office door. I was looking around to see Nicholas but apparently he wasn't upstairs just yet.

She came from behind her desk and greeted me warmly. "It is so good to see you. Are your accommodations alright?" I gave her a thirty-second synopsis of the past five hours and she asked if I would like cup of tea or coffee before meeting Nicholas. I said I'd love a cup of coffee. My mind was ready for action but my body needed a caffeine kick-start. We entered her office and sat down. Several of the staff stood in the hall smiling at me and talking softly in Hindi. I recognized two of them from my first visit.

The coffee arrived and gave me what I needed to calm down and enjoy the moment at hand. Mohini told me that another family was arriving today to adopt one of Nicholas' playmates. I heard commotion from the next room. Mohini said something in Hindi to her on-looking staff and they smiled and nodded.

"Are you ready to meet your son, David?" she asked with a smile that filled her face.

"I certainly am, but just a moment," I said as I remembered the video camera. "Raghu would you please film me meeting Nicholas so we have a permanent record of this moment?"

David R I McKinstry

I handed Raghu the camera and he fiddled with it for a few seconds, looked into the viewfinder and said, "Ready when you are."

I walked around the corner of the office and out into the hallway before entering into an adjoining office. As I crossed the threshold I could see the shadowy outline of a little boy hiding behind the legs of one of the staff. The lady staffer pulled Nicholas from his hiding spot behind her and pushed him forward to me.

I looked at Nicholas in total wonderment. He looked frightened, curious, and excited all at once. For so long I had wondered if it was possible to love this little boy in the instant we met or would I have to grow into loving him? Was it reasonable, let alone sane, to expect that fate would snap its fingers and instantly an orphan and its new adoptive parent would look into each other's eyes and love one another? What were this little boy's expectations? Standing there in front of him, tall, fair skinned and fair haired, was I what he expected? He still probably had strong memories of the life he'd known, albeit briefly, with his family and now this white man was going to be his father and take him to a far away place. Heavenly Father, give this little boy the armour to survive this.

We had only been staring at one another for ten seconds yet everything was happening too fast. I wanted to freeze this special moment in time. I had lived most of the past year of my life waiting for this moment to arrive.

Nicholas looked similar to the boy in the photographs I'd been receiving from Mohini, but different enough that it momentarily startled me. He was extremely thin and lanky. I noticed the absence of his two front teeth as he smiled graciously yet nervously up at me. Nicholas' eyes were dark and piercing which for a brief second truly unnerved me.

I tried to imagine what he must be thinking as I walked toward him, this white-faced stranger, larger than life towering over him. No longer were either of us just some obscure impersonal photograph in a file. I hoped with all my heart that Nicholas wouldn't be permanently affected in some negative way by the experience of meeting me for the first time.

A Swim *Against* The Tide

Dad and Nicholas en route to Taj Mahal, March 1999.

I was petrified he wouldn't like me.

I knew Mohini and her staff had tried to prepare Nicholas for this day. Whenever I'd raised my concern about how Nicholas might react to me, Mohini gently say, "Just give it time. Children are much stronger than we adults think they are. Nicholas knows he is one of the lucky ones to get a family."

Knowing children were dying on their city streets from disease, malnutrition and abandonment, Mohini wasn't going to worry too long over any fears Nicholas might have of a future in Canada with me, far from the life he'd known as a beggar and street urchin in the back alleys of Delhi.

Mohini had often said to me during our many telephone calls, that Nicholas had watched longingly as many of his young friends celebrated the arrival of new white parents from foreign lands. Nicholas

David R I McKinstry

had told Mohini how he longed for the day he'd get parents and have his going-away cake at the front of their classroom. Finally the time had arrived for him to leave the orphanage, his friends, his interim family, and go to some far away land in the arms of a white total stranger. I couldn't imagine the myriad of feelings he must be was experiencing. Our eyes locked onto one another and we just stared back wide-eyed. My eyes were moistening by the second and I was only semi-aware of huge tears avalanching down across my cheeks.

Twenty seconds after first laying eyes on each other, Nicholas outstretched his hand, walked up to me with down caste eyes and said, "Hello Poppa."

If ever words were heavenly it was what I heard from his lips. I stooped to his eye level and hugged him and said, "Yes Nicholas, I'm your father."

Nicholas looked at me with a nervous half smile and then ran back behind the skirt from whence he'd come. Mohini was watching us meet and I could see a few happy tears rolling down her cheek.

"This is incredible," I said with tears constricting my voice. "You can't imagine how happy I am to finally meet my son." I ached to bring Michael and Kolwyn into this celebration. I desperately wanted to share news of Kolwyn and Daddy with Nicholas, but knew it couldn't happen now and wouldn't until we arrived on Canadian soil.

Mohini and Raghu hugged one another in the doorway and smiled sweetly at me. Mohini said, "We have all become so fond of you, David. I am most excited by your reaction to Nicholas. He will love you. Give it some time. He will be a good son."

Just then we all became aware of Nicholas sobbing from the corner of the room. I walked over to hug him but he wanted nothing to do with me. Mohini told me to give him time to get used to me, after all I represented not only his future but also the end to his past and present. She said he would need time to mourn that loss of everything he knew and that it might take a while for him to warm up to me. Mohini put her hand on my arm and said, "Be patient. It has taken a year for the two of you to meet. Give him a few weeks to adjust. Every child from here must

A Swim *Against* The Tide

pass through these same experiences. We have seen it happen many times before. It will pass and you will have the loving son you always wanted."

The staff took Nicholas to the washroom while I followed Mohini back to her office. Raghu said he would go downstairs and prepare breakfast. Mohini suggested I wait in her office until Nicholas returned and then just sit with him and let him adjust to my presence. Alone in the office with my thoughts waiting for Nicholas to reappear, I felt numb from fear, insecurity, and immense happiness. I loved Nicholas from afar, and seeing him in person was one of the happiest moments of my life. We would survive and conquer the adjustment period that lay ahead of us. I had such a mixed bag of emotions running through my head during those reflective minutes alone. Was it fair of me to take him away from his orphanage home, his culture and his country? Was my adopting him more of a selfish act than an act of selfless parental love to provide a home for child?

Nicholas re-entered the room where I was sitting and came over toward me and stopped just a few feet away. With his deep dark eyes cast downward he slowly shuffled forward and stood purposely centimetres away from my knee. I wanted to grab him tightly, hoist him onto my lap and hug him. But I realised he had to come to me when he felt comfortable and I couldn't force him to jump into my arms and smother me with the hugs and kisses I'd waited an eternity to receive. Before breakfast, cake and candy was served downstairs in the living room. This had been the moment Nicholas had longed to experience. This was his celebration and he was the centre of attention. It was his cake to cut and share with his playmates.

Nicholas slowly began to warm up to me. He'd bring one playmate after another over to meet me. He wouldn't come too close but he would point to me and say "Poppa." My fears began to fade as I watched my son interacting with his friends. I felt in my soul a reassurance that everyone in Heaven was cheering me on and destiny was unfolding as it was meant to be.

Once again I was unfortunate to have purchased airline tickets with

David R I McKinstry

specific arrival and departure dates. Although I could travel anytime during those dates if seating was available. If seating wasn't available then I was out of luck. My options were to stay on in this hotel for another fourteen days at $250 US per day (without the cost of food, siteseeing, etc.) or purchase new tickets.

Mohini told me we should leave quickly once Nicholas' paperwork was finalized. I called the airlines but I couldn't get two economy seats on any airline for two weeks. However one unscrupulous agent, recommended by the Front Desk clerk, suggested that he might be able to get me two tickets out of Delhi on First Class. He made a few calls and spoke in Hindi so I wouldn't know what he was talking about.

"There are two seats on First Class out of Delhi late tonight. A cancellation just happened. These tickets will get you to Frankfurt, Germany where you can use your Air Canada economy tickets from Frankfurt to Toronto. It will be easy for me to get you on a connecting flight to Toronto on Air Canada within hours of landing in Frankfurt. But if you want them I must call my friend back immediately. He has other people who want these tickets. It will cost you $2,466 US dollars to get out tonight as far as Germany." He smiled and waited for me to answer.

I did some mental math and realized that it would cost me $3,500 US for Nicholas and I to stay in this hotel for another two weeks before heading home on my already purchased economy tickets. I calculated it would probably cost me another $1,200 US just to eat, do some siteseeing and keep purchasing toys and clothes for Nicholas. These First Class tickets sounded like a bargain.

"I'll take them," I replied. I hadn't even factored in a bribe for this agent, but figured it would only be a few hundred US dollars.

The travel agent spoke again for several minutes on the phone to his connection with the two First Class tickets up for grabs. He kept looking up at me and shrugging and talking in Hindi.

"Sir, my friend has to pay so many people to get his hands on these tickets for you. He needs $2,500 US on top of the ticket prices to make sure I can get these tickets for you. Do you still want these tickets?"

A Swim *Against* The Tide

I just wanted to get Nicholas home. As mad as it made me to pay bribes, I knew I was out of options. I had exhausted all quick escape routes. I agreed to pay for the bribe and the tickets, knowing it only left me with a $800 US in case of an emergency. Two hours later I had the tickets in my hand.

My heart bled for Nicholas and his traumatic past. This little boy had been found clutching the corpse of his deceased mother in a back alley of the refugee section of Delhi. When we left the familiarity of the orphanage the night we drove to the airport, Nicholas was inconsolable. Arriving at the departures area, he went into hysterics and became hell-bent he wasn't leaving on any aeroplane with me. Nicholas was unaware I had crushed and stirred two Gravol pills into his apple juice in the airport waiting lounge. He slept most of the way to Frankfurt.

Awakening shortly before we touched down in Frankfurt, the stewardess offered him some Hagen Daze strawberry ice cream. Never tasting anything like, and loving it, Nicholas's sounds of delight could be heard from one end of the plane to the other. After a six-hour wait for our connecting flight to Toronto, we boarded and Nicholas slept for five hours. At one point, about an hour out of Toronto, he indicated he needed to go to the bathroom. I took him to the lavatory and ushered him in to do his business. Within a minute it dawned me that toilets were something new for Nicholas and I discreetly opened the door and there he was crouching in the corner to defecate. Coming from a background of abject poverty, the likes of which no one in Canada could imagine, Nicholas was bound to be in sensory overload in a land where microwaves make popcorn, food and sweet treats are available 24 hours of the day, having his own bed in his own room, his very own bathroom, lots of pets to call his own, a bike, schooling, and not the least, the love of two parents and a brother and a huge extended family.

The day after Nicholas arrived at Sandy Lake, he met his Grandma McKinstry, learned how to ride a bike on training wheels and discovered the need to wear winter galoshes in the snow, rather than his simple

David R I McKinstry

sandals. We tried to get Nicholas to put on his new Kids Kodiak winter boots but he stubbornly refused.

Michael assembled the boys' bikes and readied them for their first riding lessons. We decided to let Nicholas learn the hard way and sensed that once his feet hit the snow it wouldn't take long for him to change his mind. It took about ten minutes and lots of snow between his toes for Nicholas to humbly indicate he wanted to go inside, ditch the sandals and put on Canadian winter boots.

We couldn't understand a word this chatty little boy was saying; all we could do was guess. He just rambled on, talking a mile a minute in Hindi as if we understood every syllable he spoke. I had learned a

Nicholas' first morning in Canada, surrounded by Christmas gifts we'd kept for him, March 1999.

A Swim *Against* The Tide

smattering of Hindi phrases, such as asking him if he was hungry, thirsty, had to go to the bathroom, or was tired. Other than that, we just nodded happily and hoped he would learn English quickly!

Nicholas was wary of me for the first week. He gravitated to Michael more easily. On one hand I was thrilled for Michael, but on the other hand I was envious that Nicholas chose him over me. I'm sure Nicholas had lingering thoughts of me being the big bad man who stole him from his country. About one month later, he gave me my first hug one night at bedtime and within a few months Nicholas was giving me unprompted hugs and kisses at bedtime.

The joy in my heart the first time he reached out for me was indescribable. Not being a naturally patient type of man, the long wait for Nicholas to show his affections to me was difficult.

Kolwyn was frustrated that he couldn't communicate easily with Nicholas. He had waited so long for his brother to arrive and desperately wanted to be able to talk to him in English. Kolwyn and Michael had found Nicholas to be quite the odd little fellow that first weekend in Canada. Our days were filled with the constant, high-pitched squeals of delight from the mouth of our Hindi-speaking son.

From the day he arrived, Nicholas began to hoard things in his room. Paper wrappings from chocolate bars, pins, dog collars, fruit, banana peels, garbage from the wastebasket such as bunched up used Kleenex tissues, brochures, juice cartons. Nicholas obsessed about finding things to hoard in his room. We finally gave him an empty pillowcase into which he stuffed all his treasures. He kept everything in his billy sack and carried it around the house refusing to let it be out of his sight. It accompanied him to the bathroom, under the covers of his bed at night and rarely was it ever out of the tight grip of his hand.

Nicholas even took the billy sack with him on his first day of school. When he proudly shared the highly prized contents of his pillowcase with his senior kindergarten classmates, they laughed at the garbage he thought was valuable. Confused by their reactions, he became even more possessive about his billy sack and wouldn't show anyone

David R I McKinstry

anything. By his second week of school, Nicholas would go to school without his bulging pillowcase. Every afternoon when he returned home, he'd run to his room to open, check and count every treasure to be sure not one item had been touched or stolen in his absence. A grim reminder of the life he'd left behind on the streets of India.

Kolwyn very proudly introduced Nicholas to his classmates at Buckhorn Public School as his brother. It didn't take long for Kolwyn to become fiercely protective of Nicholas, frequently scolding classmates if they laughed at Nicholas or made fun of his language and inability to understand English.

I attended school with Nicholas for the first week, just to be sure he was comfortable. His kindergarten teacher was made to order for our two sons. Herself an adoptive parent, she became a valuable source of information for us and had just the right mix of maternal mothering and gentle discipline our boys both needed. Nicholas was trying so hard to learn new English words every day. The first word we taught him was "no" and he would walk around the house saying no, no, no, no to dogs, people and inanimate objects like doors and pillows.

Every day since arriving in Canada had been a day full of firsts for Nicholas. He learned to use the indoor toilet rather than just squat when the need arose while outside in the school playground or on our laneway. Both boys were enrolled in swim lessons at Trent University. Kolwyn was like a fish in the water. Nicholas cried pathetically as I dragged him out onto the pool deck for his first swimming lesson. I had arranged for private lessons so both boys would be together and hopefully inspire one another. Kolwyn soothed Nicholas' fears by jumping into the water and showing him how much fun it could be. After ten minutes of squirming, Nicholas allowed himself to be carried into the water, holding tightly onto the neck of his instructor. By the end of that first class, Nicholas was bobbing under the water, laughing and squealing with delight over the joy of being submerged in the water; all that fussing and within minutes he loved the water. Unfortunately, his paper-thin body provided little insulation from the cool pool

A Swim *Against* The Tide

temperatures. His brown skin turned almost blue by the end of his swim lessons and he would huddle under the warm spray of the hot showers until thawed.

The boys could see I was passionate about them, their daddy, our dogs, their schooling, providing our guests with a great vacation and loving life in general. I was passionate about many things and was forever ready to take someone to task over anything I perceived to be mean or prejudiced. It wasn't easy for Michael to live with someone whose passions were always ready to strike their mark, like a silent barracuda charging up from the depths of the ocean to bite him on the ass when he least expected it.

The boys going to church,
April 1999.

First fish, June 1999.

David R I McKinstry

After a swim at Woodhaven, 1999.

Kolwyn, Daddy and Nicholas at Woodhaven, Victoria Day 1999.

A Swim *Against* The Tide

No Price Too High

Adopting two sons had been both exhausting and a labour of love, flying in the face of all those nay sayers who told me to stop wasting my time and money trying to adopt children.

Michael remained very worried about our financial instability. The entire adoption saga had cost us every cent we had saved, could borrow and more. We were on the brink of disaster in the spring of 2000. I reluctantly agreed to put Woodhaven, our home, on the market. Michael had made a huge financial and personal sacrifice toward our effort to adopt our children. Although our accountant felt that within twelve months Woodhaven would finally be in the black, our on-going finances were abysmal. More often than not, Michael acquiesced to my optimism for a better future just around the bend. It was time for me to give in, sell Woodhaven and let Michael feel some relief from the constant pressure of bills and payments. We listed the lodge in the winter of 2000 at $449,000. I had consciously set the price high. If I had to sell my beloved Woodhaven then someone would have to pay through the nose!

Advanced reservations for the late spring and summer of 2000 were filling up our reservation book quickly. Unfortunately in early May we got an offer on our property which excited Michael more than I'd expected. I was sick at heart when the real estate agent called us back to say they had accepted the strict terms of our counter offer. We wouldn't leave until mid-September so we could enjoy one last summer on the lake and profit greatly from the guest income. I was tied at the hip to Woodhaven in more ways than the obvious. Nick's legacy was in the walls of Woodhaven and his ashes under the Maple tree I had planted eight years earlier. Family pets were also buried on this property. We had become a fixture around the lake for organising the summer regatta and cross-the-lake swim. Our neighbours had become close personal friends and extended family to us. This was home for our sons. Selling meant saying goodbye to their legacy, and the emotional anchor that was my home.

Michael didn't want to spend his summer holidays house hunting and seemed to think that another house would fall into our laps easily. I wasn't prepared to give up on the hospitality business or philosophy so I insisted we look for a place we could convert into a downsized Woodhaven Bed and Breakfast. With a hectic summer being full to capacity every day for three months, we hardly had time to breath let alone find a new home, pack up and move out by mid September. With only three weeks to go before we had to vacate, I finally located a farm about 45 minutes west of Sandy Lake, and we bought it, paying full price as the vendors knew we were desperate and needed a place that would accommodate a smaller version of Woodhaven.

We finished serving breakfast on Sunday September 10th and our guests packed up and left Woodhaven for the last time. We had five days to dismantle seven bedrooms, two living rooms, a huge dining room, assemble tools, outdoor furniture and boats, bedding, games, paintings, and 2,500 books from Nick's library. Our new home had a tenant whom we had been assured by the agent would be out of the lower level of the house, that was being used as a two bedroom separate apartment, by the night prior to our taking possession.

It was terribly emotional to pack the dogs into the van and drive away in the late afternoon. The drive past all the funeral markers of our

A Swim *Against* The Tide

pets was gut wrenching and I knew we had just made a horrible mistake in selling our beloved property, especially to the new owners whom we had recently discovered weren't going to be made-to-order replacements for us in this community. Driving away from Woodhaven that day, I had a heavy heart knowing I'd just made the worst judgement in my life in agreeing to sell this wonderful property.

An hour later we arrived at our new farm to discover that the real estate agent had double-ended the sale of this property and had lied to us about it being empty. The main-floor tenant hadn't been given her 60-day notice by the previous owners. This notorious agent, who for weeks had told us he had sold a house to the tenant and that she would be moved out, refused any culpability for this fiasco, nor did his employer. No apologies, no financial assistance for storing truckloads of furnishings, nothing. We had 7,000 square feet of furnishing arriving the next morning on the moving trucks with only half this 4,000 square feet of house ready to receive us.

It took a few weeks to buy our tenant out of the lower level. The day she moved out our contractor began the necessary challenge to turn this farm into a charming weekend Bed and Breakfast.

The boys had been attending the local school for two weeks when we moved into the farm. They liked the new school but missed their friends at Buckhorn Public School. They missed their bedrooms at Sandy Lake so we tried to make their rooms inviting by doing our own version of the Decorating Challenge while they were out at school. Slowly the boys adjusted to their new surroundings and by mid-October we could see an end to the construction.

I'd told Michael that once we got settled into this new house I wanted us to get married, with the boys participating in the ceremony. Tom Harpur, the Toronto Star ethics columnist, had agreed to co-officiate the wedding with our United Church minister from Peterborough. Unfortunately our minister's enthusiasm for calling our ceremony a wedding was very tentative for a United Church minister. Thankfully I had lived with an intellectual Jesuit who had made a point

David R I McKinstry

of reading all the research on same-sex marriages throughout recorded history. There were certain irrefutable facts about the history of marriage that were of my ace in the hole on this argument. Jesuits and other intellectuals of Catholic Church doctrine know, but don't publicise, that marriage vows used today in most Christian ceremonies had been written for the joining of same-sex nuns and priests into romantic and spiritual unions in the 7th Century AD. It took 400 more years before heterosexuals began regularly using those vows. It was our happy day and we were calling it a wedding!

November 11, 2000 arrived on the tail of an incredible sunrise. Over 120 guests crowded into the newly renovated loft of the barn for our wedding. The boys were decked out in matching outfits and acted as ring bearers. We'd hired a terrific soloist who performed masterfully and delighted our guests with her Broadway sounds. It was a perfect weekend, warm for November, and sunny. Three days later winter arrived and stayed with a vengeance until late April.

Kolwyn and Nicholas had attended Saturday morning Hindi classes for eighteen months in Peterborough; Kolwyn excelled at the language whereas Nicholas hated Hindi classes and just wanted to be left alone to be Canadian, Caucasian and English speaking. During one of my many frequent phone calls to India to keep Mohini current on Nicholas progress, I mentioned his reluctance to speak Hindi. She told me that in her experience 90% of Indian children adopted internationally refuse to speak their native tongue because they just want to fit in, rather than feel like the odd-person out. She convinced me to end the Hindi lessons and just let Nicholas get on with being Canadian and no longer torn between two cultures and two languages.

The new Woodhaven Bed and Breakfast was slow to get off the mark. The location, a modern farmhouse situated on flat farm fields hardly had the charm of our previous place. Small group bookings kept us afloat but it soon appeared we had jumped too quickly to buy this property and we had wasted any profit from the Sandy lake property on unnecessary renovations to make this sows ear into a silk purse.

A Swim *Against* The Tide

We marvelled at our luck to have found a good rural school and the administrative and teaching staff were second to none. On bad-weather days the boys rode the bus to school but on good days preferred to walk two kilometres down the abandoned railroad tracks along the side of our property, past grazing draft horses and hundreds of cattle. The boys loved our rural setting and quickly adapted to life on the farm far from the shores of our beloved Sandy Lake.

Alas, my efforts to develop a rural farm-style Woodhaven Bed and Breakfast failed and again Michael was worried sick over mounting bills. With restricted finances we remained a one-car family. Michael had the car in Toronto during the week which nixed me finding work as I had no transportation for job searching, let alone getting to and from a job. After eighteen months on the farm, we declared bankruptcy in the spring of 2002. Somehow our bankruptcy agent was able to keep the house from being included in the bankruptcy.

It was time for us to move closer to Toronto and be a family seven days of the week. We put the house on the market for a quick sale and within weeks a conditional full price offer was signed. We decided to search for a farm north of Toronto. With two sons, three dogs and Nicholas' newly adopted barn cat and her four newborn kittens, we needed country property to accommodate our zoo.

Michael had dreams of Kolwyn and Nicholas attending the private school where he taught. For eighteen months he had been waffling over my desire to adopt more children. I agreed to move closer to the city so our boys could attend classes at Michael's private school. But that agreement came with a proviso: Michael had to agree to stop dragging his feet about us adopting a daughter. With his promise in hand, I quickly found an affordable older farmhouse outside of Queensville, that would accommodate our sons, dogs and cats. We moved into this house in early July but then our conditional offer on the farm fell through ten days later and we were stuck with two houses.

Michael's insecurity about being openly gay and his internalized homophobia had always been a sore spot for me. Many gay men carry

David R I McKinstry

their own unique brand of internalised homophobia – the effect of a lifetime of hearing people say its OK to hate gays, homosexual means child molester, being gay isn't normal and to leave the dirty family secret locked in a closet.

Some gay people only take this hate-mongering so long, and then stand up and become militant soldiers of the cause, loudly rebuking the accusers. While others put up with the barrage of abuses with defeat hidden deep behind their stoic faces, preferring not to stir the pot or cause undue attention to themselves. This is a common reaction of most minorities facing discrimination.

In September 2002 Kolwyn and Nicholas became our little preppy private school sons. They had only been in school a few days when Michael, out of the blue, said he felt our sons should tell their classmates that they had a mom and dad at home, not two gay dads. I exploded like a firecracker. I would not tell our sons to lie nor would I directly or indirectly tell them we weren't proud of who we were.

"Telling them to lie about the gender make-up of their parents would be telling them we aren't proud of who we are and that we're ashamed of ourselves and of our family. I'm damn proud to be the man I am, to love another man and to have the family we fought hard to adopt and I refuse to pass along your fears to our sons."

The next day I called the headmaster of their school and asked him to speak to Michael about the possibility of our kids being teased or Michael's concern over job security. I carefully explained that Michael was afraid our boys would be teased if their classmates found out they had two dads at home. He was also petrified to think of staff or students knowing too much about his private life. Michael worried that if his male students knew he was gay then they could blackmail him for better marks by threatening to lie and tell the world he had molested them. He felt sick about all the obscure improbable situations that could develop if his students knew he was gay. Michael believed that having our boys tell their friends that they had a mom and dad at home then it would be

A Swim *Against* The Tide

safer for them and the issue of his sexuality would never be the subject of ugly mean gossip.

This astute headmaster, eloquently told me how much he and the rest of the schools' staff appreciated Michael's expertise and teaching talents. He went on to say that should any molestation allegations ever arise against him from a student, the entire staff would be solidly behind Michael. I suggested he repeat his sentiments to Michael. Two days later Michael walked in the front door with a sheepish grin. The school's headmaster had paid him a visit to quell his fears and concerns regarding anything to do with him being gay and emphatically told Michael, "We're really pleased to have your Kolwyn and Nicholas attend the Lower School and it goes against everything this school stands for if you instruct those boys to lie about having two dads at home."

The issues we dealt with week to week such as picking the boys up from after-school sports programs, getting them to practise piano, teaching them to be responsible team players in the house by picking up after themselves, seemed to fill our free time as a family.

Michael and I would calmly sit with the boys to discuss family relations, how to avoid conflicts and how necessary it was to apologise when wrong. On weekends when the boys were asleep Michael went to the TV to get lost in sci-fi programs and I'd get lost in the pages of a book. We had, like many couples, both found solace in something other than ourselves. When we could have been sitting and talking about issues common to us, instead we'd chosen to have down time in solitude. We were conscientiously instilling in our children a sense of spirituality by being members of a church community and teaching them by example that sharing with others less fortunate is infinitely better than always being the one to get presents. But as parents, we had forgotten to share with one another.

One Sunday the boys watched a Foster Parent Plan program on the TV and told us we should sponsor a child. We had a family meeting to discuss this suggestion and the boys agreed to give up half their monthly allowances to help support a little child. We were doing lots of things right, but we had forgotten to nurture our relationship amidst all the daily responsibilities of being a family. I remembered some professor telling me long ago that a whole is only as strong the parts that make it whole. I'd neglected to make Michael a daily priority and I felt horrible.

Although we faced unique challenges as a gay couple with children in a community of mostly heterosexual families, the day to day issues of raising children was anything but unique and we drew on the advice of experienced parents to cope with common child-rearing issues.

Prejudice was something we knew we'd encounter, and so would our sons. As parents we just hoped the good would outweigh the bad.

I'll never forget the day Nicholas came home upset that someone in the gym class had made fun of his brown penis in the shower. I told him that he did have a brown penis and if he were orange his penis would be orange or flesh coloured if he was Caucasian. We didn't feel there was any merit in masking what was obvious. We wanted Nicholas to be proud of his heritage, not be embarrassed because of it. But that is an adult way of thinking about things, to an eight-year-old still learning English and trying to fit into a white world those remarks only highlighted his racial differences. In some cases I just hugged him close and comforted him silently.

While they attended their second country school I had to intervene on their behalf when bullies taunted them on the school bus ride home. The boys got off the bus one afternoon and took a long time coming into the house. It was obvious something was wrong so I asked what was up. Kolwyn spoke up first and said they didn't want to tell me because it would make me sad what some kids had said. I told him that I wouldn't be sad if he was just repeating something said by one of the kids on the bus. The boys looked at one another and Nicholas told me, "Dad, the boys call our house a faggot house."

I wasn't sad – I was mad! In gay circles it is often said in jest that hell hath no fury like a pissed off homo! I called our very supportive principal and those Grade 5 students were hauled down to his office first thing the next morning. While waiting for one of their parents to arrive

A Swim *Against* The Tide

to escort them home for a one day suspension, the boys had to apologise to Kolwyn and Nicholas face to face, one on one in the principal's office. The sad thing was that two of the boys hadn't even known what the word meant and had just gone along naively with the crowd shouting, "faggots house, faggots house."

Thankfully almost every parent whose kid was suspended because of gay taunts towards our sons was in concert with the action taken by the school. However, one parent appealed loudly for clemency, unable to understand the uproar over a child using the word faggot! Kids aren't born with prejudice, they learn it from the adults in their home.

Another time the boys got off the school bus and started to tell me how a penis goes into a c— to make a baby. Incredulity and shock shot across my face hearing this word from their young mouths, as we had taught them proper names for the human anatomy. I asked where they had learned that word. They told me a Grade 8 girl on the bus was telling them about sex on the way home and a few of the older kids were using that word. The moment we walked into our house, I called the principal (it seemed like I had a direct line to him after 4 p.m.) to report this indiscretion. I wasn't looking for extra favours for my children, but I wasn't going to sit quietly and let them and their friends be influenced by a pre-pubescent hormonal 13 year-old-girl on the bus home from school. My kids' innocene was at stake.

I was as active a parental influence in my children's school as my parents had been in mine. I was over to the school on a regular basis and had met most of the staff at various school meetings or local events. Kolwyn and Nicholas knew they couldn't be naughty at school without me being informed by someone.

In some ways our sons had a "Beaver Cleaver-like" life. I was at home as a full time parent and if the boys forgot to take their lunch or gym clothes to school, they would telephone and ask me to bring what they needed to school. If they were sick I was there, and my daily routines weren't upset by them staying home in bed. The boys invited their school classes over in winter for skating parties on the pond

David R I McKinstry

followed by hours of hot tubbing and hot chocolate. In June we'd host an end-of-term swimming party in the pond followed by hot dogs, pop and games in the yard. My presence in the school on a regular basis diffused most of the prejudice from fellow classmates or from parents about our homosexual household.

On cold days or warm days Kolwyn and Nicholas would invite friends over to play at our house. The homosexual component of our family didn't enter the equation with the children. Only on a few rare occasions did we discover through the gossip mill that some parents weren't at ease having their children attending parties at our house. Most of the time those were parents whom we hadn't met and they let their preconceived prejudices about gay people prevent their kids from partying at our home with all the other neighbourhood kids. I didn't want to see our family as being different from other non-descriptive families *or* those who had obvious cultural or racial differences.

In a perfect world our family's uniqueness wouldn't be much different from the immigrant Indian family moving into an Italian neighbourhood, or a Nigerian Black family moving into an Icelandic white bread community. But being a homosexual in a heterosexual world, I knew the world wasn't perfect.

Divorced parents could blend into any community without much of an issue being raised, so could a single white parent, but two gay dads was just about as obvious as racially different families in a white community. Fortunately many of our neighbours didn't give a second thought about our homosexuality. Most of them appeared more interested in what we could add to the fabric of the community, specifically would we stop and help a neighbour who was stuck in a snow drift. Thankfully that was the measuring stick by which 90% of our neighbours gauged our similarity or difference from them.

In early November 2002, I was given the opportunity to do some supply teaching at a private school. During one senior class, the students were discussing which universities they had applied to for the following September. I asked if anyone had applied to Trent University for the

A Swim *Against* The Tide

small campus experience it provided. One student, Caucasian and obese, sitting directly in front of the teacher's desk promptly sat up and said loud enough for a few to hear, "Only gays go to Trent. I wouldn't want to go there and be touched by gays in the shower room." This 17-year-old had no idea his supply teacher was gay, damn proud and incapable of letting that remark slip by.

I told the class to be quiet so they could listen to his statement. I then asked him to repeat what he had said about Trent. He stood and repeated his comment with gusto, smiled confidently and sat back in his seat. A few classmates yelled "Homophobe" at him while others just laughed and shrugged off his prejudice. I wondered if I dared to tell him I was gay? Could I turn his stupid remarks into a learning lesson for the class? Or should I just annihilate him silently with a venomous stare?

"Who told you Trent had a large gay student population?" I asked. He told me he had heard his dad telling his older brother that only gays go there.

I asked him if he could always pick out who was gay in a crowd. He snidely remarked, with an exaggerated flick of his wrist, "It's easy to tell fags by the way they walk and talk. It's always real obvious if someone is gay. Like waiters in restaurants, decorators and socialists, my dad says they're all gay."

Most gay men are closeted drama queens at heart and I decided to be dramatic! Lights, camera, action.

"Is that so. I'm happily married to another man and we have two adopted children attending a private school. I've been an acclaimed athlete and was a Toronto Sun SUNshine Boy. I'm educated with a Physical Education degree and an MBA. I've been a businessman for the past fifteen years and now am writing a book. Did you know I was gay?" I stared at him in front of the now very alert class of eighteen teenage boys.

He looked at me, his chubby white cheeks twitched and turned beet red. I looked directly into his eyes and wondered how this confrontation would end. Being an obese teenager, he should have been sensitive to people's prejudice. I was sure, if asked, that his non-fat

David R I McKinstry

classmates would say it wasn't cool to be obese. Had he come this far in life without having heard mean, hurtful comments about his weight somewhere along the way?

"And by the way, it's both mean and wrong for you to stand before your classmates to try to get a laugh at the expense of other people. To imply that gay men at Trent, or anywhere, hang around shower rooms waiting to pounce on unsuspecting heterosexuals is reprehensible. That would be as wrong as me saying, 'Here comes the fat kid, lock up the fridge or we'll be eaten out of house and home.' A raucous round of laughter erupted just as the bell sounded for the end of class. It was obvious at least some of the class held less caustic views of homosexuals for as they passed by the desk of the chubby student they shook their heads and called him a homophobe.

I had lunch with several teachers and told them about the smart-ass kid who had made prejudiced remarks about gays at Trent. I was unaware that the man sitting at the end of the table was the headmaster. He laughed, introduced himself and said, "Apples don't fall far from the tree. That student's father is a real piece of work, and his son comes by his prejudices by osmosis."

Alone in the staff room for the next period I questioned my reaction to this teenager's commentary on gays. I had been harsh and should have handled it better. Slowly I began to feel like an ogre for having centred him out in class so coarsely. Forty minutes later as I walked down the corridor to my next class, the student I'd so badly maimed came around the corner. He was equally startled to see me and put his face down and hunched his shoulders into a contrite stance. To my amaze-ment he came directly over to me and apologized for his comments in class. He said being overweight meant he only got attention being the class clown and he had only been trying to get a laugh.

Now I felt horrible. Here was this courageous seventeen-year-old apologizing for making me feel badly in class. How many times had I been wronged by society and politicians over the gay issue and never once received an apology! I was astonished that a child could wound me

A Swim *Against* The Tide

and also heal me. Wounding and healing, wasn't this a metaphor for my journey to parenthood? This obese boy with a man-sized heart had taught me a real lesson.

"I too was wrong. Forgive me for lashing out and trying to humiliate you." He looked up surprised at hearing me apologize. "I hit you with twenty years of my anger over people making jokes and poking fun at the expense of gay people. I've seen prejudice in many forms and I've known people who have committed suicide because they're gay, or because they are fat or just feel left out because they don't act or look like everyone else. When you remarked about only gays going to Trent, I couldn't help but wonder if anyone in the class was feeling distraught and confused about their sexuality issues and cringing at the sound of your prejudice – just like you have, I'm sure, when people have made mean remarks about your weight just to get a laugh."

I got a reassuring smile from this young lad and I reached out my hand to him and said, "Making fun of anyone for any reason isn't nice. Maybe we both learned a good lesson today." He shook my hand and walked me down the hall to my classroom.

In the silence of the near empty hallway, he asked if I would be back tomorrow as their supply teacher. I said yes and he smiled and replied, "Great. See you tomorrow, Sir."

It was I who had become contrite. I was very moved by his willingness to forgive me. I felt terrible for having pounced on him in class. Sage advice is often softly spoken out of the mouth of a child. I had been taught a great life lesson. I would be more vigilant about not letting my wounded emotions go from my brain to my mouth without due process, and in doing so I hoped I would become a better parent.

David R I McKinstry

CHAPTER EIGHTEEN

Our Family

It is 2003. Since adopting our two sons we have celebrated five birthdays with each of them. We moved twice in five years and consequently Kolwyn and Nicholas have been taught in three school districts. They are thriving in smaller size classrooms, which is the norm at most independent schools.

Kolwyn has learned coping skills to handle his anger over the many personal losses he experienced prior to his fifth birthday. He loves to swim and ski, read, play the piano, and has become a terrific comic book maker. He spends hours each week drawing pictures and writing the dialogue for each of his new action heroes. These comics are very popular with his nine-year-old classmates.

Nicholas is very athletic. Whether it is throwing a baseball, kicking a soccer ball or snowboarding down intermediate slopes, he has a natural gift for balance, strength and speed. He loves to play the piano, collect things, and his room often looks like a country flea market. Nicholas is a wiz at math, spelling – and talking!

A week in our lives isn't unique, it's just busy. The boys each have a list of daily and weekly chores for which they are paid an allowance. We encourage them to put a significant percentage of their allowance in a savings account and monthly they must each contribute money to the sponsorship of our family's Foster Parent Plan child.

Sometimes I stop the car on country roads (especially when I'm cross over fights in the backseat) and we make a family outing of picking up litter in the ditches to do our part for the environment. Every Saturday after they finish their morning piano lessons I present them with an oversized Tim Horton fruit muffin.

Sunday morning means its time for me to take them to church. The boys enjoy Sunday school and have met neat friends from all walks of life. Every night, they get to read in bed for twenty minutes and then we say our prayers. I am pleased they both have a keen sense of having guardian angels looking out for them. They are really great kids.

We taught them, as we had been taught by our parents, never to address adults by their first names but always respectfully as Mr., Ms or Mrs. Nicholas recently had an overnight at a friend's house and his classmates mother called to ask what kind of politeness pills we gave our son! Considering they can be hellions at home, I'm glad to hear they are polite when visiting their friends.

Michael and I agreed that the boys shouldn't watch TV during the school week and on weekends for no more than five hours. Instead, we play cards or chess together and occasionally have controlled water fights in the kitchen.

Kolwyn cleans out the kitty litter every day for one week then switches with his brother. On alternate weeks they have to vacuum. Twice each week one of them must go out and stoop and scoop up after the dogs. Both boys have learned to load and unload the dishwasher and carry in groceries from the car. By the time they are twelve, they'll be doing their own laundry and by the time they turn fifteen years old, I expect both boys will know how to change a tire and do an oil change on the car.

We are teaching the boys about sharing with others. At Christmas we continue to open our house to families living at a women's shelter. It took a few years for the boys not to covet what we'd bought for the

David R I McKinstry

Nicholas and Kolwyn, their first day at school, September 2002.

Kolwyn and Nicholas, downhill skiing at Devil's Elbow, February 2002.

A Swim *Against* The Tide

shelter children. This past Christmas they showed their true colours and eagerly donated some of their own gifts to those children.

My sister, Karen, has become a good aunt to our sons. She lavishes gifts on them at special times of the year and the boys enjoy spending time at the cottage with her. Being a devout Pentecostal, she believes her Saviour condemns homosexuality and we are going to Hell on a red carpet. Obviously our doctrines clash but she has promised not to discuss her religion with our children.

As fate would have it, Louise, Michael's mother, never has exercised her option to vsist us without her husband. Our children will probably be her only chance for grandchildren but our boys wouldn't recognise her if she walked past them on the street. We lived 10 minutes from her house for two years, yet she never once visited. I even offered to vacate ny home so she could visit her son and his children, but she never answered my invitations. How sad that she purposefully passed up this opportunity to be a grandparent to our sons.

Michael's sister and brother don't play any role in our lives, only Michael's father, who lives 90 minutes away, makes any effort to connect with us.

Kolwyn and Nicholas love to explore the attic in Grandma McKinstry's house, just as I did when I was a child. The boys frequently spend Saturday nights over at Grandma's and every few weeks, depending on the weather, 88-year-old Grandma McKinstry will visit us for a few days. Mum has often said that becomig a grandma later in life means she can't afford to pass up on one opportunity to be around her two grandsons.

The boys put all their mending in a box so Grandma can sew up fabric tears and adjust pant hems or sew on knee patches. She taught them to thread a needle over the holidays and now they think they can compete with Grandma. Nicholas wants to learn how to bake Grandma's buttermilk tea biscuits while Kolwyn is bugging Grandma to make him a quilt for his bed. The boys are determined to keep Grandma alive until she is 103 so she lives longer than the British Queen Mother.

David R I McKinstry

All in all, we are just another family living next door. Doing our best to raise our children to be happy productive members of the community with a strong social conscience about what kind of behaviour is acceptable or not.

Kolwyn was chatting with me from the back seat of the car one night as we drove home from purchasing new jeans at the mall. He was curious about love and told me that he loved Amy, a girl in his class. Kolwyn asked, "How do you know if someone loves you back?"

I told him that love wasn't a guessing game and that when he became an adult and fell in love he would have to tell his partner every day that she/he was deeply loved and respected. I told him that love stops growing and getting better when two people in love stop telling each other how much they love one another. Kolwyn wanted to know what it was about Daddy that I loved. Whatever it was I told him, caused Kolwyn to become silent for a few minutes and then he said, "Dad, when I grow up I hope I marry a girl who loves me just like you love Daddy."

Out of the mouth of a child ... what better testimonial could any father wish to hear from his nine-year-old son! This was a kodak moment and I realised that Kolwyn and Nicholas believed in their hearts that our family unit was their definition of normal and they had adjusted well to life with Dad and Daddy.

Swimming against the tides of injustice toward homosexuals in this country during the last quarter century was every citizen's burden to carry. Some fought loud and carried big sticks. Others stemmed the tide with peaceful demonstrations. I owe a huge debt to gay trail-blazing brothers-in arms, like George Hislop and Svend Robinson, who took up the unpopular task of demanding equal rights and dignities for all citizens in this country long before it became a popular avocation of the urban masses.

I have learned from others how important it is to volunteer and contribute something back to community organisations. We all have particular causes close to our hearts. I've had strong male mentors and equally strong motivating female mentors, like my cousin Elizabeth McKinstry and dear friend Lindalee Tracey.

If a troubled gay or bisexual person reads my book, realises how precious they are to the broad community of human beings and that being gay isn't the end of the road, then I will have done my part to change the world one person at a time. If in reading *A Swim Against The Tide* one adult (single, married, gay, straight) is moved to open their heart to adopt a child, then I will feel my honesty and openness about our family has been worth it.

My social battles have been about championing equal rights for all people, improving and expanding the obligations of our social networks to defend and save battered women in this country and living proud as one-half of a same-sex couple being legally married and able to adopt children. Obviously my long struggle to adopt children became my most committed effort. It was an often lonely and always frustrating campaign being forced to take baby-steps instead of jumping by leaps and bounds.

I am very aware that this crusade to change adoption laws had gay soldiers across the country working alone, with little or no solidarity. Unfortunately many other adoption pioneers became discouraged or were forced, because of circumstances, to abandon their goal of becoming parents.

I was blessed to have had lovers, family and friends, mentors near and far, who buoyed me up against the waves of resistance. Our children are a miracle that many around us can rejoice in, knowing they contributed prayers, money and time to help us adopt Kolwyn and Nicholas. The list of contributors is long. Our boys are a blessing to the world and most certainly to us. Getting Kolwyn and Nicholas was the result of a huge community effort.

Reflecting back on twenty years of being a thorn in the side of adoption officials, walking in their offices but being told not to let the door hit me on the ass as I left, I wonder how I survived. I know I had angels on my shoulders.

David R I McKinstry

Michael is my best friend, lover and confidante. We're total opposites … he says no and I say yes. Fate played a major role in our becoming a couple and I have no doubt he is the left to my right. He has never been a replacement for Nick. Working through my grief helped me to understand that I didn't have to live the rest of my life as part of a ghost partnership.

Michael and the boys are my present and future focus. Our sons are the answer to my prayers. With all my heart and soul, I believe that the universe put them into our arms for safekeeping. I hope their mothers are looking down from Heaven happy and confident in the master plan being unveiled for their sons as Nicholas-Eric Rattenbury McKinstry and Kolwyn Irlam Rattenbury McKinstry.

I have a few suggestions to our country's politicians who purport to be interested in child welfare in Canada. First and foremost, WAKE UP! You have lost sight of thousands of children's reality – every hour a child somewhere is being abused and in need of good parental love. It's time to make the rights of children a priority. Child welfare organizations are stuck in quagmires of rules and regulations that assuage the egos of the legislators who made them. Provincial governments need to provide hundreds of millions of dollars to hire child advocate watchdogs who have the time to make children their focus. Wouldn't it make sense to eliminate the wasted months and years children spend in foster homes before becoming eligible to be adopted into permanent families?

The Children's Aid Society and the judicial system need to change their primary focus away from reunification of families wherein parents have sexually, physically or emotionally abused their children. Parenting isn't some insignificant laboratory experiment. Abuse in childhood leaves an impact on a child for life. Parents who abuse their kids shouldn't be given a second chance to re-offend. Ninety percent of

A Swim *Against* The Tide

social workers within the CAS are responsible, dedicated, underpaid, over-worked and desperate for a moment's respite from the horrific cases they face every day. Like good teachers, some social workers put in sixteen-hour days while only being paid for eight hours of work. These people are charged with the responsibility of looking after minors who have been neglected, hurt or abused ... and like teachers, nurses and day care workers they get paid peanuts for the jobs they do because society undervalues the role of these front-line workers.

Can we expect understaffed social agencies to police child abusers, transplant children into temporary foster homes, monitor parental visitations with minors, and finish the mountain of paperwork and interviews necessary to place a child into a permanent adoptive home ... all in a regular work week? The evidence speaks loud and clear every day in our cities across Canada, that it is impossible. Meanwhile no government in power puts its money where its mouth is in terms of giving a damn about the perils of children at risk in this country.

There are people in Canada who ache to be biological parents but infertility renders them incapable or the expense of IVF or other modes of assisted pregnancies are prohibitive. Imagine how unfair the world must seem to those wanna-be parents who hear stories of adults who simply act as studs and bitches procreating at random with no perceivable responsibility or love for the baby they unwantingly create. There are too many children caught up in the bureaucracy of our social and legal networks, lost in the courts and stuck between parents who fight to keep them as chattel not persons.

Having the biological capability to produce a child doesn't mean anyone has the right to be a parent. What if biological parents had to go through the same scrutiny as adoptive parents? Would our jails still be overflowing with men and women who tried to live outside our community value system? What's the dollar value of rehabilitating valuable lives unfortunately born into irresponsible loveless homes? Isn't it about time all parents in this country had to take courses, pass exams and be licensed to parent children?

David R I McKinstry

One brave federal politician needs to stand defiantly before governmental peers and initiate legislation that would give mammoth tax credits to men and women who complete parenting courses, long before they couple up and procreate. Money impacts people's decisions, so have the government make an investment now for the children of tomorrow. The time is nigh for children to be made society's highest priority, not tax breaks for big business, not waging war and not paying out-of-sight salaries to athletes or company presidents.

Infertile couples are everywhere in increasing numbers. They are drowning in tears and anguish over the absence of children in their lives. Remove parental rights from adults who have abused their children. The courts and child welfare organizations must be given the tools to act swiftly and decidedly regarding the placement of children into the waiting arms of those who really want to be good parents.

We must adjust our attitudes toward children needing to be in loving and responsible homes with one or two parents, heterosexual or homosexual, who understand that parenting isn't a *right*. Child rearing is a *privilege* only for those who are truly committed to being the best parent their child could ever wish to have.

I received a note from an old friend (himself a father of five) who wrote, "I recently heard a couple give a speech at a YMCA dinner about family-life and I was struck by their conviction to make parenting their primary priority. They said there are two important things good parents give to their children, one is roots and the other is wings."

I'm Joe-average, your next door neighbour, and I'm living proof that dreams can come true. With tenacity, anyone can swim against the tide and reach the destiny of their desires.

David McKinstry

In 2003 I finally confessed my homosexuality in a letter to the orphanage director in India. I told Mohini that Nicholas and Kolwyn have two fathers. This was her warm reply:

Dear David and Michael,

It is the basic goodness of heart and soul which is the abiding principle in this trouble-torn existence of humans. Michael is as much welcome as David. I will not add anything more but I hope this conveys my acceptance.

Lots of love to you all,
Mohini

David R I McKinstry

About the Author

David McKinstry is a fighter and has been since his days protecting stray animals and volunteering with charitable organizations, the YMCA, Parkinsons Disease and Adult Training Centres (ARC) for mentally challenged adults, etc. Ten years later he would face his greatest challenge as an Olympic-trained swimmer, a cross-lake swim attempt, not just once, but three times! The win by Lake Ontario against his attempts at crossing that thirty-two-mile expanse of water was the last time he let anything or anyone stop him from achieving his goal.

Hence the title of his book.

The author's introduction to the literary world brings a story to us about his longtime desire to adopt children into a loving home that he shares with his companion, Michael. But that choice came with a mountain of prejudice to overcome in having his orientation as a gay man respected as well as breaking new ground as he sought equal treatment for same-sex couples under the law.

His venture into ownership of a most unusual B&B (Bed and Breakfast) and its development into a family lodge is a lesson of sharing with those who have naught.

David's book is the first of many that he will be writing on social issues expressing his ever-deepening concern that everyone in society be treated as an equal and that children be love and raised by caring parents without bureaucratic entanglement.

His determination to adopt children has brought together a wonderful, loving, unique family as only a person of his talent and attitude could accomplish.

A Swim *Against* The Tide

Special Offer

VISIONTV

To celebrate the publishing of David R I McKinstry's book, *A Swim Against The Tide*, VisionTV is offering, at a special price, copies of a real heart-warming documentary about David McKinstry produced by Kevin O'Keefe. The rare and sensitive theme of "Destiny's Children" will be enjoyed during every second of the 22 minute documentary. It brings out the beauty of human nature by showing the development of David's dream to adopt children into the loving home provided by him and his companion.

VHS copies of **"Destiny's Children"** are available for $39.95 (taxes, shipping and handling are included). To obtain a copy of the documentary, please send a cheque or money order to *VisionTV* at the following address:

VisionTV
Audience Relations
80 Bond Street, Toronto, ON M5B 1X2

With your payment, please include the following reference:
"Destiny's Children."

Together with the tape, VisionTV will include a receipt for the above-mentioned amount.

Please allow 4-6 weeks for delivery.

Thank You